The Spirit within Me

THE ANCHOR YALE BIBLE REFERENCE LIBRARY is a project of international and interfaith scope in which Protestant, Catholic, and Jewish scholars from many countries contribute individual volumes. The project is not sponsored by any ecclesiastical organization and is not intended to reflect any particular theological doctrine.

The series is committed to producing volumes in the tradition established half a century ago by the founders of the Anchor Bible, William Foxwell Albright and David Noel Freedman. It aims to present the best contemporary scholarship in a way that is accessible not only to scholars but also to the educated nonspecialist. It is committed to work of sound philological and historical scholarship, supplemented by insight from modern methods, such as sociological and literary criticism.

John J. Collins
General Editor

THE ANCHOR YALE BIBLE REFERENCE LIBRARY

The Spirit within Me

Self and Agency in Ancient Israel and Second Temple Judaism

CAROL A. NEWSOM

YALE AYBRL

Yale UNIVERSITY PRESS

NEW HAVEN AND LONDON

Yale University Press books may be purchased in quantity for educational, business, or promotional use. For information, please email sales.press@yale.edu (U.S. office) or sales@yaleup.co.uk (U.K. office).

Set in Adobe Caslon and Bauer Bodoni types by Newgen North America.
Printed in the United States of America.

Library of Congress Control Number: 2021932817
ISBN 978-0-300-20868-9 (hardcover : alk. paper)

A catalogue record for this book is available from the British Library.
This paper meets the requirements of ANSI/NISO Z39.48-1992 (Permanence of Paper).

10 9 8 7 6 5 4 3 2 1

To the memory of

Brandon M. Newsom
1971–2018

and

R. Terrell Finney, Jr.
1953–2020

Contents

Preface

Like many academic projects, this book was not the one I set out to write and took much longer than I anticipated. I had been intrigued by three quite different models for reflecting on the nature of good and evil in ancient Israelite and early Jewish literature. The origin, nature, and end of evil is an explicit topic in many apocalyptic writings. Less often discussed are the assumptions about goodness and evil in the wisdom books of the Hebrew Bible, assumptions that differ sharply from those found in apocalyptic literature. Both of these perspectives, however, frame the issues in cosmological or ontological terms. That is obvious for much apocalyptic literature, with its cosmic drama of suprahuman conflict. In wisdom literature the conviction that evil is ephemeral (e.g., Ps 1, Job 20), in contrast to the lasting, resilient quality of good, tacitly assumes that this dynamic is based on transcendent reality, namely, the way in which God created the world "by wisdom" (Prov 3:18). The third perspective, however, the one most memorably represented in the mythic account of the first humans in Genesis 2–3, is radically mundane. Through an apparently unplanned sequence of events, human beings come into possession of a type of agency that they are ill equipped to use well. The rest, as they say, is history. Even though the origin story in Genesis 2–3 itself may be a late composition, much of the literature of the Hebrew Bible, including the prophets, Deuteronomy, and the historical books, assumes that often unreliable human moral agency is the central factor in the creation of good or evil states of affairs.

Oddly, when I began to look for research on moral agency in biblical literature, I found surprisingly little. The reception of Genesis 2–3 in Christian reflections on moral agency and the development of the Rabbinic models of the evil *yēṣer* were well attested, but little had been written on the assumptions undergirding moral agency in biblical texts themselves. Consequently, I took advantage of my Society of Biblical Literature Presidential Lecture in November 2011 to present a sketch of what seemed to me to be models of moral agency in biblical and Second Temple texts. There appeared to be not only multiple models but also a dynamic history of development. The issues involved were too broad and complex and too little researched simply to be part of a larger study. Consequently, my focus shifted to moral agency in particular. Even that has turned out to be a project too vast for one book, especially since the issue of moral agency is so intimately connected with the development of introspective subjectivity in Second Temple Judaism. What follows is only a partial exploration.

In certain ways the book has developed into a kind of broader companion piece to my earlier work, *The Self as Symbolic Space: Constructing Identity and Community at Qumran*. That work, however, was both more narrowly focused on a sectarian context and more oriented to the interplay between self and society. The current work is broader in scope, attends where possible to historical development, and is more focused on the individual. One dimension of analysis that is not explicitly present in either work is gender. Although it is possible to discern gendered differences in moral psychology and general agency in certain Israelite and Second Temple texts, I did not find gender to be a salient category in reflections on moral agency. Even with respect to Genesis 2–3, reflection on gender appears to be largely a feature of the reception of that text, and even there it tends to be marginal except in texts that are significantly influenced by Greek culture and its views on women's moral agency. Although women are at times presented as models of prayer and piety in biblical and Second Temple literature, I think it likely that most of the literature I discuss assumes a male subject, and so where personal pronouns are necessary I have referred to the subject as "he."

Two other issues of terminology require comment. Many of the texts I discuss in chapters 4–6 come from the discoveries at Khirbet Qumran. The community that resided there is now properly understood to be part of a larger movement that referred to itself as the Yahad, "the community." When I refer to "Qumran texts" or "Qumran literature," I mean the sectarian literature of the Yahad community, as we have come to know it from the texts discovered at Qumran. The sociological provenance of the nonsectarian literature found at Qumran, though representing perspectives congenial to the sectarian community, generally cannot be determined with specificity. The provenance of that portion of the Community Rule known as the Two Spirits Teaching is disputed and will be briefly discussed in chapter 4. In referring to the Hodayot, I capitalize the term when designating the work as a whole, one or more manuscripts (e.g., 1QH[a], 4QH[a–f]), and groupings of compositions (e.g., Hodayot of the Teacher, Hodayot of the Maskil) but use lower case (hodayah/hodayot) when referring to individual compositions.

I wish to thank the many people who have generously shared with me their insights and expertise as I found my way into new issues. These include but are not limited to Sam Adams, Yitzhaq Feder, Christian Frevel, Steve Kraftchick, David Lambert, Ingrid Lilly, Hindy Najman, Eileen Schuller, Ben Wold, and Christine Yoder. This project probably would not have happened without the encouragement of John Collins, who believed in it before I did. The anonymous reviewers for Yale University Press were both encouraging and insightful, and I have attempted to respond to their suggestions, especially in the closing pages of the book. Jennifer Banks, senior executive editor for religion and the humanities, Yale University Press, Abbie Storch, editorial assistant, Ann-Marie Imbornoni, senior production editor, and Harry Haskell, copyeditor, have made the process of publication a true pleasure. In this project, as in all others, my wonderful husband, Rex Matthews, has been not only a supportive presence but also a computer wizard, guiding me through technical problems I would never have navigated on my own. No one deserves more thanks than Evan Bassett, my indefatigable research assistant and copyeditor. More than that, he has been an invaluable conversation partner.

My research has also been generously supported by the Luce Foundation, the Candler School of Theology and Dean Jan Love, the Emeritus College, and the Fox Center for Humanistic Inquiry of Emory University. The year that I spent in residence at the Fox Center as this project was beginning was an academic idyll. I am deeply grateful to the director, Martine Brownley, and the executive director, Keith Anthony, for the supportive and welcoming academic atmosphere they nurtured there.

As most of us do, I developed this project in significant measure through a series of presentations and essays in various venues. I am grateful to the Society of Biblical Literature, E. J. Brill, Mohr Siebeck, Walter de Gruyter, and Westminster John Knox for permission to include reworked portions of the following articles (see list of abbreviations in the back matter):

"Genesis 2–3 and 1 Enoch 6–16: Two Myths of Origin and Their Ethical Implications." Pages 7–23 in *Shaking Heaven and Earth*. Edited by Christine Roy Yoder et al. Louisville: Westminster John Knox, 2005.

"Deriving Negative Anthropology through Exegetical Activity: The Hodayot as Case Study." Pages 258–74 in *Is There a Text in This Cave? Studies in the Textuality of the Dead Sea Scrolls in Honour of George J. Brooke*. Edited by Ariel Feldman, Maria Cioată, and Charlotte Hempel. STDJ 119. Leiden: Brill, 2017.

"In Search of Cultural Models for Divine Spirit and Human Bodies." *VT* 70 (2020): 104–23.

"Models of Moral Agency: Hebrew Bible and Second Temple Judaism." *JBL* 131 (2012): 2–25.

"Moral 'Recipes' in Deuteronomy and Ezekiel: Divine Authority and Human Agency." *HeBAI* 4 (2017): 488–509.

"Toward a Genealogy of the Introspective Self in Second Temple Judaism." Pages 63–78 in *Functions of Psalms and Prayers in the Late Second Temple Period*. Edited by Mika Pajunen and Jeremy Penner. BZAW 486. Berlin: De Gruyter, 2017.

"Predeterminism and Moral Agency in the Hodayot." Pages 193–211 in *The Religious Worldviews Reflected in the Dead Sea Scrolls: Proceedings of the Fourteenth International Symposium of the Orion Center for the Study of the Dead Sea Scrolls and Associated Literature, 28–30 May, 2013*. Edited by Ruth Clements, Menachem Kister, and Michael Segal. STDJ 127. Leiden: Brill, 2018.

"Sin Consciousness, Self-Alienation, and the Origins of the Introspective Self." Pages 225–37 in *Rhetoric and Hermeneutics: Approaches to Text, Tradition and Social Construction in Biblical and Second Temple Literature*. FAT 130. Tübingen: Mohr Siebeck, 2019.

Finally, I wish to dedicate this work to the memory of two members of my family who are deeply loved and profoundly missed—my nephew, Brandon Newsom, and my brother-in-law, Terrell Finney.

The Spirit within Me

1 The Self in Israelite Culture: A Preliminary Overview

What *is* the human self? Part of the difficulty in talking about that thing we conveniently call "the self" is that we can be torn between two conflicting insights, both of which seem to have a claim on truth. On the one hand, since all humans belong biologically to the same species with the same types of bodies and the same types of brains, then whatever it is that neurophysiologically constitutes the self should be structurally and functionally the same in all humans. To be a functioning human being requires a certain set of capacities both to engage the world and to monitor and direct oneself. Each individual has to have a sense of its differentiation from other agents and from forces outside itself. It seems eminently reasonable to posit that these exist in all times and places.[1] On the other hand, anyone who has read anthropological accounts of different societies and their folk theories of the self can easily come away overwhelmed by the extraordinary number of different ways in which various cultures conceptualize and talk about the self, its nature, and its components. Whatever one may posit is going on neurophysiologically in terms of "self functions," this phenomenon is open to a wide variety of ways of being figured, and, I would say, experienced. The neurophysiological self and what we might call the cultural self are related but need to be distinguished from one another. While it is appropriate to assume that all persons have the capacity for conscious self-monitoring, for example, only in some cultures will this capacity become the focus of cultural attention, description, and cultivation. But that is only part of the complexity. Our individual consciousnesses are mediated to ourselves largely in language and other symbolic forms. That is to say that in a profound sense our "selves" are largely accessible to us by means of culturally constructed forms. Moreover, cultural symbolizations and practices themselves can have an effect on the organization of neural functions and in some cases even brain structure, so that to a certain extent culture shapes not just the symbolizing mind but the brain itself.[2] Thus it is important in talking about the nature of the self or person in different cultures to keep in mind both the neurophysiological and cultural dimensions. The fact that self functions can be represented and symbolized in a nearly unlimited fashion also makes it highly likely that in any given culture multiple ways of representing the self may be in use at the same time, even ways that are logically contradictory. These different folk theories of the self are most likely to be employed for different purposes in different social situations. They may also be the domains of specific subcultures or the products of older and newer models of the self that overlap, as traditional ways of talking and conceptualizing are retained alongside emergent models.

The task of the historian who seeks to recover cultural models of the self is hermeneutically similar to that of the anthropologist, though the sources of information are rather different. But for the historian who works with materials that are not just ancient artifacts but also parts of traditions that have profoundly shaped western culture, there are additional difficulties. It is easy to implicitly modernize the meanings and referents of words and concepts from antiquity that have come into our own language and thinking as linguistic and mental calques, and so to subtly assimilate them to contemporary meanings and referents.[3] The recognition of the otherness of past cultures is one of the major achievements of the modern historical consciousness. Nevertheless, the otherness of ancient cultures has sometimes been exaggerated, especially where evolutionary or progressivist models of culture are employed, models that posit ancient societies as having primitive, collectivist conceptions of the self that contrast with the more individualized and interiorized forms of later cultures. Such schematizations distort the complexity of the representations of the self in antiquity. Similarly, anxiety about hegemonic projection of the modern western conception of the self (as though there were only one) onto nonwestern and premodern cultures can lead to overcorrection, creating a falsely exoticized model of the ancient self. The challenge is to recognize and analyze cultural differences reflected in the textual evidence without resorting to dichotomies that exaggerate and distort.

Indeed, even framing the concept of the "self" as object of inquiry might itself be seen as a potential source of confusion, but I do not think it need be, so long as the category is defined with sufficient clarity and specificity. First, consider the various possible uses of the term. It can refer to the physical, sensory, emotional, volitional, and noetic experience of an individual *as it is apprehended by that individual*, not simply as a transitory experience but as part of an autobiographical continuity.[4] Since we have only texts and cannot conduct subtle and probing interviews with subjects, we have no access to that experience for ancient Israel. Nor, in my opinion, given the nature of our sources, do we have much if any access to a closely related phenomenon, namely, the *self-representation* of an individual to him or herself. Deeply personal diaries, for example, might provide such evidence, though even such sources are complicated to assess. In any event, that genre was not employed in ancient Israel. We do have, however, a variety of first-person texts that can be said to be *self-presentations*, that is, communicative representations of the self to others, including the deity. Whether these are or are not congruent with self-representations is impossible to say, given the nature of the evidence. They tend to be fairly stereotypical, though occasionally one can identify ways in which they are individually inflected.[5] These self-presentations are best understood as examples of the culturally normative models of the self that can occur in a variety of narrative, didactic, and poetic genres. Sometimes these models are explicit in their modeling of the self and sometimes they disclose implicit assumptions.

The nature of the relationship between cultural models embodied in the symbolic forms of culture (linguistic and nonlinguistic) and self-representation or individual experience has been variously evaluated. Clifford Geertz famously assumed that the relationship was simple and direct:

> I have tried to get at this most intimate of notions . . . by searching out and analyzing symbolic forms—words, images, institutions, behaviors—in terms of which, in each place, people actually represent themselves to themselves and to one another.[6]

He thus assumed that by knowing the symbolic forms one also knew both the forms of self-presentation (a reasonable assumption) and self-representation (a more contested matter). Subsequent anthropological research has brought into serious question such an unproblematic relationship between symbolic forms—that is, cultural models—and actual self-representation or subjective experience. Unni Wikan's anthropological study of Bali, *Managing Turbulent Hearts: A Balinese Formula for Living*, is exemplary, since she began her research as an attempt to extend and deepen Geertz's observations and ended by putting his assumptions in question.[7] As her work showed, though agents are aware of cultural expectations for how persons are to conduct themselves and how, subjectively, one is *expected* to experience things, people often struggle to actualize the cultural norms and are often aware of a gap between self-experience and normative models. They may even be critical or dismissive of the cultural model.[8] That is certainly not to say that the cultural models are unrelated to self-representation and subjective experience. Even informants who report struggling to embody cultural norms feel their force. But it is equally important to remember that cultural models of the self are also not simply attempts to summarize "how our culture wants people to experience themselves." Cultural models of the self are often complex products of efforts to negotiate many other aspects of culture and society, for example, the desire to maintain social hierarchies, control conflict, adapt to population densities and limited resources, or, from the individual perspective, as a strategy for avoiding sorcery or seeking status.[9] Cultural self-models are parts of the larger dynamics of society and world. The self is often "symbolic space."[10] Once again, in dealing with the textual remains from antiquity it may be possible only in some cases to identify these connections, but it is important to be aware of them, even as possibilities.

In this book I am not trying to provide a comprehensive study of cultural models of selfhood in ancient Israel and Second Temple Judaism. There are simply too many possible issues and approaches for any one book to address.[11] My efforts will focus on two often related areas of self-representation. One is the issue of agency, in particular, moral agency. This is a common topic of discourse in the texts from ancient Israel and is often a place where assumptions about the self are accessible and where innovations in ways of thinking about the self emerge. The closely related topic is the development of cultural forms that model and support introspective practices and self-representations. To a certain extent changes in models of moral agency and increasing evidence for introspection and metacognition (that is, thinking about one's thinking) can be related to cultural responses to the national trauma of the Babylonian destruction of Judah in 586 BCE. These new patterns of self and agency, however, come to serve a variety of functions within the society and become rich resources for the development of novel forms of spirituality. Before turning to these matters, however, it is useful to survey some of the recent discussions of the ancient Israelite self, to see both where consensus lies and where certain relevant disagreements occur. Two major foci for discussion that are particularly pertinent to the issues I wish to examine are the role of the body in representations of the person and the relation of the individual self to larger social units.

The Body in Israelite Anthropology

If there is any point of consensus in Israelite anthropology, it is the fundamentally somatic character of the language used to represent the human person in all its dimensions. Although he was not the first to draw attention to the prominence of the body,[12] the publication of Hans Walter Wolff's *Anthropologie des Alten Testaments* in 1973 marks an important reorientation in scholarly understanding of the cultural models of the self in ancient Israel.[13] Wolff was concerned that translation practices, beginning with the Septuagint, had unintentionally assimilated the biblical models of the self to those derived from Greek philosophical formulations.[14] By way of correction, Wolff drew attention to the physicality of the terms most frequently used to represent the individual in biblical texts. Since one of his concerns was to combat the impression that the biblical texts assumed "a trichotomic anthropology, in which body, soul and spirit are in opposition to one another,"[15] he focused in particular on four key terms—*nepeš*, *bāśār*, *rûaḥ*, *lēb*—though he considered a wide variety of body terms in the course of his discussion.

Wolff's approach was to examine uses of the critical terms in context, arranging the evidence from those contexts in which the more physical nuances of the term were prominent to those in which the terms were used for more abstract concepts. Thus *nepeš* in its physical sense refers to the throat, but also in some contexts can connote hunger and thirst, desire, soul (in the sense of "the seat . . . of other spiritual experiences and emotions"),[16] life, and person. It can even serve as an equivalent of the first-person pronoun. To be sure, Wolff's chapter headings ("*nepeš*—Needy Man," "*bāśār*—Man in His Infirmity," "*rûaḥ*—Man as He Is Empowered," and "*leb[āb]*—Reasonable Man") may suggest a certain semantic essentializing of the physicality of the terms even in their more abstract uses, though his discussions are generally more nuanced. But one of the important insights of Wolff's work was his perception of the deeply integrated way in which, as Bernd Janowski phrases it, "physical and psychic/cognitive aspects and functions" are represented in ancient Israelite conceptions.[17]

Ironically, as Andreas Wagner has pointed out, the attempt to differentiate ancient Israelite from Greek philosophical conceptions of the person was carried out largely by means of focusing on those terms that could most clearly be correlated with their supposed Greek counterparts: *nepeš*, *rûaḥ*, *bāśār*.[18] Even the addition of *lēb* does little to correct the narrow focus. The result was an analysis that was still in some ways dominated by a focus derived from Greek philosophical concepts about the relation of body, psyche, and soul. Wagner makes a strong case against thinking of the four terms *lēb*, *bāśār*, *rûaḥ*, and *nepeš* as a closed system of privileged terms for the self. Representing the self in its various modes draws on a variety of terms, including *kĕlāyôt* (the kidneys) for emotion, *yād* (hand, forearm) for effective power, and *regel* (foot) for constancy, presence, or control. Each of these terms can serve as the equivalent of the personal pronoun, as can *ʿayin* (eye) or *ʾōzen* (ear) when the aspect of seeing/recognizing or hearing is the foregrounded mode of the self. Nor is even this list exhaustive but merely illustrative.[19]

Though Wagner's caution is a good one, the various terms are, of course, not equivalent in significance, and *lēb* and *nepeš* do seem to have a particular role to play in the representation of the self in Israelite discourse, with *rûaḥ* taking on an increased significance in some Second Temple texts.[20] A recent dispute about the conceptualization of *lēb* in relation to other body parts is helpful in framing some of the questions I wish to pursue in this book. The role of the heart as the locus of feeling, willing, and thinking is well established. It is the organ that has a role both in what we might term the subjective experiential aspect of the self and in its agential aspect. But it is also the case that various other organs of the body can be spoken of in some passages as though they had intention, appetite, attitude, and agency. For example, Prov 6:17–18 refers to "haughty eyes, a lying tongue, hands that shed innocent blood, a heart that devises evil plots, feet that hurry to run to evil." How seriously should one take what appears to be disposition and agency distributed throughout the body? Are these expressions indications of a somatic psychology in which the self is thought of as a site of multiple subindividual impulses? Or is this simply a form of synecdoche, in which the self as a whole can be represented as active in the organ that represents the disposition or behavior in question? Most scholars favor the latter interpretation, and Janowski, in particular, has argued strongly that the prevailing biblical conception of the human is holistic, manifested in a "principle of relationality" between the heart and other organs.[21] In a recent essay, however, Thomas Krüger took issue with the consensus, arguing for a less integrated view of the person. While he attributes the same basic functions to the heart, he sees the representation of the heart as "distinguishing between different parts or aspects of the human being—such as his inside and his outside, his center and his periphery, his reason and his affects."[22]

It may be helpful to recast the issues about the representation of the self in this debate by means of a heuristic originally formulated by William James in *The Principles of Psychology* (1890) and in *Psychology* (1892).[23] James differentiated the self as subject of experience ("I") from the self as object of experience ("Me"). The "I" is "that which at any given moment *is* conscious, whereas the 'Me' is only one of the things which it is conscious *of*."[24] This fundamental ability of consciousness to engage in self-referential cognition is fundamental to human psychic existence, and James's distinction, variously nuanced, is frequently used in contemporary neuroscientific studies of consciousness and the phenomenal self.[25] Human beings, of necessity, represent ourselves to ourselves, and in so doing we construct ourselves as object. Some of these "Me" representations have to do with our social self ("my family," "my possessions," "my reputation"), some have to do with our bodily self ("my arm," "my pain"), and some have to do with our mental, volitional, and emotional self ("my thoughts," "my fears," "my willpower"). The self as subject of experience or the self as knower ("I") turns out to be quite an elusive concept, since as soon as one attempts to represent it, it, too, has become an object, a "Me." Granted that state of affairs, there are some self-representations that are close stand-ins for the "I" in our discourse about the self.[26] Other "Me" terms, however, may construct the self more as an other-object. Such representations have also been examined from the perspective of cognitive metaphor by Mark Johnson and George Lakoff, who use the terms "subject" and "self" or "selves" to distinguish between the "I" and the "Me."[27] Although the existence of this phenomenon is certainly universal for humans, particular formulations may be flexible and dynamic both across cultures and within cultures.

Both Janowski and Krüger would agree that the heart is one of the primary representations of the "I" of a person. But they disagree—in my reformulation—about the extent to which other body terms (e.g., "eyes," "lips," "mouth," "hands," "feet") are better thought of in terms of "I" or as object-aspects of the "Me" that have to be acted upon by the "I." Having reviewed the discussions, I think that Janowski has the better of the argument, at least in most cases.[28] To be sure, in a proverb like Prov 16:23 ("The heart of the wise makes his mouth effective, and adds persuasiveness to the lips," *lēb ḥākām yaśkîl pîhû; wĕʿal-śĕpātāyw yōsîp leqaḥ*) a basic "I-Me" trope is used to describe the relation of thinking and speaking. The use of *yaśkîl* and *leqaḥ* may suggest an implicit teacher-pupil metaphor for the relation of heart and mouth/lips (cf. Ps 16:7). But the proverb appears to describe a unified agential act, which I take to be the point of Janowski's claim about the "holistic" self. There are, however, a few instances that Krüger notes in which the rhetoric constructs a more differentiated psychic self. Job 31 provides two of the best examples: "I have made a covenant with my eyes, so how should I gaze upon a maiden" (v. 1), and "If my heart followed after my eyes . . ." (v. 7). The image of making a covenant recasts the desiring and constraining aspects of the psyche in social terms, much as Laban and Jacob make a covenant to regulate their relationship and set limits to the actions of both (Gen 31:44–54). In Job 31:1 the image clearly alludes to the setting of a limit to the freedom of the eyes to do what they wish. "Following after" typically describes the action of a person in pursuing a course of action with respect to an external object. Although it may be positive or negative, the rest of verse 7 indicates that the referent is to a wrongful action ("so that a stain clung to my hands"). Here the eyes and the heart represent different impulses within the same person, and the act of moral self-control is represented by means of an "I-Me" differentiation.

Clearly, the somatic anthropology of ancient Israel establishes a rich vocabulary full of potential for articulating inner self-relations. Although it is certainly the case that ancient Israelites experienced inner conflict about proper courses of action, intuitively engaged in self-monitoring, and exercised effortful control in subordinating certain impulses, they appear not to have been particularly interested as a culture in *representing* these inner-psychic phenomena. In Second Temple literature, however, especially in the middle Second Temple period, one can identify a much more marked interest in exploring the experience of a nonunified psyche and inner conflict, as I will discuss in later chapters. In various texts the *bricoleurs* of Second Temple Judaism exploit some of the previously undeveloped potential in traditional somatic anthropology. Even the heart can find itself sometimes displaced from its role as stable "I" and recast as the problematic "Me." These developments of the "I-Me" relationship become one of the tools for constructing a more self-reflexive form of thought, a form of introspective practice.

Sociocentric and Egocentric Models of the Self

Though there has been more agreement than disagreement about the somatic anthropology in ancient Israel, the issue of how to assess the significance of the socially embedded nature of the Israelite self has generated significant controversy. One of the most common modes of classifying the self-models of cultures is according to the extent to which the self is conceptualized as an individual or in strongly social or relational terms. An older cultural evolutionary perspective current in the first half of the twentieth century posited that ancient and "primitive" societies possessed minds that were not fully developed and so did not grasp realities in the same way as modern minds, including the nature of the self and its relation to the social group.[29] In biblical studies this stance had its most influential expression in H. Wheeler Robinson's notion of "corporate personality."[30] The term is actually drawn from a legal concept in which corporate responsibility could be attributed to all members of a group for the malfeasance of one (e.g., the punishment of all of Achan's household for his guilt in Josh 7). Robinson did not restrict the understanding to legal matters, however, but extended the notion to suggest that the mentality of the ancient Israelite did not differentiate between the individual and the group but merged the one into the other. Robinson's model found its way into a variety of scholarly analyses through the 1960s. A vigorous critique by John Rogerson largely discredited Robinson's reconstruction of ancient Israelite corporate personality,[31] though Christian Frevel has suggested that Robinson's ideas continue to influence contemporary descriptions of Israelite cultural models of the self in subliminal ways.[32]

Analogously, in the fields of anthropology and social psychology, even though notions of "the primitive" or "the savage" were rejected at an early stage,[33] a keen interest remained in identifying cultural variations in the anthropology of the self. One major focus from the 1970s onward was reflected in a variety of attempts to distinguish between sociocentric and egocentric models of the self.[34] Oftentimes these were framed as distinctions between a "western" and a "nonwestern" self. Though these labels are highly problematic in themselves, the "nonwestern" model was deemed to be characteristic of eastern, traditional, and premodern cultures. One of the most influential formulations is that of Clifford Geertz, who characterized the egocentric or western self as a

> bounded, unique, more or less integrated motivational and cognitive universe, a dynamic center of awareness, emotion, judgment, and action organized into a distinctive whole and set contrastingly both against other wholes and against a social and natural background.[35]

Geertz contrasted this western self with the sociocentric self as he perceived it in Bali, which is less a "person" than a "persona":

> . . . it is the dramatis personae, not actors, that endure; indeed that in a proper sense really exist . . . the masks they wear, the stage they occupy, the parts they play, and . . . the spectacle they mount remain and constitute not the facade but the substance of things, not least the self.[36]

Although not all societies are as "theatrical" as Bali, Geertz's general perception of the difference between western and other societies was widely shared. In the "western" model, it was argued, the self is centered in the individual ego; in other societies it is invested in the social role. One of the most influential attempts to give social scientific grounding to this differentiation is the study by Hazel Rose Markus and Shinobu Kitayama, "Culture and the Self," which contrasted Japanese and American self-construals. Though their preferred categories are the "interdependent" and "independent" self, their analysis complemented that of Geertz and others. As they characterize these two types, the interdependent self

> is viewed as *inter*dependent with the surrounding context, and it is the "other" or the "self-in-relation-to-other" that is focal in individual experience. . . . Thus one's actions are more likely to be seen as situationally bound, and characterizations of the individual will include his context. . . . [T]he expression and the experience of emotions and motives may be significantly shaped and governed by a consideration of the reaction of others.[37]

By contrast, the independent self in western cultures presents

> a view of the individual as an independent, self-contained, autonomous entity who (a) comprises a unique configuration of internal attributes (e.g., traits, abilities, motives, and values) and (b) behaves primarily as a consequence of these internal attributes.[38]

One of the implications of the typology embraced by Markus and Kitayama is that the cultivation of what one might call inner experience would be more characteristic of the independent rather than the interdependent self, and thus of the modern western self more than the eastern, traditional, or ancient self.

In biblical studies a strikingly similar analysis appeared in the influential essay by Robert Di Vito,[39] although Di Vito oriented his work less to the anthropological tradition than to the work of the moral philosopher Charles Taylor and his analysis of the origins and development of the modern western self.[40] In contrast to the modern self, which is characterized by "radical disengagement from one's personal and social location in the world,""sharply defined personal boundaries,""inner depths," and "a capacity for autonomous and self-legislative action," the construction of personhood in the Old Testament, Di Vito argued, is one in which

> the subject (1) is deeply embedded, or engaged, in its social identity, (2) is comparatively decentered and undefined with respect to personal boundaries, (3) is relatively transparent, socialized, and embodied (in other words, is altogether lacking in a sense of "inner depths"), and (4) is "authentic" precisely in its heteronomy, in its obedience to another and dependence upon another.[41]

In Di Vito's view the ancient Israelite self would be a classic instance of the sociocentric self.

Though the basic perception of a difference between cultures with a more interdependent model of the self and a more independent one is widely accepted as a generalization, criticism of the positions as articulated by Geertz, Markus and Kitayama, and others making similar arguments has been sharp. The critiques can be grouped under several headings: (1) conceptual confusion about the category of the "self" or "person," so that the distinction between cultural models, self-presentation, self-representation, and subjective experience is overlooked; (2) caricature and reductionism in describing the cultural models, especially the "western" model, which overlooks extensive evidence for the social embeddedness and other-directedness of many cultural norms for selfhood in modern western countries; (3) the tendency toward reification of the types such that cultural diversity, historical and social change, and individual negotiation of and resistance to cultural norms are obscured; and (4) the inadequacy of a typology with only two types.[42] Charles Lindholm pointed the way toward a more nuanced understanding of the self in culture, arguing that rather than reified cultural types, "the differing actions, beliefs, and motivations of individuals in the East and the West can best be understood not as due to a mysterious 'self' but as reasonable and predictable human responses to divergent patterns of power and constraint."[43] Similarly, Dorothy Holland and her coresearchers developed a "practice theory" of self and identity. Culturally normative models of the self are certainly one important influence on the development of self-identities, Holland argues. These are only some of the "living tools of the self," however, and one must recognize that "the loci of self-production or self-process" are plural.[44] Thus a person is always negotiating and codeveloping a sense of self and identity in a dynamic fashion. It would be a mistake to assume that culturally normative models are themselves static or that they are simply replicated in individuals.

Just as the "culturalist" theories about the self in anthropology have been questioned, so Di Vito's discussion of the Israelite self has been the focus of significant critique by Christian Frevel, among others. Frevel sees in Di Vito's sociocentric account a persistence of the old notion of "corporate personality,"[45] though it is more immediately the heir to the exaggerations of the sociocentric accounts of anthropological and social psychological studies of the 1970s and 1980s. Like those studies, Di Vito's model tends to merge the individual into the social to such an extent that "apart from the place in society one occupies there is no marker of personal identity, no 'inner depths,' to provide identity with characteristic content."[46] As Frevel notes, however, such an account is neither sociologically plausible nor ethnologically supported. If one does not posit personal identity, then it is not possible to account for how a social role would even get unified with the I-identity.[47] Moreover, ample textual evidence from the Hebrew Bible makes the more extreme articulations of the Israelite self as radically sociocentric implausible. The biblical narratives repeatedly feature accounts of social strife within family units (e.g., Jacob and Esau, Joseph and his brothers, the sons of David), protagonists who seek personal advancement or make personal choices that challenge or disrupt social ties (e.g., Jacob, Ruth), or protagonists whose identity and significance are developed in ways that are almost wholly separate from that of family (e.g., Samuel, Nehemiah, Daniel). These narratives do not condemn such expressions of individual self-assertion. Most interesting in this regard is the book of Nehemiah. Its first-person sections have been compared to Egyptian "autobiographies," to the structure of lament psalmody, and more broadly to the cross-cultural development of various forms of biographical writing in the Persian era. Whatever its generic links,[48] the composition uses first-person narration to construct a form that Susan Niditch rightly refers to as a "memoir," whether or not the historical Nehemiah is its author. Both in content and in style, it is, as she terms it, a "self-story." Nehemiah is presented not simply as person but as personality.[49] Overall, the narrative tradition of ancient Israel can only be understood as the product of a culture that was aware of the ways in which persons have to negotiate between individual and social identities, individual desires and social expectations.

Problematic also is Di Vito's characterization of the way in which moral identity is configured in Israelite culture. One can certainly agree with him that "the community provides the *raison d'être* for individual action and concrete behavior."[50] Indeed, given that all humans in all cultures are fundamentally social animals, it is difficult to envision a society in which that would not be the normative ideal. But to conclude that "individual Israelites, disengaged from the socially determined roles which form the basis of their responsibility, are not 'selves' about whom one can speak meaningfully or whose actions one can meaningfully evaluate . . . , [that] only the socially embedded self, identified by membership in a 'father's house,' is a morally intelligible agent"[51] is both implausible on the face of it and simply not consistent with the textual evidence. The legal literature, for example, though it incorporates many references to social and familial structures, figures the individual agent ("whoever," "the one who," "if a man") as the one with whom the law is primarily concerned. It generally does not configure the agent in terms of his social role.

The wisdom literature also is difficult to square with Di Vito's characterization of moral identity. It is precisely because the individual *is* a moral agent with genuine personal choices to make that the literature of moral formation, such as one finds in Proverbs, is cast as strenuous persuasion. Moreover, though one can agree that the society was strongly hierarchical and that heteronomy was the cultural ideal, Proverbs' own rhetoric offers ample evidence of how difficult it was to establish. Though the various kinds of fools are negatively described, they provide indirect evidence for significant resistance to the cultural norms, much as recent ethnographies have shown the tensive relationship between sociocentric cultural norms and actual individual agency. But the Israelite evidence goes beyond this, as both Job and Qohelet provide examples of personae who model and explicitly defend autonomy of experience and judgment. Though Job does recognize the limits of his understanding in his final words, this confession in no way obscures the bold epistemological challenge he makes to the champions of tradition throughout the dialogues. As with the narrative literature, the evidence of the wisdom tradition suggests a more complex interplay between the claims of the social group and the agency of the individual.

Much the same could be said of Di Vito's claim that Israelites did not possess "inner depths" or exhibit self-conflict. Of course, one first needs to be clear as to what one means by that somewhat obscure term "inner depths." I take it to mean the capacity for self-reflexive investigation of one's own emotions and thoughts, and also an awareness of the possibility that one may not fully understand oneself (or, as it might be figured, one experiences a belated recognition that one has previously been ignorant of one's own motives, thoughts, or nature). Even before Augustine, there are impressive examples of the examination of one's thoughts and emotions in Greco-Roman literature.[52] But it is an overstatement to deny the existence of a sense of inner self in Israelite antiquity, even if it is not culturally salient to the same degree as in Greco-Roman elite traditions.

Cultural Practices of the Self in Poetic and Narrative Genres: An Overview

The focus of my attention in the following chapters is largely on the ways in which changes in understandings of moral agency develop and become the vehicle for new models of the self and self-experience in Second Temple Judaism. This approach is only one of many trajectories one might follow in exploring self-models in Second Temple Judaism, and I would not want to give the impression that it is *the* account of Second Temple Judaism's growing interest in the self. Thus in the final section of this chapter I want to sketch three contexts in which one can document the interest in representing mind and self in early Second Temple literature that differ from the trajectory I am primarily investigating. Perhaps they can serve as encouragements for research in different directions.

Recollections of Distress as a Vehicle for Retrospective Introspection: Psalm 73

In most of the psalter the expressions of distress in laments and the recollection of distress in thanksgiving psalms are, of course, performances of self designed to elicit response from the addressee (God) and perhaps from others who form an audience for the psalm.[53] They are thus *social* performances and not primarily designed as self-examinations. The structure, however, lends itself readily to an examination of psychological and cognitive distress, an option that perhaps first appears in Jeremiah 20:7–13, and then in more elaborate didactic psalms in the early Persian period, notably in Psalms 32, 39, and 73. In these psalms acts of metacognition are made central to the drama of the composition.[54] Psalm 73 is the most elaborate example.[55]

Opening with a proverbial saying (v. 1), Psalm 73's depiction of a recollected time of distress and its resolution forms the body of the psalm (vv. 2–20). The crisis it recalls, however, is one of inner spiritual conflict. The account begins with a retrospective judgment by the psalmist on his own previous views and mental states. "As for me, my feet had almost stumbled, my footsteps had nearly slipped" (v. 2). What he now judges wrong was that he had envied the arrogant and the wicked (v. 3), a perception that he describes for twelve entire verses (vv. 3–14), concluding with a vivid first-person-singular citation of his past emotion of cynical bitterness: "Truly it is for nothing that I have kept my heart pure and washed my hands in innocence, as I am afflicted every day, and each morning brings me punishment" (vv. 13–14). Since these are no longer (v. 2) the speaker's views, one must consider the purpose of such an extended passage, recreating the past mental state of the speaker and drawing him back into the experience. In effect, it functions as something like a spiritual exercise, creating and resolving a moral challenge by means of emotional engagement with the thoughts now judged to be wrongful and dangerous. In her essay "Prayer as Metacognitive Activity," anthropologist Tanya Luhrmann describes this process as one of framing and reframing an emotionally charged experience, so that it can be encountered through "imaginative immersion" but within a reframed narrative in which the danger is overcome. Thus the critical part of the account is how the improper thoughts were dispelled or resolved.

This part of the narrative begins in verse 15, a verse that presents one of the most psychologically and rhetorically complex moments in the psalm. The counterfactual introduction ("if I had said . . .") removes the speaker from full immersion in the past and resituates him as a critical observer of his own past state of mind. The verse appears to depict both his own impulse to speak and the counter inhibiting thought that caused him to refrain ("If I had said, 'I will say these things'—see! I betrayed the circle of your disciples," *'im-'āmartî 'ăsapĕrāh kĕmô; hinnēh dôr bānêkā bāgādtî*). Though it is possible that the understanding of the potentially negative social and ethical effects of the subversive speech is only now registered in retrospective awareness, some consideration kept him from speaking, and so this verse appears to recall his own inner debate at that time. This is an extraordinarily sophisticated representation of past thoughts, including the depiction of the inner processing of psychological conflict by means of the evaluation of a hypothetical subsequent state of affairs.

The psalmist has not yet said *how* he came to change his mind. He begins by recalling a failed attempt, again presented as a recollection of a past psychological state. "But when I considered how to understand this, it seemed a wearisome task in my eyes" (*wā'ăḥašbāh lāda'at z'ōt; 'āmāl hû' bĕʿēnay*, v. 16). Although the sentence is somewhat elliptical, the expression *ʿāmāl* ("wearisome task") suggests that the speaker refers to the difficult mental process of arguing with oneself, of dividing the mind so that one is aware of one set of thoughts and beliefs and then sets up a heuristic alternate self who thinks and believes differently and can argue against one's presenting thoughts.[56] The effort does not prove successful in resolving the tension. The change in cognition comes "when I entered the sanctuary of God, and I reflected on their fate" (*ʿad-ʾābôʾ ʾel-miqdĕšê-ʾēl; ʾābînāh lĕʾaḥărîtām*, v. 17). The text indicates nothing more specific than the change of location as responsible for the change in thoughts.[57] But the power and persuasiveness of thoughts and beliefs are often conditioned upon environmental and social-contextual cues. In ordinary public places where the wealth, good fortune, arrogance, and violence of the impious are prominently on display, the idea that their lawlessness is rewarded seems more persuasive. In the sanctuary, where the symbolic reminders of the divine are present in physical and sensorial immediacy, the thoughts congruent with ideals of divine justice are simply easier to think. The *ʿāmāl* of resolving the cognitive dissonance itself dissolves, and the speaker can reframe his thoughts (vv. 18–20).

The psalmist concludes the exploration of his cognitive experiences with one final contrast. Verses 21–24 are variously construed as part of the speaker's retrospective reflection, general statements, and future affirmations, or reflections that begin with the past but continue to describe present reality and future expectation. The negative critique the psalmist gives of his own cognitive capacities in verses 21–22, however, is best understood as part of his self-critical retrospective. If one takes verse 23 as also referring to the conditions of the past, then the speaker acknowledges a second, at-the-time unrecognized agency that was guiding him in the right direction. "Yet I was always with you, you held my right hand; you guided me by your counsel, and afterward you received me in honor" (*waʾănî tāmîd ʿimmāk; ʾāḥaztā bĕyad-yĕmînî; baʿăṣātĕkā ḥanḥēnî; wĕʾaḥar kābod tiqqāḥēnî*, vv. 23–24). Since these verses immediately follow the psalmist's description of his subhuman state of understanding and confused emotion (vv. 21–22), they appear to describe why the speaker did not utter his despairing words (v. 15) and why, in the midst of his mental struggle, he went to the temple and experienced relief (vv. 16–20). If so, then these words represent another sophisticated representation of a complex mental state. The speaker is saying that he is *now* aware of a past divine assistance that was at the time unknown and unknowable but that was in fact operative in directing him.[58]

The speaker recognizes that he was not the sole agent in his own mind and actions, though now he acknowledges the process of shared agency and cognition that brought him to his present insight into reality. Although only a small number of psalms make representation and analysis of prior mental states central to their representation of self-experience, the sophistication exhibited by Psalm 73 suggests that the author of this psalm had some prior models upon which to draw. Indeed, the speaker presents himself and his experience as a model from which others can learn, an instantiation of the proverb of God's goodness to the pure of heart with which he began the psalm. His psalm is itself a fulfillment of his intent to "recount all your works" (v. 28). The rhetorical framing is much the same in Psalm 32. Public presentations of this sort direct cultural attention to and increase cultural fluency in certain ways of attending to one's own thoughts and dispositions. They are not simply reflections of but also tools for changing the nature of subjective experience.[59]

Representing Mental States: Dramatizing Cognitive Dissonance in Job

If one uses formal criteria to compare the dialogues of Job with the dialogue in the Babylonian Theodicy, they are strikingly similar. But if one looks at the dramatization of emotional and cognitive suffering, including inner conflict, then Job stands in stark contrast to the Babylonian Theodicy. The elaborate vividness and verbal inventiveness in the Joban speeches are striking. This difference suggests that a cultural taste for the representation of complex emotional states had developed by the early Persian period, when Job was most likely written.[60] One could choose almost any speech by Job to illustrate the interest in depicting extreme psychological distress. Although the author of Job was able to draw on a tradition of rather formulaic cultural traditions for representing psycho-physical distress found in the psalmic lament traditions, the novel and often bizarre ways in which such distress is represented in Job suggest that the author was deliberately transcending the received aesthetic conventions and seeking new forms of representation that render states of mind more complex than those presented in lament psalms.

One of the recurring literary devices in the book of Job is the use of what one might call emotional gapping. The abrupt shift in Job's self-representation between chapters 1–2 and 3 opens up a gap in the emotional psychology of the character and gives him dramatic depth. How is it that Job moves from saying, "Should we accept only good from God and not accept what is bad?" (2:10) to saying, "Damn the day on which I was born" (3:3)? All the author offers is the statement that Job and his three friends had been sitting for seven days in silence before Job's outburst in 3:3. Withholding representation of Job's mental processes only draws attention to their existence. The narrative is bookended by a similar profound change that is also signaled but not described in the notoriously enigmatic 42:1–6 that is then juxtaposed with the narrative in 42:7–17, in which Job's actions perform his acceptance of the comfort and consolation that he had resisted from the friends' efforts (2:11). Lest one dismiss the psychological interest in abrupt changes of mental states as simply an unplanned effect of a hypothetical redactional process, it should be noted that one of the frequent dramatic devices in the author's representation of Job in the dialogues is the rapid transition from one emotional state to another—from confident hope to deep despair to defiance and back again (e.g., 13:17–28; 14:7–22; 19:1–27; 23:1–17). Though the psychological changes at the beginning and end of the book serve narrative purposes and initiate rather long-lasting mental states, the ones within Job's speeches are repetitive and so appear to represent a different psychological phenomenon—cognitive dissonance. Martin Buber brilliantly articulated the theological content of this aspect of Job's words when he observed that "[Job] believes now in justice in spite of believing in God, and he believes in God in spite of believing in justice."[61] But the aesthetic problem for the author was how to represent cognitive dissonance in a character's speech. Israelite anthropology did not allow for the solution available to the Egyptian author of the Dialogue of a Man with his Ba, in which the dialogue form could be transferred to the different aspects of the self. Nor did the author attempt a version of self-reporting of thoughts, as in the presumably later Qohelet. Instead, he dramatizes thoughts in the process of being thought.

In some of the passages Job's contradictory ideas simply appear to be abruptly juxtaposed, but in others one can discern how one thought invites a counterthought, often through the multivalent potentialities of central images. In chapter 23, for example, the trope that runs through the chapter is that of presence. The desire for presence before God ("O that I knew where I could find him," v. 3) leads to imagining presence and the testimony that would clear Job (vv. 4–7). But the counterfactual nature of his longing reasserts itself in the denial of the possibility of presence, leading to despondency (vv. 8–9). This, in its turn, is displaced by hopefulness as Job reverses the perspective on seeking presence in the recognition that God "knows the way I take" (v. 10a), allowing Job to envision a successful examination by God (vv. 10b–12). But even if Job is transparent to God in such an examination, God's intentions remain opaque ("whatever he desires," "what he appoints for me," vv. 13–14). Consequently, it is God's very presence that terrifies Job (vv. 15–16). Whether there is a final swerve is uncertain, since the semantic and grammatical difficulties in verse 17 can be resolved in quite different ways, but the double repetition of *pānîm* in that verse suggests that some additional play with the governing trope is involved.

In chapter 13 the organizing trope is the trial at law. As Job explores the idea, he builds an image of God's justice that emboldens him (vv. 3–12), though in verses 13–16 the dissonant ideas of God's justice and arbitrary power are jammed against one another, however one resolves the ambiguity of verse 15. Beginning with verse 17, however, as Job articulates his case, he grows increasingly confident. But at what point does his confidence flag, so that by the end of the chapter he is in despair? As he begins to make his accusations against God (vv. 24–27), he constructs an image of a God in pursuit (v. 25) who obsessively watches (v. 27), using the image of "windblown leaf" and "dried up straw" to characterize himself (v. 25). His difficulty is that in giving voice to his accusation, he gives voice to the problem, which then takes over his imagination. In the last verse of chapter 13 and throughout chapter 14, the imagery shifts to the ontological difference between God and human and between the relentless divine scrutiny and power and human ephemerality and susceptibility to judgment (e.g., 14:1–6). The resurgence of hope comes by envisioning a way of blocking the coming into contact of these two opposites ("hide me . . . conceal me" [v. 13]; "would not count . . . or keep watch," "sealed up, coat over" [vv. 16–17]). The final set of images even envisions the human with the image of something immeasurably strong—a mountain—yet even that is destroyed by the relentless erosion that takes place when divine and human come into contact (vv. 18–22).

There are, of course, other places where one can identify Job's cognitive dissonance, perhaps none more disorienting than in the third cycle of speeches, where Job appears to articulate the "fate of the wicked" speeches that his friends have given (24:2–17, contrasting with vv. 18–25 and 27:13–23), even as he swears to speak the truth, taking an oath by "God who has deprived me of justice, Shaddai who has embittered my life" (27:2). Scholarly attempts to dissolve the head-spinning dissonance are misplaced. The contradiction is at the heart of Job's emotional and cognitive experience.[62] Though this contradictoriness has most often been examined through the lens of the content of what Job says, one can learn much about the interest of Second Temple culture in the psychology of cognitive dissonance by attending more closely to the ways in which the author of Job attempted to find an aesthetic means of representing such experience.

Theory of Mind in Israelite and Second Temple Narrative

A growing interest in the examination of mental states also appears in narrative literature of the early Persian period. In most of the narratives that are typically dated to the First Temple period, characters seldom speculate about the thoughts and beliefs of other characters.[63] Occasionally, especially in narratives about deception, where the engendering of false beliefs in another is of the essence, the effects of the false beliefs are dramatized. When Jacob deceives Isaac, for example, narrative interest is created through depicting parallel scenes in which Isaac doubts, but overcomes his doubts about the identity of the son who serves him food ("The voice is the voice of Jacob, but the hands are the hands of Esau," Gen 27:22), only to realize when Esau comes that he has been deceived (27:33). But for the most part, even in the deception narratives, little attention is given to the psychology of the deceived.[64] A more sophisticated use of theory of mind (that is, characters speculating on the mental states and beliefs of other characters) occurs in the narrative of David's rise in a scene when David and Jonathan discuss Saul's disposition toward David (1 Sam 20). When David asks what he has done to make Saul wish to kill him, Jonathan protests that Saul tells him everything and would not conceal such a matter from him. But David then tells Jonathan what *David* thinks *Saul* is thinking about what *Jonathan* would think if *Jonathan* knew *Saul's* state of mind, an extremely complex example of theory of mind. "Your father knows well that you are fond of me and has decided: Jonathan must not learn this or he will be grieved" (1 Sam 20:3; NJPS here and below). Jonathan undertakes to learn Saul's true state of mind at the feast of the new moon. The narrator, too, demonstrates interest in depicting Saul's own uncertain state of mind as he attempts to assess David's absence. "'It's accidental,' he thought. 'He must be unclean and not yet cleansed'" (v. 26). Yet it is clear that Saul is not successful in persuading himself with this explanation of David's absence. The following day, when Jonathan lies to Saul about the reasons for David's absence, Saul's reply also indicates his own projection of what he takes Jonathan's motives to be: "I know that you side with the son of Jesse—to your shame and to the shame of your mother's nakedness!" (v. 30). One could find additional examples of this kind of sophisticated representation of theory of mind in other episodes of the David narratives. Such practices of theory of mind are, in fact, essential to the complex social life that humans enjoy and played an important role in the evolution of early humans. There is no reason to think that actual Israelites were any less adept at them than modern persons. So it is not surprising to find occasional attention to the phenomenon in narrative literature. But by and large, preexilic Hebrew narrative does not make mindreading the focus of narrative interest.

Increasingly, however, in Persian and Hellenistic period narratives, one can see an interest in depicting and enjoying scenes involving theory of mind. Both Tobit and Judith engage the audience by depicting a state of affairs disclosed to the audience but unknown to one of the characters. Readers take pleasure in knowing that Tobias interacts with Raphael without understanding who Raphael is. Similarly, readers join Judith in enjoying the fact that Holofernes misconstrues her motives and tactics and is taken in by her misrepresentation of God's intentions toward the people of Bethulia (Jud 11). When Holofernes expresses concern that the meager provisions she has brought will not last, she replies truly but in a manner that plays on the false assumption she has created in his mind—because *she* understands what *he* wrongly thinks to be the case: "As surely as you live, my lord, your servant will not use up her supplies before the Lord accomplishes by my hand what he has determined" (Jud 12:4; NABR). The audience's pleasure derives precisely from the author's constructing a character's mistaken state of knowledge with the audience being "in the know." So, too, in Esther, Ahasuerus's misunderstanding of Haman's throwing himself upon Esther as attempted rape depends upon the audience's grasp of how comedy (or sweet revenge) often depends on mental misunderstandings. In Daniel 2 the (im)possibility of reading the king's mind concerning his dream is key to the development and resolution of the conflict.

A more central role for theory of mind informs the entire premise of the book of Job. The plot of the prose story of Job turns on the fact that Job's state of mind—whether he "fears God for nothing" or not—is unknown and unknowable to the characters of God and the Adversary. Nor does the audience know, though the audience may initially think it does. The prose tale seems to confirm one supposition, only to have that surmise increasingly complicated by the dialogues. The ambiguity of Job's final answer in Job 42:6 may be an intentional tease of the audience's desire to finally resolve the state of Job's mind. In Ruth and Jonah also, authors play with the reader's desire to discern the characters' mental states and intentions. In Ruth, the enigmatic exchanges between Ruth and Naomi at the beginning and end of chapter 3 and between Ruth and Boaz on the threshing floor in the middle of the chapter appear to be intentionally designed to require the reader to work at making hypotheses about the thoughts and intentions of characters who are presented, as often in real life, through ambiguous forms of disclosure. In Jonah, the entire premise of the book is based on the author's setting the reader up to make an inaccurate judgment about Jonah's mental state, an assumption that is suddenly overturned at the very end of the story. The clever ways in which authors of the early Second Temple period make use of theory of mind to create narrative pleasure, construct characters who are difficult to know, and even pull surprises on the audience suggest a growing cultural appetite for thinking about thinking.

Although there is ample evidence for a basic cultural model of the self in ancient Israel, including dimensions of interiority, it is also the case that in First Temple literature only modest attention is given to describing aspects of or cultivating practices for self-observation and introspection. As I have attempted to demonstrate in a preliminary fashion, however, a noticeable increase in interest in the cultural significance of the self appears to be a feature of Second Temple literature, even in texts from the Persian period. Although such an interest is attested in diverse ways in a variety of genres, a particularly significant strand of attention focuses on the self in relation to the problem of moral agency. Before examining moral agency, however, it is necessary to look at the phenomenon of agency in general.

2 Agency in Biblical Narrative

Agency in Cross-Cultural Perspective

It is impossible to talk about the self without talking about agency. But just as the self is both a transcultural, neurophysiological phenomenon and a culturally inflected one, so is agency. At its most basic, agency is both the capacity to act and the sense of being able to act. It is a fundamental property of the sense of "Me" that all humans possess.[1] At the same time agency is commonly a social phenomenon, involving coordination with others.[2] Agency, even when it subjectively feels autonomous, may nevertheless be exercised within the sphere of various influences of which the subject may be conscious or unconscious.[3] Given the complexity of the phenomenon, it is not surprising that various cultures develop a wide variety of ways of representing agency.

In a helpful study Paul Heelas and Andrew Lock suggested a way of mapping various cultural theories of self and agency according to two fundamental coordinates. One has to do with *location*, that is, where agency is thought to reside. The other has to do with *control*, whether the self is "in" control or "under" control.[4] That is to say, is agency "in" the person who acts? Or does agency come from a force outside the person? If it is inside the person, is it thought to be simply an expression of the whole, undifferentiated person? Or is the source of agency envisioned as some objectified entity within a person, such as the ancient and medieval theory of the humors or certain Greek models that conceive of the forces acting within the self as divided among reason, passion, and appetites? In such cases agency is envisioned as a complex phenomenon, one that may or may not include some sort of executive function that negotiates among the different internal forces that would act upon or through the person. But agency may also be envisioned as located outside the person, as in cultures such as the Dinka, which considers the world of spirits to be the source of agency and the person as the object acted upon.[5] When agency is envisioned as external, it is most often associated with a sense of the self being under the control of this external agent. When agency is envisioned as internal, a wide spectrum of ways of thinking about control is possible. All systems, however, have some way of representing the two fundamental experiences of agency: the sense of being able to act and the sense of constraints on acting.[6] How these are represented and the balance between them allow for a large number of variations.

As helpful as this heuristic set of coordinates can be, it obviously understates the complexity and flexibility of ways of representing agency that exist in any culture and the purposes for which such representations are used in different situations. For example, deflecting or displacing agency from oneself to a supernatural agent may be a means of claiming authority for an action ("God moved me to do this") or of evading responsibility ("the devil made me do it!") or of pursuing some other socially advantageous goal. More broadly, different kinds of discourse—narrative, hortatory, legal—will represent or feature different aspects of agency that are relevant to the purposes of that discourse. In order to build up a thick account of agency in the Hebrew Bible, it is best to begin with a particular type of discourse and to be mindful of how the purposes of that discourse will bring into focus certain aspects of the culture's thinking about agency.

Agency in Narrative

As an attempt to render events as a meaningful pattern, narrative is by its nature concerned with agency. Narrative is given its momentum by tracing the arc of agential acts and how they interact with other such acts, whether in coordination or in conflict. In addition, the act of narrating is itself an agential act, as the shape and sequence of events and the degree of information provided or withheld are coordinated by the author. Within a given narrative or narrative tradition, however, agency may be simply part of the taken-for-granted nature of reality, or it may be made the focus of dramatization or reflection. In the narratives of the Hebrew Bible, agency largely functions as a simple presupposition. Characters have desires, form intentions, make and execute plans, and deal with the consequences. But agency itself is only occasionally the focus of the drama or the subject of second-order reflection.

Who, however, counts as an agent? Humans are certainly agents, and God, too, is an agent, though one who acts in certain distinctive ways. The agential status of angels is less clear, since their narrative function is largely to carry out the intentions of God, though in Gen 6:1–4 they seem to act on their own intentions, and in Second Temple literature their agential nature will be exploited in fuller fashion. Animals are only rarely represented as agents in narrative—Balaam's ass being the notable exception. In the legal literature it appears that animals are sometimes treated as agents in that they are held accountable for their actions, as in the case of the goring ox in Exodus 21:28. It is not merely killed but killed by stoning, a means of executing humans; moreover, its flesh is not eaten, suggesting that its being treated as an agent removes its body from the category of meat. In general, though, animals do not seem to be treated as agents in Hebrew tradition. Natural forces are a more complicated issue. Joshua addresses a command to the sun and the moon to stop and stand still, and they do (Josh 10:12–13). In poetic literature natural phenomena are more frequently described in possibly agential terms. Heaven and earth may be called as witnesses (Deut 4:26; 30:19; 32:1), and mountains, hills, and the foundations of the earth are called to hear a judicial case (Mic 6:1–2). Mountains and hills may shout, and trees clap their hands (Isa 55:12), though it is possible that some of these descriptions are merely poetic personifications. Basic cosmic structures and meteorological phenomena, however, may have been thought to be spirit-agents (Ps 104:3–4). Certainly in later Second Temple literature they were conceived of as either spirit-agents or entities directed by spirits (Jub 2:1–3). In narrative, however, such representations are very rare. Also to be considered is whether one should attribute agential nature to certain entities that play a role in ritual. How should one think about the blood Moses dashes upon the altar and the people in the covenant-making episode in Exodus 24:6–8? It seems to "do" something that could not be effected without its presence or by some other entity. Similarly, the ink of the curses that are dissolved into the water of bitterness in the ritual of the suspected adulteress in Numbers 5 seems to do something in response to the woman's innocence or guilt. Examples in narrative literature would include Aaron's rod (Exod 7:17–21), and the salt and flour Elisha drops in the spring and the pot (2 Kgs 2:19–22; 4:38–41). Though some scholars of ritual do wish to use the term "agency" for such entities or at least the rituals of which they are a part,[7] I choose not to include the blood and the water of bitterness and similar entities within the category of agents. Such things are more than mere instruments; they have *potency*. But I wish to restrict agency to those things that are represented as having intentions that they attempt to carry out. If Hebrew narrative or ritual texts had an entity comparable to the "sorting hat" in the Harry Potter novels, I would call that an agent. But I prefer to say that the blood and the water of bitterness, Aaron's rod, and Elisha's flour have potency but not agency. For the most part, the agency that will be the focus of my discussion with respect to narrative will be restricted to human agency and divine agency.

Subtypes of Agency

Although the body of narrative that runs from Genesis 12 through 2 Kings 25 is itself heterogenous with respect to date of composition, social location, and subgenre, its treatment of agency is more or less uniform, with certain exceptions (e.g., the narratives in Judges and in the Elijah-Elisha cycle). The same is true for the shorter narratives of the Second Temple period (e.g., Jonah, Ruth, Esther, Daniel 1–6, Tobit, Judith). For the time being I largely leave aside Genesis 1–11, which is more speculative in nature and will be the subject of a separate chapter.

Agency can be divided into subtypes in a variety of ways. For my purposes it is helpful to distinguish among *primary* or *individual* agency (a character intending and acting), *proxy* agency (characters attempting to get others to act on their behalf or in a desirable way), and *coordinated* or *co*-agency (characters acting together to achieve a goal). In addition, some narratives assume what one might call *dual* agency, in which divine agency shapes or coordinates human agency. This, too, is a form of co-agency, but one in which the human agent may not be aware of divine agency at work. Although the narratives frequently speak of corporate characters (e.g., "the Israelites," Joseph's "brothers"), little if any attention is given to specifically *corporate* agency, that is, agency that is vested in a supra-individual body, such as "the elders," where the agential action is taken by the body, whether or not all of the members are in agreement. The lack of such agency is probably incidental to the nature of the stories rather than reflecting the absence of corporate agency in ancient Israel. Corporate agency may be assumed when the nation is described as an entity (e.g., "all the tribes of Israel") and depicted as taking an action. More significantly, what one tends *not* to find in the Hebrew narrative tradition is what Laura Ahearn describes as subindividual agency, "as when someone feels torn within herself or himself."[8] One can find perhaps one or two possible examples (arguably but not definitively, 1 Sam 24:6–8; 1 Kgs 18:21). This absence of descriptions of inner conflict recalls the debate discussed in chapter 1 about the presence or absence of "interiority" in the ancient Israelite concept of the self. It is certainly not the case that ancient Israelites failed to experience conflicts within themselves about what actions to choose. Both at the neurophysiological and at the cultural level, intrapersonal conflict is a constituent of the human condition.[9] But it seems to be the case that, culturally speaking, ancient Israelites were simply not very interested in the phenomenon, at least not in representing it in narrative contexts. It will, however, become a topic of considerable interest in certain Second Temple didactic and prayer genres.

Proxy Agency

What does interest the authors of these narratives about human agency? Notably, proxy agency is represented multiple times. In proxy agency the actor cannot secure his or her goal directly but can only succeed by means of the agency of another. This attention is not surprising. One would expect an interest in proxy agency to be prominent in social contexts with a strong social hierarchy or gendered distribution of power, where structural features restrict direct agency for some individuals. One of the primary tools of proxy agency is persuasion. Thus Daniel and his friends wish to eat only foods that will not defile them, but in order to do so they must both persuade the officer in charge of them to look the other way and the guard who tends to them to exchange their food (Dan 1). Quid pro quo is another tool of proxy agency, as when Rahab hides the Israelite spies so that they are not captured (a goal they cannot achieve themselves) and in turn persuades them to spare her family when the Israelites attack Jericho, a goal she cannot secure without their action (Josh 2). Prayer is, of course, one of the primary means of proxy agency, as individuals ask God to act on their behalf to achieve an end they cannot achieve on their own, as when Isaac or Hannah asks God for children (Gen 25; 1 Sam 1).

More striking is the number of times that deception substitutes for persuasion in proxy agency. Abram does not want Pharaoh to kill him but cannot secure his own safety directly; thus he and Sarai lie about their relationship in order to influence Pharaoh's actions (Gen 12). Rebekah wishes to secure the primary blessing for Jacob, so she enlists Jacob to trick Isaac into giving him the blessing intended for Esau (Gen 27). Laban wishes for Jacob to marry Leah, though he knows Jacob has asked for Rachel, and so he deceives Jacob on his wedding night (Gen 30). The examples could be multiplied. Though there are many reasons for the attention given to proxy agency in the narratives, including imbalance of power, some of these narratives also illumine the issue discussed in chapter 1 about the relation between self-interest on the part of agents and the demands of a sociocentric society. Thus it is not surprising that the dramatic situation is repeated so frequently in narrative. Cultures often explore in fiction the type of issues they have to negotiate in life.

Although proxy agency can be identified as a focus of narrative interest by means of the level of detail in which the strategies of the actors are described, there is little or no secondary reflection on it. It is an important but well-understood phenomenon of social life. What attracts even more attention in the narratives, at the level of both plot and explicit comment, is the relationship between divine and human agency. This topic requires more attention in narrative because it is more elusive, more complex, and more important. Although Yhwh is represented in strongly anthropomorphic ways, Yhwh's means of acting are not coextensive with those of humans.

Divine Co-agency

Divine agency is most often featured in complex contexts where considerable contingency exists. In these situations people act as agents but are aware that, though their actions are necessary, they are not sufficient to achieve their outcomes. Thus the situations are implicitly conceptualized as divine agency acting in concert with human agency. Perhaps the most frequent occasion for the invocation of divine agency in contexts of contingency in the narrative literature is the outcome of battles. In the narratives about the judgeship of Gideon, human agency is explicitly minimized in order to highlight the role of divine agency. For example, in the narrative of Gideon's call, Gideon asserts his own insignificance as an objection, which is overcome through Yhwh's statement "I will be with you and you will strike down Midian to the last man" (Judg 6:16). When Gideon prepares to attack the Midianite camp, God instructs him to dismiss most of his troops, "lest Israel boast against me, saying, 'my own hand brought me victory'" (Judg 7:2). The narrative is not unaware of the psychological play of fear and confidence in swaying the course of battle (e.g., the anxious dream of the Midianite overheard by Gideon in vv. 13–14, the strategy of cacophonous noise and disorienting sudden lights that produces panic in the Midianite camp in vv. 16–22). But all of this is understood as an expression of the agency of Yhwh (cf. 1 Sam 14:6–15). Similarly, despite David's claim to Goliath that "Yhwh can give victory without sword or spear" (1 Sam 17:47), the narrative clearly describes David's own clever strategy for inflicting death from a safe distance (vv. 40, 48–50). Both agencies, the human and the divine, must act together to produce victory. When unexpected defeat occurs to well-armed troops, then inquiry is made into why God was not with the army, as Joshua 7 illustrates. A more complex narrative in which divine assurances must be trusted even when they do not seem effective and in which sophisticated human strategies are employed to turn the tide of battle is described in the eventual rout of the Benjaminites in Judges 20.

Divine co-agency also operates in the lives of individuals and families. Pregnancy is one such case. Though intercourse is a necessary action for pregnancy to occur, the highly contingent nature of pregnancy led to the conclusion that pregnancy is ultimately an act of divine agency in "opening the womb" (Gen 21:1–2; 25:21; 29:31; 30:1–2, 17, 22; Exod 1:20; Judg 13:2–5; 1 Sam 1:2–20). The tense exchange between Rachel and Jacob in Genesis 30:1–2 illustrates the ambiguity of agency in such cases. Rachel does seem to hold Jacob responsible for her childlessness, whereas his invoking of divine agency deflects this responsibility. Similarly, the role of divine agency in Leah's fertility (29:31) addresses an unresolved family tension. Agriculture, too, is a contingent matter, as anyone knows who has farmed or even planted a garden. Thus good agricultural yields and abundant flocks, even though they are in part the result of skill and hard work, are also seen as the result of the agency of divine blessing (Gen 24:35; 26:12–13).

One particularly instructive narrative demonstrates how the theme of interwoven divine and human agency serves overall narrative purposes and illustrates the usefulness of appeals to divine agency in social situations. Genesis 24 describes Eleazar's mission on Abraham's behalf to secure a wife for Isaac from his relatives in Paddan-Aram. Eleazar raises the issue of uncertain outcomes and how to deal with contingencies when he is assigned the task ("What if the woman does not agree to follow me to this land? Shall I take your son back to the land from which you have come?" Gen

24:5). Abraham seems to say two contradictory things. He assures Eleazar that God "will send his angel before you, and you will get a wife for my son from there" (v. 7), but in the next sentence entertains the possibility that the woman may refuse. When Eleazar arrives, he prays to God for a sign that will serve as an assurance of God's proxy agency to ensure success (vv. 12–14). A modest amount of suspense is added to the narrative as the young woman waters his camels and he wonders whether "Yhwh had made his journey successful or not" (v. 21), and when she identifies herself as daughter of Bethuel, Eleazar concludes that "Yhwh has indeed led me on the way" (v. 27). But nothing is yet assured. Within the story world it is assumed that Bethuel and Laban are free to refuse consent and that Rebekah is also free to refuse to go with Eleazar (vv. 39, 41, 49). Since he cannot simply take Rebekah, Eleazar must secure the proxy agency of the parties through persuasion. This he does by and large by constructing his narrative of the mission in terms of how divine agency has been present in Abraham's own flourishing (vv. 35–36), in Abraham's assurance of divine assistance (v. 40), and in the answer to his prayers at the well, confirming that his mission was divinely guided (vv. 42–48). Invoking the presence of divine agency so strongly serves as a powerful piece of persuasion. Though Eleazar notionally suggests that Bethuel and Laban are free to refuse, to do so they would either have to refute his claim of divine co-agency or risk opposing the will of God. Eleazar's rhetoric is presented as successful, for Bethuel and Laban frame their agreement not as their own decision but as a matter that has been determined by God ("the matter has been decreed by Yhwh; we cannot speak to you bad or good," v. 50). That is to say, they represent their own agency as having been preempted by God's. They suggest that it is not really in their power now to agree or disagree so much as to acknowledge. Clearly, one of the narrative's purposes in featuring divine agency so prominently is to persuade the reader of divine guidance in the events that led to the origins of the people of Israel. Thus one cannot assume that the narrative is a fully realistic depiction of the social uses of discourse about divine agency. But it is suggestive. All of the parties seem to assume that there may be problems in securing the outcome. Despite the advantages of the kinship marriage, the distance is formidable. Several different wills are involved—Abraham and Eleazar's, Bethuel and Laban's, Rebekah's, and the rest of the family's. Invoking divine co-agency in Abraham's plans not only gives Eleazar a persuasive strategy for overcoming reservations by Bethuel and Laban, but also gives Bethuel and Laban "cover" in the event that other family members object. Deferring or displacing one's own agency onto that of a divine actor creates a social space for things to happen that might be difficult to negotiate directly. It also legitimates the course of action that the actors desire.

An arguably more cynical instance of this appeal to divine agency is the account in Genesis 30–31 of Jacob's acquisition of wealth while in Laban's service and his subsequent flight. The story begins by highlighting Jacob's own shrewdness and cleverness in using sympathetic magic to produce the type of sheep and goats that he and Laban have agreed will be Jacob's wages (30:37–43). When Jacob needs to persuade Leah and Rachel to return to Canaan, however, he represents the events as wholly God's agency, obscuring his own role in the quite complicated strategy for producing the flocks (31:4–16). As persuasion, this account undoubtedly works better with Leah and Rachel than one that would set Laban over against Jacob in a contest of wits. While Jacob's speech certainly looks like cynical manipulation, and trickery is a prominent theme in his characterization throughout the narratives, it is also possible that both accounts would be understood as equally true, if the production of the flock was understood as a co-agency that might be described with focus on either the human or the divine participant.

A more nuanced example of the relation of human and divine agency is presented in the immediately preceding verses. The narrator describes an increasingly tense situation between Laban and his sons and Jacob. Clearly, it is time for Jacob to go. But rather than report that Jacob "decided" to leave, the narrator reports that "[t]hen Yhwh said to Jacob, 'Return to the land of your ancestors where you were born'" (v. 3). Biblical texts, unfortunately, do not reflect on the psychology of hearing the divine voice. The divine voice may be introduced into narrative without much contextualization (e.g., Gen 12:1; 15:1), but the frequency with which biblical narrative introduces the divine voice at moments where crucial and oftentimes socially controversial decisions must be made suggests that the divine voice may have served a variety of functions. Though it certainly serves literarily to justify and authenticate a writer's perspective on the right course of events, as in the story of David's rise (see, e.g., 1 Sam 15:16; 16:1, 7, 12; 23:2–12; 24:5), it is likely that the literary use is an extension of the way in which the divine voice functioned psychologically in ordinary life. That is to say, the divine voice may be the way in which the resolution of many complex considerations, uncertainties, and inner conflicts into a sense of certainty was experienced. I do not mean to be reductive or to "demythologize" but simply to note that where a modern secular folk psychology[10] would describe the process of coming to a momentous decision as a resolution of internal conflict or calculation of alternatives, the Israelite narrative tradition describes it differently. For the ancient Israelite author and audience, Jacob's consciousness in pondering what to do is merely implied. It is not a subject that they consider particularly interesting to explore in detail. The narrative, however, suggests that what this resolution felt like—and was taken to be—was a direction from an authoritative external source.[11] That the ancient writers understood the psychological dimensions of this phenomenon, however, is reflected in passages in which a character *wrongly* assumes he has discerned the divine intention (e.g., Saul in 1 Sam 23:7: "Saul was told that David had come to Keliah, and Saul thought, 'God has delivered him into my hands, for he has shut himself in by entering a town with gates and bars'"; NJPS). Notably, in these cases the narrator refrains from using the locution "Yhwh said," even though that might well have been Saul's perception. The complexities of false assumptions about the divine voice, including subjective experiences of divine direction, are examined more explicitly in narratives about prophetic claims, as I discuss below.

Unrecognized Divine Co-agency

Other narratives provide even more subtle and nuanced understandings of an agency that is shared between the person and God. One might pose the issue by asking why characters do certain things that turn out to have been very fortunate or very unfortunate, or that have ramifications beyond what they could have been aware of. The case of Abimelech of Gerar, Sarah, and Abraham in Genesis 20 can illustrate. Acting on the basis of his own desire and Abraham's misrepresentation, Abimelech takes Sarah into his household. But he does not have intercourse with her at the first opportunity. Why not? The narrative initially does not say. In the night God threatens Abimelech for having taken Sarah. He protests that his action was done in innocence. God acknowledges as much and says, "and so I held you back from sinning against me" by having intercourse with Sarah (v. 6). Abimelech acted agentially in not having sex with Sarah and undoubtedly could have given reasons for his decision had he been asked at that time. But he now learns that his actions were not in fact wholly his own. The decisive source of his inclination not to have sex with Sarah that night was actually God's agency subtly directing him. This situation is not a form of determinism but is better described as a form of subconscious co-agency. Other examples can be added. Samson's parents are mystified by Samson's preference for Philistine women and try to argue him out of his desire for the Timnite woman. Samson, however, is obdurate, though all he can say about his desire is "she is the one who pleases me" (Judg 14:3). The narrator, however, explains that it was "from Yhwh," because God was seeking a pretext against the Philistines (v. 4). There is no indication, however, that Samson was ever made aware of this motivation, as Abimelech was. Why do Eli's sons not listen to him when he rebukes them? "Because Yhwh wished to kill them" (1 Sam 2:25). Why does Absalom not listen to Ahitophel's counsel when he has David at a disadvantage? David has sent Hushai "undercover" to Absalom's camp in an attempt to undermine Ahitophel by giving contrary advice. So there is considerable human intentionality and agency at work. But why is Absalom persuaded by Hushai rather than Ahitophel? The story does not explain Absalom's reasoning, though doubtless he could have given a reason, if asked. Instead, the narrator explains that it was because "Yhwh had decreed that Ahitophel's better advice be nullified, in order that Yhwh might bring ruin upon Absalom" (2 Sam 17:14), apparently in response to David's prayer, "Please, Yhwh, frustrate Ahitophel's counsel" (2 Sam 15:31). And finally, why does David take the inexplicable act of ordering a census of the people and insist on it, even against Joab's advice to the contrary (2 Sam 24:1–4)? Even David himself later seems shocked at his own action ("his heart struck him," v. 10).

Narrative, of course, has a vested interest in constructing patterns of meaning out of the varied choices and actions of the characters, so it is not surprising that these moments when the course of action stands at a crossroads are declared to be governed by divine intentionality. But from the point of view of the characters, the implied psychology is perceptive. Humans often do not have full conscious access to their own motives for the impulses they feel and the choices they make, though we are all quite adept at supplying reasons when asked. But there is an unexplainable residue, an unsettling mysteriousness about the full sources of our desires and decisions. David knows that he has "acted foolishly" but does not know why he has done this inexplicable action. The Chronicler was so troubled by this story of divine entrapment that he not only displaces the source of the unconscious motive to "an adversary" or "Satan," depending on one's interpretation of the word, but also makes God's action in "striking" Israel precede

David's recognition that he has done something wrong (1 Chron 21:1–8). Second Samuel is the more psychologically intriguing account, since David apparently finds his own mind strange even before he is aware of the full consequences of his actions. The perception that one does not always understand one's own motivations and impulses is not limited to narrative, though it finds its most frequent representation there. Psalm 73, briefly discussed in the previous chapter, gives a thoughtful and detailed account of retrospective reflection on just such a psychological state. In the literature of the mid–Second Temple period, other genres will also take up the issue of belated understanding of one's own impulses.

The most notorious of these narratives of subconscious co-agency with disastrous results for the human agent is, of course, the hardening of Pharaoh's heart. The basic dynamics are announced to Moses in advance in Exodus 4:21: "When you return to Egypt, see that you perform before Pharaoh all the marvels that I have put within your power. I, however, will stiffen his heart so that he will not let the people go" (NJPS).[12] What seems to offend modern sensibilities is that our own sense of agency defaults to autonomous free agency. Thus the prior constraint of Pharaoh's agency seems manifestly unfair. Yet as folk models go, untrammeled, autonomous free agency is one of the most inadequate ever developed. It captures well the sense of being able to act, but it is poor in being able to address constraints on agency. Though this model may still enjoy a measure of popular acceptance, it has been significantly challenged not only by those masters of suspicion Marx and Freud but also by more recent social scientific experiments that indicate how deeply situationally constrained human choices actually are.[13] Neuroscientists, too, have documented the extent to which what prompts our choices is not consciously accessible ("motivational amnesia"). Thus both the reasons individuals give to themselves for their actions and, more broadly, the cultural folk theories, ranging from free will to karmic cause and effect to a theory of humors or divine determinism, are attempts to rationalize a process that is to a large extent opaque.[14] In Israelite folk psychology, as in much of modern western folk psychology, individual moral agency is assumed, even when there are larger forces at work influencing a person's choices. The individual experiences himself or herself as willing or intending an action, even if there is a known or unknown divine co-agent. One "owns" one's decisions, both experientially and morally. In the narrative about Pharaoh, his decisions are alternatively described as the result of God's hardening his heart (external causality) and Pharaoh's hardening his own heart (internal causality). Though it is not clear that Pharaoh is ever aware of the influences that have affected his agency, he takes responsibility for his actions: "I stand guilty before Yhwh your God and before you. Forgive my offense . . ." (10:16–17). To a certain extent this may reflect the way in which guilt was judged objectively rather than subjectively in antiquity, but even Abimelech protested at the discrepancy between his innocent intentions and his guilt, and Israelite law also made exceptions for a person who killed another and yet who did not premeditate or intend the death (Num 35:9–15; Deut 19:4–13; Josh 20:1–9). Pharaoh's case is more complex. He did intend the obstruction of the Israelites, even if he did not fully comprehend the origins of his intentions, and so he deems himself responsible.

One of the additional ways in which divine co-agency functions is to account for the charisma, good fortune, or unusual abilities of a character. An upward turn in Joseph's fortunes is described as occurring because "Yhwh was with Joseph, and he became a successful man" (Gen 39:2). This is not only information shared by the narrator with the reader but also represents Potiphar's assessment of the source of Joseph's success (v. 3; cf. v. 23). Closely related is the explanation for the positive attitude of others to the person, as when Yhwh "gave him favor in the eyes of the officer in charge of the prison" (v. 22). A similar explanation is given for the favorable disposition of the chief eunuch toward Daniel in Daniel 1:9, the Egyptians' attitude toward the Israelites as they prepare to depart Egypt in Exodus 3:21; 11:3; 12:36, and the captors of the people in Psalm 106:46. Those who are favorably disposed may or may not be aware of the role of the divine in prompting their dispositions.

A somewhat different aspect of the relation of divine and human agency is also addressed in the narrative about Joseph and his brothers. Although the narrative gives considerable attention to the various reasons behind characters' motives for actions (Jacob's preference for Joseph, the brothers' hatred of him, Potiphar's wife's spurned advances, etc.), at the end of the narrative Joseph explicitly addresses the phenomenon of dual agency, in which free, individual human actions are complexly orchestrated so that they come together to achieve a goal that none of the human actors intended or could have envisioned but that was the divine intention. In Joseph's words, "though you intended me harm, God intended it for good, so as to bring about the present result—the survival of many people" (Gen 50:20; NJPS). There is no minimizing of individual human agency. The brothers' intentions and actions (and, implicitly, those of all the other actors) are explicitly recognized as their own. Nor is there any suggestion here of direct divine direction of particular dispositions or actions, as in the case of Pharaoh. But even as individual agency is exercised in genuine freedom, an unperceived force draws these actions into a pattern that is determined in advance. The perception bears some resemblance to the ancient Greek notion of fate and its dramatization in Greek tragedies. Somewhat more explicit, since the fated outcome is couched as a divine oracle rather than an ex post facto reflection on events by one of the characters, is the response to Rebekah's inquiry about her difficult pregnancy. Even before birth, Jacob is fated to be stronger than Esau, who will serve him (Gen 25:23). The narratives then show how the choices made by each of the brothers lead to this foreordained end.

One should remember, however, that these statements are not *the* ancient Israelite model of agency. Rather, they pertain to one of a variety of ways of representing divine and human agency. The various models are conceptual options, tools available for specific purposes. Emphasizing the divine role serves well to authorize a special identity or destiny, as in Genesis, or to authorize the Davidic dynasty, as in the stories of David's rise to kingship. In other contexts, where narratives function in didactic, hortatory, or theodical fashion, the autonomous role of human agency may be described to emphasize human resistance, as one sees, for example, in Deuteronomistic narratives. Even if the different models are variously distributed, however, they are all part of the repertoire of available folk models and may be developed in new ways in new contexts.

Divine Spirit, Human Agency, and the Agential "Boost"

In the narratives described so far, reflection on the mechanisms by which a person acquires basic human agency or the means by which divine agency acts to specially influence human agency has been largely missing. There are other texts, however, both narrative and nonnarrative, in which one can see some of the cultural cognitive models by which these phenomena were understood to occur. The most important models are those that involve divine and human spirit/breath (usually *rûaḥ*). At times these cultural models will be more or less explicit, but at other times they may be implicit and require a bit of detective work to uncover. This type of inquiry has been developed in the field of cognitive anthropology. Although most of the research has been conducted with contemporary communities, it can also be fruitfully applied to historical texts,[15] since it is, fundamentally, a form of text or discourse analysis.[16] The goal, as Dorothy Holland and Naomi Quinn put it in their programmatic essay, is to identify "presupposed, taken-for-granted models of the world that are widely shared (although not necessarily to the exclusion of other, alternative models) by the members of a society and that play an enormous role in their understanding of the world and their behavior in it."[17] And, as Quinn has formulated it in a later essay, "I came to see my analytic approach as the reconstruction, from what people said explicitly, of the implicit assumptions they must have in mind to say it."[18] The search for cultural cognitive models pays close attention to keywords that occur in discourse about a particular topic, but also to embedded metaphors and even syntactic and grammatical features that may offer clues to cognitive models. Claudia Strauss, in particular, has investigated the way in which a person's discourse may switch between models, even those that are logically incompatible with one another.[19] As should be evident, this approach is not only compatible with forms of textual analysis used in biblical studies but also overlaps many of our standard practices. It does, however, shift attention to certain aspects of discourse that may be neglected in our typical approaches, and so may offer some new insights.

Rûaḥ—Spirit

In biblical scholarship it is common to distinguish between a life-constitutive *rûaḥ* that animates beings with the basic agency of living creatures and a charismatic *rûaḥ* that provides some sort of agential "boost."[20] John Levison, however, has rightly cautioned against a too radical dichotomization,[21] and while I think he is correct to identify the distorting effects of some theological commitments and, more pervasively, anachronistic imposition of modern categories onto ancient conceptualizations, the distinction remains valuable. Moreover, one can identify two different cognitive models based on the verbs and prepositions used to describe the operations of *rûaḥ*, though these models can and do intersect with each other, especially in Second Temple literature. Before turning to the relationship between *rûaḥ* and agency, some general context is required.

To begin to analyze the complex cultural models of "spirit" in ancient Israel, one needs to start with the fundamental recognition that *rûaḥ* refers to air in motion. In the external world this includes wind or breeze, and probably also vapors or miasmas. Not surprisingly, the breath of the body is also understood to be a type of wind with properties similar to those of *rûaḥ* in the world. Physical phenomena that can be readily experienced often lend themselves to analogical extension for the understanding of phenomena that are less immediately accessible, and *rûaḥ* is used to explore not only various issues concerning agency but other phenomena as well. Whether in these cases one is dealing with the extension of a physical theory or a conceptual metaphor that transfers reasoning about one realm to a quite different one can often be difficult to judge in cross-cultural context.[22] Thus when *rûaḥ* is used to refer to what we would call emotional or psychological states, it is not always clear which process is in play. It is possible that expressions like a "bitter spirit" or a "steady spirit" may be allusions to physical phenomena. Much as a theory of humors in ancient Greek thought used a model of the balance of certain bodily fluids as a way of thinking about what we call emotions and psychological states, so it is possible that ancient Israel had an implicit theory of bodily winds.[23] Alternatively, it is possible that conceptual metaphor is at work, such that emotions and psychological states are grasped as in some respects but not others "wind-like." For example, the social discord that results between Abimelech and the citizens of Shechem in Judges 9:23, when God sends a "bad *rûaḥ*," might be understood literally as a kind of miasma; but it might also be a conceptual metaphor for the discord that "blows through" the community. Although it would be desirable to be able to distinguish between folk theories about the physical properties of *rûaḥ* and conceptual metaphors involving *rûaḥ*, one can still learn much about implicit cultural cognitive models without resolving those matters.

The easily experienced characteristics of wind—that it is invisible, can move, has force that can be felt, can in some cases penetrate solid objects either forcefully or by seeping through, and so forth—also make it useful, either by logical extension or conceptual metaphorical transfer, for understanding categories of things that lack fleshly bodies, such as divine, angelic, and demonic beings. Although exegetes often disagree whether to translate *rûaḥ* as "wind" or "spirit" in Eliphaz's account of his nocturnal experience in Job 4:12–16, he is simply describing an encounter with a transcendent being that manifests itself to him as wind in motion that becomes still and that, like a vapor, has a visibility but not a clearly defined shape. Although not every encounter with a divine or demonic being exploits this phenomenology, the windlike nature of *rûaḥ* is critical in developing cognitive models for how beings that lack fleshly bodies interact with beings that are made of flesh—with significant implications for how the agency of fleshly beings is understood.

Life-Constitutive *Rûaḥ*

Several texts understand the creation of sentient beings with agential capacity as resulting from the insertion of *rûaḥ* into an inert material entity. Genesis 2:7 gives the most graphic description, though there the term used for animating breath is *nĕšāmāh* rather than *rûaḥ*. Although *nĕšāmāh* and *rûaḥ* are not strictly synonymous, a part of their range of meaning overlaps when it comes to that which animates a sentient being.[24] In Genesis 2:7 Yhwh forms a person from the dust of the earth, as though making a pottery vessel, and then puffs into its nostrils the *nišmat ḥayyîm*, so that it becomes a *nepeš ḥayyāh*. The model is of an external spirit or breath from God that is placed into bodies as one might place something into a container. This model is also assumed in Ezekiel 36 and 37, which describes a form of new creation. In 36:26 God removes the heart of stone and replaces it with a heart of flesh and also says, "I will put [*wĕnātattî*] in you a new heart, and a new spirit [*rûaḥ*] I will put [*'ettēn*] into your body [*bĕqirbĕkem*]." This spirit is specifically identified in verse 27 as God's own spirit ("my spirit," *rûḥî*). Similarly, in chapter 37 the revivification (v. 3, *ḥāyāh*) of the dry bones is announced as follows: "I am causing *rûaḥ* to enter you, and you will live again. . . . I will put *rûaḥ* into you" (*wĕnātattî bākem*, vv. 5–6). As befits the high view of God in Ezekiel, there is no puffing into the nostrils but rather the summoning of the four winds to animate the bones, suggesting again that wind and breath are part of the same conceptual category. Apparently, this model was also assumed to be similar to the process of the animation of the fetus when it quickens, as Qohelet 11:5 suggests: "Just as you do not know what is the way of the *rûaḥ* into the bones in the belly of the pregnant woman . . . ."[25] The comatose are similarly revived. Even though Ezekiel uses expressions describing external spirit possession when he is transported in a vision (cf. 8:3; 37:1), when he faints in response to his encounter with the glory, God revives him by means of a *rûaḥ* that enters into him (*wattābō'*, 2:2; 3:24).[26]

Some exegetes argue that because the text of Genesis 2 does not explicitly note God's blowing breath into the nostrils of nonhuman animals, therefore the text marks an ontological distinction between the *'ādām* and the *ḥayyat-haśśādeh* and the *'ôp haššamāyim* that God creates in verse 19.[27]

But this is to overread what is merely a convention of storytelling, in which it is not necessary to repeat every detail of a repetitious scene. Moreover, such a reading runs contrary to the essential plot of Genesis 2–3, in which what *does* make humans more "like God/gods" than animals are, occurs specifically through the eating from the tree of knowledge (3:5, 22).[28] Other texts, too, assume that humans and animals alike belong to a category of "breathing beings," as in the references to the death of all such creatures possessing the breath of life (*rûaḥ ḥayyim*) in Genesis 6:17 and 7:15, 22.[29] Breath is what gives life to matter. Without it, all creatures are dead and "return to dust" (Gen 3:19; Ps 104:29; 146:4; Job 34:15; Qoh 3:19; 8:8; 12:7).

What, however, does the *rûaḥ* actually contribute? In Genesis 2:7, Ezekiel 37:4–6, Job 32:8; 33:4; 34:14–15, and Qohelet 11:5, the breath from God is simply the source of vitality, sentience, and agency. These are qualities that appear to distinguish human and other animal beings from plants and soil.[30] None of these texts seems to suggest that any additional qualia are communicated to dust or bone by the implantation of the *rûaḥ* from God.[31] Is life-constitutive *rûaḥ* then simply an alternative way of describing what is elsewhere referred to as *nepeš*? Although these terms do overlap in part of their range of meanings, there is one context in which it is evident that the cognitive model that associates *rûaḥ* with animating spirit retains the sense of its essentially divine nature. This assumption becomes clear in references to what happens to *rûaḥ* at death, especially when one compares passages about death that use the alternative conception of breath as *nepeš*. This difference is germane to understanding why and how *rûaḥ* functions in order to explore the manner in which divine agency interacts with human agency.

Excursus: *Rûaḥ* and *Nepeš* as Alternative Cultural Models

One should not think of ancient Israelites as possessing a "doctrine" of anthropology or even a single cultural model for thinking about the life-death relationship. Most likely there are several that come into play in different discourses and contexts. Although *nepeš* and *rûaḥ* overlap in some ranges of meaning, when the topic is what happens at death, the accounts are largely distinct. Both terms can represent the breath of the living person,[32] but the term *nepeš* derives from a cultural cognitive model of life and agency in relation to the body. It is, in physical terms, the "breathing throat,"[33] though it takes on a wide variety of other connotations that somewhat overlap and somewhat diverge from the range of meanings and contexts of *rûaḥ*.[34] Following Aubrey Johnson, most scholars accept the sense of *nepeš* as "vitality."[35] In only one instance does *nepeš* appear in connection with the cessation of the breath at death, in Genesis 35:18. There, when Rachel dies, it is simply said that "her *nepeš* went out." While some have assumed that the *nepeš* dissipates,[36] Joachim Schaper has persuasively argued that it lodges in the *maṣṣēbāh* that Jacob sets up above her grave (35:19–20).[37] How to understand the references to the *nepeš* in Sheol in a number of psalms remains contested, given the fluidity of the boundary between life and death, but the fact that *nepeš* can be associated with Sheol is clearly linked with the notion of the ultimate placement of the body into the grave and the body's gradual decomposition.[38] The directional and locative imagery associated with *nepeš* is guided by that associated with the body. The close association of the *nepeš* with some form of body may also be indicated in the stela of Katumuwa, which appears to be an object that hosts or facilitates the presence of the king's *nbš* in a cultic and social setting, whether because his own body has been cremated, as David Schloen and Amir Fink suggest, or whether it is simply a "pied-à-terre for visits from the netherworld" or is a permanent residence.[39] A final bodily context for *nepeš* can be discerned in references to cultic defilement from the *nepeš* of a dead person (e.g., Num 5:2; 6:6; 9:6–7; and especially 19:14–15). Pollution is not limited to direct physical contact with a dead body (Num 19:13) but, if the person dies in a tent, then anyone who enters into the tent and any open vessels without lids in it are also rendered unclean by the dead *nepeš* (vv. 14–15). Frevel suggests that the reason the *nepeš* pollutes is tied to its liminal status, as it "has left the body, without being totally detached from it" and so exposes an ambivalence between life and death that is marked as dangerous.[40] But the mode of pollution also underscores the conceptual connection of *nepeš* with the body. Based on the logic of the text and cross-cultural parallels, Yitzhaq Feder cogently concludes that "the spread of this form of defilement was modeled after the dissemination of the stench of a decomposing corpse."[41] That does not necessarily mean that the odor was *identified* with the pollution; but it does indicate that the physical phenomenon formed the conceptual analogy for thinking about how the *nepeš* of the dead pollutes—it pollutes in the same way that the smell of decomposition fills an enclosed space. All of these examples suggest that the bodily associations of *nepeš* provide a set of conceptual pathways for the development of ideas about human vitality in life and in death.

When death is described in terms of the *rûaḥ*, however, a very different model appears, because *rûaḥ* is understood in terms of its origins with God. Although Psalm 146:4 superficially resembles Genesis 35:18 in its terse formulation "his *rûaḥ* goes out" (at death), the parallel line, "he returns to his *'ădāmāh*," indicates that the verse is a gloss on Genesis 3:19 and the model in that narrative of God's breath puffed into the vessel of "dust of the earth." Although Genesis 3:19 does not comment on the fate of the *rûaḥ/nĕšāmāh* at death, Qohelet 12:7 does: "the dust returns to the ground as it was, but the *rûaḥ* returns to God who gave it" (cf. Qoh 3:19–21). So, too, Elihu observes that if God "gathers up his spirit and his breath to himself, then all flesh together would expire, and a human would return to dust" (Job 34:14b–15). The model of "gathering" (*'āsap*) breath is similarly present in Psalm 104:29–30, using the same terms as in Job 34: "if you gather up their *rûaḥ*, they expire, and to their dust they return. If you send forth your *rûaḥ*, they are created, and you renew the face of the earth" (cf. 4Q416 2 ii 2–3 and 4Q419 8 ii 7–8). In the enigmatic Genesis 6:3, also, God seems to express a kind of possessive concern for the fate of "my spirit" as it pertains to its presence in humankind, for the reason that humans are also "flesh." However this difficult passage is understood, it also appears to refer to a reclaiming of divine spirit from the bodies of humans.

What I am suggesting is that the debate about whether the ancient Israelites envisioned the person as a psychosomatic unity[42] or, as James Barr has forcefully suggested, as more of a dual constitution[43] might be more helpfully reframed by recognizing that more than one cultural model existed for thinking about human vitality as manifested in the breath, models that are in significant ways inconsistent with each other. Having more than one cultural model for an area of concern is quite common. As the studies of anthropologist Claudia Strauss have shown, the most common pattern for negotiating such alternative models is compartmentalization, so that logically conflicting ideas are held "in separate, largely unconnected cognitive schemas."[44] Moving from one to another is the conceptual equivalent of linguistic "code switching" and can be done quite rapidly. At least in the case of discourse about death, this seems likely to be the case for most of the occurrences of *rûaḥ*-based and *nepeš*-based models in the biblical text. When the focus is on the body or the human experience more generally, the *nepeš* model comes to the fore. When the focus is on God's role, the *rûaḥ* model comes to the fore. Because of its associations with the divine, *rûaḥ* can also be employed in other contexts to describe various divine-human relationships in which human agency is controlled or enhanced by divine *rûaḥ*.

Charismatic *Rûaḥ* and Divine Co-agency

In contrast to the model of life-constitutive *rûaḥ* as a substance placed in a container and then gathered up again when the container disintegrates, texts that speak of the role of spirit in situations of divine co-agency usually represent divine *rûaḥ* as an external phenomenon that has a contiguous or metonymic relation to the person. This model is employed primarily in texts about the judges, the most ancient of Israel's kings, and certain prophets. Most commonly, the relationship is expressed by the preposition *ʿal*, and the inception of the contact is often highlighted. Thus the *rûaḥ* from God may "be upon" (*hāyāh ʿal*, Judg 3:10; 11:29; 1 Sam 19:20, 23; 2 Chr 15:1; 20:14; *ʿal*, Isa 61:1) or be "placed upon" (*śîm ʿal*, *nātan ʿal*, Num 11:17, 25) or "rest upon" (*nûaḥ ʿal*, Num 11:25; Isa 11:2) a person. It may "fall upon" (*nāpal ʿal*, Ezek 11:5) or "rush upon" someone (*ṣālaḥ ʿa*, Judg 14:6, 10; 15:14; *ṣālaḥ ʿal*, 1 Sam 16:13). Not only is it external and contiguous, but it is often also described as exercising external agency, as it "impels" (*pāʿam*, Judg 13:25), "carries off" (*nāśaʾ*, 2 Kgs 2:16; Ezek 8:3), and "takes away" (*hôṣîʾ*, Ezek 37:1). In some cases, especially in connection with the actions of the judges, with instances of translocation by the spirit, and prophetic inspiration in Numbers and Chronicles, the presence and effect of the spirit appear to be transitory and enable the person to do something that he would otherwise not be capable of doing. Even when there is a more long-lasting presence of the spirit, the *rûaḥ* is said to "rest upon" or be "put upon" a person (Isa 11:2; 42:1), or even to "rush upon" (1 Sam 16:13), underscoring the conceptualization of the spirit as external but contiguous.

The representation of spirits in the Saul and David narratives is particularly instructive because of the parallel way in which the operations of the "spirit of Yhwh" (*rûaḥ yhwh*) and the "evil spirit from Yhwh" (*rûaḥ-rāʿāh mēʾēt yhwh*) are described (1 Sam 16:14).[45] Just as the spirit of Yhwh can "rush upon" (1 Sam 10:6, 10; 11:6; 16:13), so too the evil spirit (18:10). It can also "be upon" (*hāyāh ʿal*, 16:16) or "come to" (*hāyāh ʾel*, 16:23; 19:9). Both can "turn aside from" (*sûr mēʿim/mēʿal*, 16:14, 23). Although the evil spirit causes what we would call psychological changes in Saul, the verb used to describe its action is "terrify" (*bāʿat*, v. 14), implying an objectified otherness. The role of music in causing the spirit to depart (*sûr*) remains obscure, though music is elsewhere a means for invoking the divine charismatic power ("the hand of Yhwh," 2 Kgs 3:15). Overall, the discourse about the spirit of Yhwh constructs an implicit model of an external and independent force that acts upon humans.[46]

There are two striking exceptions to this model of an external, contiguous spirit. The most developed is 1 Kings 22:22–23, when the divine council debates how to "entice Ahab." A "spirit" stands before Yhwh and offers to "go out and be a lying spirit in the mouth of all his prophets" (v. 22). Micaiah summarizes by saying that "Yhwh has placed [*nātan*] a lying spirit *in the mouth* [*bĕpî*] of all your prophets" (v. 23).[47] Notably, the spirit in the divine council is an agential spirit-being. It is capable, however, of entering *into* human beings and functioning within the human mental capacity. The king's prophets are apparently aware that their prophecy is enabled by divine spirit and subjectively experience the presence of that spirit, since the outraged Zedekiah demands of Micaiah, "in what way did the spirit of Yhwh pass from [being] with me to speak with you?" (v. 24). Zedekiah's description also suggests that prophetic inspiration was, at least in this case, understood as a kind of inner speech. Such a model is confirmed by Yhwh's words to the spirit in verse 22, "you will seek to persuade" (*tĕpatteh*) and "you will prevail" (*tûkāl*), suggesting that the spirit's mode of presence within the prophet is experienced as inner speech or thoughts.[48]

Similarly, when Yhwh wishes to mislead the king of Assyria, he says, "see, I am putting in him a spirit [*hinĕnî nōtēn bô rûaḥ*], and he will hear a rumor and return to his land" (2 Kgs 19:7). The spirit directs the king's thoughts and judgments, so that he believes the rumor rather than dismissing it. Thus, where the action has to do with thought, judgment, and perception, the model is of a spirit entering the body, presumably acting upon the heart/mind. One sees the same model in the much later book of Jubilees. When Abram is uncertain whether to remain in Haran or return to Ur, he prays to God to "save me from the power of the evil spirits who rule the thoughts of people's minds; may they not mislead me from following you, my God" (Jub 12:20; trans. VanderKam).[49] In Israelite anthropology both heart and spirit are associated with cognition.[50] Alien spirits, whether from God or from demonic forces, can thus enter into one's body and be active within one's heart, so that the individual may have difficulty in discerning the true source of his or her own thoughts and inner discourse. The effects on human agency are similar to those in the narratives about Abimelech and Pharaoh discussed above, although in 1 and 2 Kings the mechanism of the spirit is made explicit.

Thus one fundamental aspect of the ancient Israelite cultural model for divine spirit and human bodies focuses on the mode of relationship, developing a "breathwind-in-container" model for basic animation and an external but contiguous "wind-against-object" model for most charismatic relationships. But when divine causation operates on human thoughts, the "wind-against-object" model does not work well, yielding instead to a model of a temporarily inhabiting spirit that operates like a parallel sentience to the person's own mind, though this inhabiting spirit may or may not be recognized as such. This model bears a strong resemblance to the way in which *rûaḥ* is invoked to think about the presence of knowledge and skill that exceeds the ordinary human condition.

Giftedness and the Divine *Rûaḥ*

In the model of *rûaḥ* as life-constitutive, described above, the *rûaḥ* is understood to be from God and only temporarily lodged in humans and animals until it is gathered up again by God. While it is in breathing beings it confers life, vitality, and sentience, but it does not appear to be experienced as in any sense an "alien" presence. It is simply that which makes a living being a living being. In a number of passages, however, the term *rûaḥ* does designate certain exceptional abilities, mostly associated with skill or special knowledge, that occur in particular humans. The date of many of these passages is contested, so one should not attempt too much in the way of tracing chronological development. Ordinarily, these references are distinguished from the temporary charismatic experiences of judges, kings, and prophets that one might refer to as spirit possession.[51] Syntactic analysis suggests that these cases of exceptional ability do not employ the model of the external contiguous spirit of charismatic endowment, using the preposition *ʿal* and verbs of spirit-agency, but rather employ the container model also used in accounts of creation. Some of these instances, notably those in the Pentateuch, specifically use the verb "to fill." Thus, God says of Bezalel, "I have *filled* him [*millēʾtîw*] with the spirit of wisdom" (Ex 28:3) and "I have *filled* him with a divine spirit [*rûaḥ ʾĕlōhîm*], with wisdom and understanding and knowledge in every craft" (31:3; 35:31). Joshua, too, is said to be "*filled* with the spirit of wisdom" (Deut 34:9) and someone "*in whom* the spirit is" (Num 27:18). In Micah 3:8 the prophet affirms, "I am *filled* with strength by the spirit of Yhwh, and with judgment and courage, to declare to Jacob his transgressions and to Israel his sin" (NJPS). These are all qualities of skill or leadership that are common to many humans to some degree but raised to a distinctive level in these remarkable individuals. The attention given to the divine origin is noteworthy, as it suggests an awareness of the presence of qualitative dimensions of the spirit that differ from the *rûaḥ* that makes one a living being. The phenomenon is easily recognizable. In many cultures, including those of modernity, persons with particular talent or skill may experience those talents as operating beyond the level of conscious control. That sense lends itself well to a model of endowment by divine spirit that is experienced as in some sense "other," even as it operates through one's own person. In the era of European romanticism such a model was regularly invoked by poets and artists. That this type of experience has charismatic overtones in biblical references may be indicated by one instance in which the external contiguous model is used to describe gifts similar to the ones above. Isaiah 11:2 says of the messianic king that "the spirit of the Lord will rest upon him [*wĕnāḥāh ʿālāw*]: a spirit of wisdom and insight, a spirit of counsel and acuity, a spirit of knowledge and fear of Yhwh."[52]

The figures of Joseph and Daniel also belong to the model of special endowment by an indwelling divine spirit. Joseph is described as someone "*in whom* there is a divine spirit" (or "spirit of God/the gods"; *ʾîš ʾăšer rûaḥ ʾĕlōhîm bô*, Gen 41:38). So also Daniel has a "holy divine spirit *in him*" (or "spirit of the holy God/gods"; *rûaḥ ʾĕlāhîn qaddîšîn bāk*, Dan 4:6, 15; cf. 5:11, 14). There are indications in each story that the spirit by which they are able to interpret mysterious dreams and inscriptions is recognized not simply as a talent but as due to this divine endowment. In contrast to the courtier Ahiqar, whose success at court contests is due simply to his superior intelligence, when Joseph interprets, he is at pains to say that it is "God who interprets" through him (Gen 40:8). When Pharaoh says that he has heard of Joseph's ability, Joseph directly deflects the attribution away from himself: "Not I! God will give Pharaoh a favorable answer" (41:16; NRSV, modified). In Daniel 1:17 the special capacities enjoyed by Daniel are explicitly identified as a gift of God, which is understood in 4:6 and 15 as an indwelling divine spirit. To be sure, these texts are not particularly concerned to speculate on the subjective experience of receiving such a "second wind" from God or the extent to which it is felt as a distinct presence within oneself. But the notion that divine spirit could use a person as a conduit may be implicit in the oracular last words of David in 2 Samuel 23:2, which he credits to "the spirit of Yhwh that has spoken *in me/through me*" (*bî*).[53] These instances are similar in important ways to the model of the spirits sent into the minds/bodies of the prophets of Ahab in 1 Kings 22 and into the king of Assyria in

2 Kings 19, though in 1 and 2 Kings the spirits function to direct perception and agency against a person's default inclinations, whereas in the examples of Joseph, Daniel, and David, they may be said to enhance the person's capacities beyond his own default level but in concert with his desires.

To summarize, in the texts discussed above the relation of divine spirit and human agency serves to map several important aspects of human experience. The understanding of what makes humans and animals animate beings with vitality, sentience, and agency is explored through the model of divine breathwind puffed or placed into inanimate material as into a container. That the *rûaḥ* breath is conceived of as substance rather than what we would refer to as the *act* of breathing is evident from the way the *rûaḥ* is understood to be gathered up at death and returned to God. Although in most contexts the *rûaḥ* is not experienced as conveying any qualia beyond vitality, sentience, and agency, its divine origin allows for the development of this locative model to include an account of the exceptional wisdom or understanding possessed by some persons. The godlike nature of the *rûaḥ* is more palpable in these references, though it is integrated into the psychosomatic nature of the individual. Where the context involves more of a stress on active divine co-agency, then the model shifts from being wind-breath placed into the body to a model of wind-force that is external but contiguous to the person, with one exception. When this co-agency has to do specifically with divine influence on perceptions, belief, and thoughts, then the model is closer to the insertion of *rûaḥ* into the mind/heart of the person.

What is strikingly absent from this picture of the relation of *rûaḥ* to human agency is any reflection on *rûaḥ* in relation to moral agency. For the most part discussions of moral agency in the preexilic literature focus on human capacity for exercising moral agency and an examination of the impediments to that exercise. Although *rûaḥ* as an aspect of human character and will sometimes appears in discussions of moral agency, especially in Proverbs, it is not a major topic. Nor is the relation between divine *rûaḥ* and human action a part of discussions of moral agency. The fall of Judah to the Babylonians, however, generates a crisis of confidence in the ability of Judeans to exercise moral agency in any significant manner. One of the innovations in postexilic and Second Temple Jewish religious literature is to reenvision the relationship of divine *rûaḥ* to human agency, including moral agency.

3 Moral Agency in Israelite Perspective: Three Case Studies

The entire arc of biblical narrative from Genesis to 2 Kings can be read as a meditation on moral agency, its successes and its failures. Although these narratives, especially the ones related to the Deuteronomic History, sometimes pass moral judgments on characters or portray them as good or bad, there are only occasional examinations of the underlying assumptions about what leads to the exercise of good or bad moral agency.[1] This topic is more clearly brought into focus in the wisdom literature (notably, Proverbs), the book of Deuteronomy, and the prophetic literature. Even these texts seldom engage in any deeply reflective examination of moral agency. Instead, the focus is typically on a problem in social behavior, which the text engages by means of critique, exhortation, or advice. It is possible, however, to tease out implicit cultural models of the self and moral agency that were broadly shared in ancient Israel, as well as distinctive frameworks that shape the resources for thinking about moral agency and its discontents.

Although the category of moral agency primarily refers to the capacities of individuals, it is also common in biblical literature to treat collective bodies *as though* they were individual moral agents. This, however, is a cognitive metaphor. One construes a collective body (e.g., a city, a nation) as though it were an individual with an individual's moral agency. This metaphor can have great explanatory power. A collectivity can act with intention. It seems in many respects as agential as any individual human. One can credit it with good and evil actions, exhort it, plead with it, and so forth, using an often-subconscious trope of personification. This personification is so familiar to the cultural heirs of the biblical imagination that it requires a bit of effort to recognize that the nation is *not* a person. It is rather a social entity composed of many hierarchically arranged persons and systems of decisionmaking. Thus to construe it as though it were a person with a person's intentionality and agency and moral responsibility is to construe it figuratively. And while metaphors may map certain aspects of a relationship powerfully in ways that create significant understanding, they may sometimes mislead. Moreover, the metaphor may also seed the relationship with the potential energy of unforeseen transfers of meaning back and forth between tenor and vehicle. What is recognized (and sometimes misrecognized) in treating a complex social entity as though it were a moral agent may also feed back into how a culture understands the nature of individual human beings and their moral agency.

Across the literatures of the ancient Near East one can find examples in which collective entities—cities, nations—are treated as moral agents. But ancient Israel seems to have developed this trope far beyond most other attested cultures. Why this was the case is difficult to say. Perhaps it was because the institution of kingship was never fully mythologized in ancient Israel but rather was recalled as a specific historical contingency. Thus the figure of the king could never fully substitute for the figure of the nation or serve as its privileged symbol. Certainly, the power of the covenantal model of relationship between God and people (not simply God and king) that was influential in Israelite and Judean thought from at least the eighth century BCE was a major factor in establishing the understanding of the nation as a moral agent. Political covenants in the ancient Near East were themselves dependent on metaphorical transfers from the realm of human kinship relationships. Whatever the reasons for the hyperdevelopment of the metaphor of the nation as moral agent in ancient Israel and Judah, the history of assumptions about personal, individual moral agency is inextricably interwoven with the history of discourse about the nation as moral agent.

The fatefulness of the interrelationship of ways of thinking about moral agency of the individual and the nation becomes clear as one examines the writings that pertain to the national crises, most particularly, the rich literature produced at the time of the destruction of the kingdom of Judah by the Babylonians in 586 BCE. This calamity was framed in several texts as a catastrophic failure of moral agency that resulted in a divine judgment, which manifested itself in the Babylonian conquest. In later years, however, both the general sense of moral failure and certain models for thinking about the moral agency of the nation in relation to this crisis were appropriated for the language of individual prayer and moral reflection. Such developments facilitated profound shifts in the conceptualization of self and spirituality. These were not the only factors in the evolution of Second Temple beliefs and practices, but they were a critical element. Thus it is important to track the flow of models of moral agency in both directions, from the individual to the nation and from the nation back to the individual, and to reflect on the possible significance of this transfer.

In what follows I will first examine the common cultural model of moral agency and then engage in three case studies (Proverbs, Deuteronomy, and Ezekiel) that illustrate three different formulations of the problems of moral agency.

The Assumptional Framework of Moral Agency

Since biblical texts rarely make general statements about the nature of moral agency, one has to tease out the assumptions as they are reflected in the rhetoric of indictment, rebuke, and warning on the one hand and hortatory appeal on the other. References to the failure of moral agency provide particularly useful data. Various texts across a broad spectrum of genres repeatedly focus on three areas of concern: failure of understanding, a cognitive problem; wrongly directed desire, an emotional/appetitive problem; and stubborn resistance to appropriate authority, a volitional problem. Many texts, of course, focus on the contents of morally bad actions (e.g., violence or injustice) or on particular vices (e.g., pride) or on the consequences of radical sin (e.g., defilement). When the issue is what leads people to commit such actions or indulge in such vices, however, then the vocabulary and images cluster in the three areas that I have identified. A few examples can serve to illustrate each one.

Failure of understanding broadly encompasses inadequate grasp of the dynamics of situations as well as a failure to know God. Clearly, this is not a narrowly cognitive failure but one that has to do broadly with the adequate apprehension of reality. It manifests itself in the rich vocabulary for the various categories of fools in Proverbs (e.g., *petî*, *ḥăsar lēb*, *kĕsîl*, *lēṣ*, *ʾĕwîl*),[2] as well as in Hosea's references to the failure of knowledge of God (e.g., Hos 4:1, 6), in Jeremiah's critiques of self-deception on the part of the leaders of Judah (e.g., Jer 5:12–13, 21, 31), in Deuteronomy's warnings against forgetting (Deut 4:9; 6:12; 8:11–14), and in many other contexts. As for wrongly directed desire, David Lambert has rightly cautioned that "desire" in the Hebrew Bible not be inappropriately psychologized. Instead, it must be recognized in all of its material and social dimensions.[3] I would agree. In almost all cases in the biblical literature wrongly directed desire is represented as a problem of the whole person in its social context, not as a problem framed primarily as an "I-Me" dilemma.[4] Only in Second Temple literature will there be evidence for such a shift in focus. In the prophetic literature a wide range of wrongful practices and covenantal violations are figuratively represented as lust leading to infidelity (e.g., Hos 2:15; 5:4; Jer 2:23; 3:2–4; Ezek 16). The vividly narrated desire for food in Numbers 11:5–6 ("meat . . . fish . . . cucumbers, melons, leeks, onions, garlic") is the form that mistrust and repudiation of Yhwh take.[5] In Proverbs, too, the imagery of food, drink, wealth, and sex figures desire, both as it should be directed (toward wisdom) and as it is wrongly directed (e.g., Prov 1:10–13; 4:16–17; 5:3; 10:3; 21:10). Such misdirected desire is represented as fundamentally disordered. As Michael Fox observes, the evildoer "not only speaks and does evil, he *delights* in it; he is a moral pervert."[6] Resistance to appropriate authority as a category of moral failure also underscores the fundamentally social nature of the moral concern in biblical literature. The rhetorical framing of Proverbs through a series of instructions in chapters 1–9 foregrounds the proper stance as obedient listening to the authority of the father and the mother (1:8). Resistance to the call and rebuke of wisdom lead to disaster (1:24–27). Similarly, Deuteronomy frames obedience or disobedience as life-or-death decisions (30:15–20). Frequently, the imagery of docile submission or rebellious resistance is framed in imagery from the behavior of domesticated animals. The "stiff neck" (e.g., Deut 9:6, 13) evokes an animal that resists the yoke. Hosea refers to Israel as a "stubborn cow" (4:16), an image Jeremiah reworks to describe Judah as breaking its yoke and tearing off the yoke bindings (2:20). The vocabulary of rebellion and resistance is prominent in several prophetic books (e.g., Isa 30:1–2; Jer 2:9–13; Ezek 2:3–5; Hos 7:13; Zeph 3:1–2), and in Deuteronomic assessments (e.g., Judg 2:19–23; 1 Sam 8:7–8; 2 Kgs 17:13–15).

In Israelite literature the three aspects of the moral self are not understood as distinct parts or even separate faculties that can be in conflict with one another.[7] Rather, they are deeply interconnected aspects of the whole person. Nor is any one aspect consistently privileged over others as the key to good moral agency. Although in Israelite literature certain texts may identify understanding, wrongful desire, or recalcitrant will as particularly problematic, the three are largely understood as interactive and reinforcing. Disorder in one area generally leads to disorder in the others as well. A deep understanding of the nature of things enables one to direct one's desires appropriately and grasp the importance of obedience to God and wise elders. By contrast, undisciplined desires cloud the understanding and result in rebellious behavior, whereas rightly directed desires enhance understanding of how things work and facilitate appropriate behavior. Only the one who submits to the discipline of appropriate authorities can gain understanding and learn to desire what is good. These basic principles undergird all of the discourses about moral agency in the texts of the Hebrew Bible.

In the following pages I examine selected issues of moral agency in Proverbs, Deuteronomy, and Ezekiel. Although the book of Proverbs cannot be simply taken as encapsulating the common moral culture of ancient Israel, it likely comes as close as we are able to the fundamental assumptions that grounded the formation of children and youth. Even though the book itself is the product of scribal culture, specific social-class perspectives are reflected in only some sayings. More likely, it is an elite version of shared culture. That being said, if the instructional and proverbial collections in Proverbs served as part of the scribal curriculum, as many assume, then it would have been part of the mental furniture of the scribes who composed other, more specialized types of literature. The close connection between Deuteronomy and wisdom literature has often been noted and perhaps runs in both directions.[8] In my discussion Deuteronomy is important first of all because it provides a model of distributed moral agency in which the coordinated agency of individuals is what creates the national agency. It also self-consciously examines the ways in which agency can fail and models a variety of strategies for strengthening agency. In its postexilic additions it also demonstrates a strategy for recognizing and repairing a catastrophic failure of agency. And finally, it provides a moral vocabulary and set of conceptual resources that were exceptionally influential in Second Temple literature, concerning both individual and collective moral agency. Finally, Ezekiel is featured in part because the book is focused almost entirely on the crisis in moral agency provoked by the fall of Judah, but it does so with a set of conceptual resources derived extensively from priestly traditions. It, too, creates a way of encompassing and rectifying the collapse of moral agency through a set of symbols that become critical to many Second Temple texts that deal both with individual and with collective agency.

The Moral Agent in Proverbs

Proverbs prompts a very basic question: Are all humans capable of becoming good moral agents, or are some destined to be wicked? The aphoristic style and the tendency toward rhetorical hyperbole make it difficult to determine what Proverbs assumes about innate human capacity. This issue was more explicitly raised in a number of the Egyptian instruction texts, and several different positions were argued.[9] The most extreme position was taken by *Ptahhotep*, who claims that the character of the fool is determined before birth, so that no training can make a fool wise ("He whom god hates does not listen," l. 546; such a person is "one for whom an impediment was assigned in the womb," l. 217).[10] The opposite pole is argued in Papyrus Anastasi III, 4.1–4, which maintains that, like animals that can be taught all kinds of behaviors contrary to their natures, humans can similarly be trained, whatever their given natures (cf. also the Instructions of Anii, 22.17–23.7). An intermediate view, articulated by Anii's son Khonsuhotep, argues that different pedagogies are required for different students (23.7–11).

It is not clear that Israelite sages ever considered the question explicitly. Their assumptions must be deduced from the sayings. The sharp contrast between the wise and the foolish, the righteous and the wicked, leads some to conclude that character is largely a given, and that formation plays only a limited role in wisdom.[11] To be sure, many sayings emphasize the intractable folly of certain types of fools, especially those designated as *lēṣ* ("arrogant scoffer," 9:7–8; 13:1b; 14:6; 15:12) and *'ĕwîl* ("morally perverse," 15:5a; 27:22). But were these types always thus? Or is folly the hardening of a character that was once malleable? That possibility is suggested by the saying in Proverbs 13:1b, "The *lēṣ*? He never heard reproof." It is certainly plausible that the sages acknowledged differences in aptitude for wisdom (perhaps 16:21). But to assume that character was largely fixed for all is, I think, to mistake the sometimes exasperated rhetoric of Proverbs for its core commitments. Proverbs is a strenuous and sustained exercise in pedagogy, and such commitment makes sense only on the assumption that it is worthwhile. Fox observes that the primary audience for Proverbs' teachings is the naive youth, the *petî* (1:4; 8:5), more or less synonymous with the "mindless" (*ḥăsar-lēb*, 7:7; 9:4). Such children are not simply unformed but may also have folly (*'iwwelet*) in their heart; yet the rod of discipline will drive it out (22:15). The implicit assumption about human nature that makes sense of the sayings found in Proverbs and its commitment to strenuous pedagogy is that humans are by nature impulsive, emotional, and motivated by immediate desires. Without early and rigorous formation such tendencies will indeed produce intractable folly, with all of the antisocial behaviors that attend such a character. It is, as Fox observes, the "ingrained" or "dyed-in-the-wool fool" whose character has been irrevocably set.[12] Anne Stewart articulates the project of the formation of moral agency in Proverbs well:

> . . . one's moral selfhood must be disciplined into being. Proverbs implies that moral equipment is innate, but exists in potential only. The origin of moral selfhood is both with the external aid of discipline, which serves to reorient one's concept of the good toward wisdom, *and* with an internal capacity to receive and profit from discipline.[13]

Thus while it is possible that there are some individuals who are impervious to formation, the project of wisdom makes sense only if the default assumption is that the inchoate perceptions, impulses, and desires of the young can be shaped by wisdom.

The moral agent who is successfully formed by wisdom is a highly stable construction. As discipline is internalized, one's very desires are molded into appropriate channels, and inappropriate desires become abhorrent. Cognitive training shapes the individual to perceive the logic of wisdom's moral world as an expression of reality itself. Each element feeds back to strengthen the others. Though Proverbs shows considerable concern for the dangers of those who resist or elude formation, no anxiety is expressed over the possibility that a wise person, once formed, will go over to wickedness.[14] Similarly, the fool, once formed by folly, becomes one of the wicked. And, as Sun Myung Lyu points out, "no saying or instruction is found to urge a wicked person to change his course to become righteous."[15] The character of the wicked, once formed, is as intractable as that of the righteous. Formation is forever.

Formation in wisdom takes place at the intersection among the three aspects of human capacity (will, understanding, desire) and the foundational moral values that make up the framework of wisdom's moral world. Numerous studies have documented the ways in which Proverbs schools the understanding to perceptions of the act-consequence relationship in various social and moral contexts. Michael Fox, in particular, has examined the distinctive epistemology that shapes the way in which such perceptions of the structure of reality are guided according to socially consensual values.[16] Others have documented the ways in which desires that might be unruly (for food and drink, sex, and wealth) are imaginatively coopted and redirected to the desire for wisdom itself.[17] And, of course, the prominence of physical and verbal discipline as a means of requiring the submissiveness of the subject has been frequently examined. It is not my intention to rehearse all of these investigations or to attempt to give a complete account of the formation of moral agency in Proverbs. I wish to focus on one rather narrow issue concerning how moral selfhood is "disciplined into being," and in particular the way in which this process is imagined and rhetorically presented.

In every human culture moral formation is a process of the internalization of norms. With the exception of prisons, concentration camps, and certain other highly controlled social environments where external authorities police behavior minutely, societies largely depend upon individuals to monitor and regulate themselves. The "I" supervises the "Me."[18] But the degree to which that internalization is represented varies considerably from culture to culture. Thus I want to look at the imagery and rhetoric by which Proverbs envisions the nature of discipline.

Not surprisingly, given the rather sociocentric orientation of ancient Israel, social or external imagery dominates over internalized or intrapersonal imagery, though the latter is not entirely lacking. The introductory chapters of Proverbs 1–9 establish a speech relationship in which a father instructs his son, with an occasional appearance by Woman Wisdom. As I analyzed this discursive relationship in an earlier article, "The father, who speaks, is the 'I' of the discourse. The son, addressed in the vocative and with imperative verbs, is the 'you.'"[19] The reader is thus offered the subject position of the son, who is encouraged to listen and attend but never speaks himself. Thus the rhetorical formation of Proverbs is almost exclusively external and social rather than internal or intrapersonal. Even in the chapters that have the rhetorical structure of proverbial sayings rather than instructions, sayings are presented as objective rather than subjective perceptions. The reader is invited to give assent to them, as the good son is asked to be attentive and receptive to the words of the father. Nevertheless, it is clear that the goal is not mere submission and compliance, as though the father's authority were like that of a military commander or overseer of laborers. The imagery used for discipline might initially suggest such externality, since "rebuke" (*mûsār*) or "correction" (*tôkaḥat*) is sometimes figured as physical (striking, *nākāh*; with the rod, *šēbet*), sometimes as verbal reprimand (*gĕʿārāh*, *tôkaḥat*) coming from an authority figure. But that the engagement of the son is more than submission is clear from the fact that what is sought is attentive listening and receptiveness (*šāmaʿ*, "heed"; *hiqšîb*, "pay attention"; *lāqaḥ*, "accept"; *šāmar*, "keep"). These are all responses that require the full engagement of the one addressed. Moreover, the purpose and function of rebuke is not simply to correct behavior but to lead to insight. *Mûsār* is frequently associated with *ḥokmâ* (8:10–11; 23:23), *bînâ* (4:1; 23:23), *ṣedeq ûmišpāṭ* (1:3), *daʿat* (19:27; 23:12), and *tôrâ* (1:8; 4:1; 6:23).[20] Thus the process of becoming a moral agent formed in sapiential culture is largely a matter of internalizing the dynamics of teaching and rebuke (3:1; 4:4, 21). Discipline becomes self-discipline. One becomes a social father to oneself.

But how does this happen? Proverbs does not engage this dynamic with a great deal of second-order reflection. Nor does it describe in any detail practices by which this process takes place. Much of the process is subliminal, and it is doubtful if the authors of Proverbs would even have been self-conscious of many of their implicit strategies, though some of these have been analyzed by modern scholars.[21] Since much of what Proverbs attempts to discipline has to do with actions resulting from personal impulses, desires, dispositions, and proclivities, it is attempting to construct a regime of self-discipline. Such self-discipline requires self-monitoring and thus a significant measure of what one might call tacit introspection. If one wishes not to act on greed, lust, bibulousness, impulsiveness, anger, and so forth, then one has to be able to recognize these impulses in oneself in order to keep from acting upon them. In Proverbs, however, the development of a vocabulary and a rhetoric of self-examination and self-monitoring is rudimentary. But it is not entirely absent.

Internalizing External Authority

Internalizing external authority is represented by a shift in the location of instruction in relation to the body. What was external is brought close to and even placed inside the body. One of Proverbs' privileged images is drawn from the practice of wearing amulets. "Bind them [the father's/mother's teachings] over your heart always; bind them around your throat" (6:21; cf. 3:3a; 7:3a).[22] That image represents teachings as an external protective power, but one that is metonymically related to the subject's own body. Other imagery suggests that teaching was stored in the body as a liquid was stored in a jar. Wisdom herself uses such a metaphor when she says that she will "pour forth my spirit to you; I will let you know my words" (1:23; cf. Sir 16:25; Ps 19:3a). The *rûaḥ* as breath and the *rûaḥ* as cognition are part of the same model for production of thoughts in speech. They pour forth from the container of the body through the mouth. Learning and preserving such wise speech is represented in inverse imagery, as in 22:17–18: "Incline your ear and listen to the words of the wise, and set your mind upon my knowledge. For it is pleasant when you store them in your belly, and they are always ready upon your lips."

The most powerful image draws on scribal practice, where the father commands the son concerning his teaching, "Write them on the tablet of your heart" (3:3b; 7:3b). The tablet or scroll was an aide-mémoire, normally an external repository for a text that the scribe learned.[23] The "tablet of the heart/mind" is in part an image for memorization,[24] but it is also likely a cultural model for the mind itself and the way in which the social norms of teaching become naturalized within the self. If the teaching and the heart/mind are merged, then the teaching is an indelible part of the person.[25] Memorization and recall of the text also bring into focus another aspect of the subject positions offered by the book of Proverbs. If one thinks of the text as a record of a social context involving teacher and student, then the only subject position offered to the reader/hearer of the text is that of the pupil or son, who is addressed. If, however, one considers the text as a memorized object that one then recites to oneself, then the one who has memorized it can be seen as occupying both the subject position of the father who speaks and the subject position of the son who is spoken to. That is to say, the externalized relationship of father and son stands in for the "I-Me" relationship of differentiated subjectivity. To memorize the text and to recite it to oneself is to internalize the entire relationship. In this way discipline is internalized as self-discipline. Notably, however, no attempt is made in the book of Proverbs to explore or exploit this space of the interior. Instead, internalized self-training and self-discipline are represented as though they were external social relationships. The culture simply does not seem to be all that interested in constructing a differentiated model of the self. But a few texts do begin to develop such a model.

One can see a modest sense of self-differentiation in the way the addressee relates to or is asked to control specific body parts. Self-control is often imaged as control of these organs. Control of the feet is control of actions (e.g., "Hold back your feet from their path," 1:15; cf. 4:27; 19:2; 25:17). Speech, which is of particular concern to Proverbs, is represented by the mouth, lips, and tongue, all of which must be subject to supervision and control (e.g., "The one who guards his mouth, preserves his life; the one who opens his lips wide—there is ruin for him," 13:3; cf. 4:24; 14:3; 21:23; 24:28). The capacity to direct the ears indicates the ability to orient the self receptively (e.g., "If you make your ear attend to wisdom and guide your heart toward understanding," 2:2; cf. 4:20; 5:1, 13; 22:17; 23:12). Direction of attention is also described in relation to eyes ("Do not let [my words] escape from your eyes, guard them inside your heart," 4:21; cf. 3:21; 4:25; 23:26; 28:27). In these instances, however, the body parts seem largely to function as synecdoches for the person as such. They are not particularly reified as problematic aspects of a psychosomatic self. The only expression that might suggest a mistrust of one's self is the statement about being wise, right, or pure "in one's own eyes," designating self-evaluation (3:7; 16:2; 21:2; 26:5, 12, 16; 28:11; 30:12). These expressions always represent flawed or faulty self-judgment. They do not appear to represent a congenital problem of the human composition, however, but simply a failure of formation in wisdom more generally. One can conclude that the sayings that refer to mistrust of and the need for control of various body parts are evidence for a concern with self-monitoring, but they do not suggest a highly differentiated model of the psychological self.

The most significant organ for self-representation in Proverbs is the heart/mind (*lēb*). As the organ that retains external teaching ("Let your mind guard my commandments," 3:1b; cf. 2:10; 3:3; 4:4), it is key to self-formation. Often paired with the ears, it is the organ of attentive focus and active engagement ("An intelligent mind acquires knowledge, and the ear of the wise seeks out knowledge," 18:15; cf. 2:2; 7:25; 22:17; 23:19, 26; 24:32; 27:23). Unlike the organs that negotiate the sphere of public interaction (e.g., foot, hand, eyes, mouth, tongue, lips), it is often associated with the self as private space, sometimes in dangerous ways ("Duplicity is in his mind—the one who plots evil all the time," 6:14; cf. 12:20; 14:13; 15:11; 20:5; 23:7; 24:12; 25:3; 26:23, 25), and a place of reflection ("The mind of the righteous considers how to answer, while the mouth of the wicked blurts out evil," 15:28). But its status as a place of self-privacy is limited, since the wise (20:5) and God (24:12) are able to search it out. Moreover, its role as the executive function of the self is constrained by the intentionality of God in directing speech and actions ("A man may arrange his thoughts, but what he says depends on the Lord," 16:1; NJPS; cf. 16.9). The heart/mind appears frequently in sayings that model self-reflexive action, the "I-Me" relationship. In those sayings, it may be represented either as the "I" that perceives or acts ("The heart knows the bitterness of its soul," 14:10a; cf. 16:23) or as the "Me" that is acted upon ("More than all that you guard, guard your mind, for from it come the springs of life," 4:23; cf. 8:5; 15:32; 17:16; 23:12; 24:32; 27:23; 28:14). There are limits to one's ability to act upon the self (20:9), and the heart/

mind, like the eyes, can be a deceptive instrument of self-evaluation (28:26). The fundamentally sociocentric orientation of Proverbs is reflected in the way in which what guards against deceptive self-evaluation for the wise is the receptiveness to rebuke from the social community of other sages (e.g., 6:23; 10:17; 12:1; 13:18; 15:5, 32). The *nepeš* is less prominent in Proverbs than the *lēb*, though sometimes they are paired (2:10; 19:8). Most often it is used as a quasi-reflexive term for "self" or as a term for "life." In a few cases, however, it figures self-reflexivity ("the mind [*lēb*] knows the bitterness of its soul [*nepeš*]," 14:10; "the one who acquires a mind loves his soul," 19:8; "the counsel of the soul," 27:9).

The notion of the interiority of a core self or a self that can be hidden from others is evident in the idiom "chambers of the belly" (*ḥadrê beṭen*). The metaphor likens the body to a house with a series of rooms. Social pain caused by the harsh words of others is said to "go down to the chambers of the belly," that is, to penetrate to the inner reaches of a person (18:8; 26:22). Although the overall meaning of 20:30 is debated,[26] the sense of "chambers of the belly" as the core of the person is clear there as well. Unfortunately, the gnomic syntax and our limited understanding of Israelite anthropology complicate the interpretation of 20:27 (*nēr yhwh nišmat ʾādām; ḥōpēś kol-ḥadrê-beṭen*). Even here it is clear that "chambers of the belly" represents an aspect of the self that is both its core and normally inaccessible to others. Breath does go down into the body, and so it may be that it provides some sort of access to the central part of a person. I agree with Fox that one should not gloss "human lifebreath" as "conscience" and see the breath as exercising an introspective examination of the person.[27] That would be a more developed notion of interiority than appears in the rest of the book. It is possible, as Fox and Clifford suggest,[28] that the lifebreath here is understood, as in Genesis 2:7 and Ezekiel 37:9–10, as coming from God, though there is no intertextual allusion. But in what sense is the lifebreath the "lamp of Yhwh"? The lamp is clearly something that illuminates what is otherwise dark and impenetrable. Perhaps nothing more is intended by the image than the sense that the breath is what connects the exterior and the interior of a person. Thus to follow the breath to its source is to be able to examine what a person might think is hidden.

The internalization of discipline and the issue of internal self-action also come into view in the relation of the person to his or her *rûaḥ*. As Tyler Duckworth has argued, *rûaḥ* "operates as a psychosomatic 'organ,'"[29] and thus it deserves examination alongside of the other bodily organs related to cognition, character, and action. Although a few occurrences of the word in Proverbs refer to meteorological phenomena, most refer to the cognitive domain of temperament or mental faculties, though in some instances also overlapping with the domain of physical respiration.[30] It seems quite likely that, similar to the way in which Homeric literature represents the physical organs of respiration as part of the mental faculties,[31] so, too, Israel may have associated the organs of respiration and the breath itself with personal vitality, disposition, and cognition. Both the pace and the temperature of one's *rûaḥ* were indicative of psychological disposition. A "cold *rûaḥ*" is associated with good sense, manifested in "holding back" speech (*ḥôśēk 'ămārāw*, Prov 17:27).[32] What they mean by "cold *rûaḥ*" is clarified by its opposite. Although the exact expression "hot *rûaḥ*" is not used, the association of heat with the nose is a common idiom for anger in the Hebrew Bible, and the nose, along with the mouth, is the conduit of the *rûaḥ* (cf. the discussion of Prov 1:23 above). Thus they belong to the same cultural cognitive model of anger. Elihu in Job 32:2–3 is said to have a "hot nose," and in Proverbs 29:22 the "man of nose" (*'îš 'āp*) is paralleled with the "possessor of wrath" (*ba'al ḥēmâ*). Physiologically, we would think of the phenomenon in terms of increased blood flow to the face and nose. But it seems likely that the Israelites attributed the sensation of heat to the *rûaḥ* breath.[33] Thus rash speech or speech that might appear to be rash (in Elihu's case) is associated with heated breath as it comes to the mouth and nose. Similarly, the rate of breathing or the length of breaths was indicative of different dispositions, as in Proverbs 14:29, where "shortness of *rûaḥ*" is contrasted with "length of nose," expressions that are typically understood as connoting impatience and patience, respectively. As Duckworth suggests, these differences may well be observations about "an agitated person exhibiting short breaths," as contrasted with someone whose breathing is slower and more measured.[34]

The use of "high" and "low" to describe a person's *rûaḥ*, as in 16:18b–19a (cf. 29:23), is likely not a physiological model so much as the application of another common cognitive model in which height is associated with pride or arrogance and lowness with modesty and humility. Less clear is whether references to a "shattered" (*šeber*) or "broken" (*někē'â*) spirit are thought of in physiological terms. We simply do not have enough evidence from the texts to judge. In Proverbs these expressions appear to denote depression or sadness (Prov 15:4, 13; 17:22; 18:14), though in Psalms the "broken spirit" denotes humility before God (Pss 34:19; 51:19).

Although a number of the references to *rûaḥ* as psychosomatic organ are merely descriptive, there are also sayings that presume the ability of a person to control his or her *rûaḥ*. As Duckworth points out,[35] the description of uncontrolled *rûaḥ* ("like a city breached, without walls, is a person who lacks control of his *rûaḥ*," 25:28) would be meaningless unless it were possible to exercise control. Such regulation of the *rûaḥ* figures explicitly in a saying contrasting the fool and the wise in 29:11 ("A fool [*kĕsîl*] gives full vent to his *rûaḥ*, but the wise person holds it back"). Thus an important part of the training in wisdom is the ability to monitor and control one's own temperament and impulses, and indeed, it is one of the highest manifestations of internalized wisdom: "Better is the one who rules his *rûaḥ* than one who takes a city" (16:32).

All of the sayings that speak of control of the body in its various parts and organs are part of the system of self-monitoring and control that points toward the "I-Me" self-differentiation necessary for all human social functioning. Significantly, in Proverbs no organs of the body are seen as intrinsically bad or defective. Like the person as a whole, they are educable and only become problematic when undisciplined and untrained. Those sayings that are related to the organs that represent the temperament, emotions, impulses, and cognition—what we take as the psychological domain—are the most important for estimating the degree to which a sense of interiority and self-differentiation was developed in Proverbs. Judging from the evidence, one would have to say that while the potential was certainly present, it was not developed. In part this may be because the inherited literary forms of instruction and gnomic saying do not give much scope for the development of discourses of introspective consciousness. Indeed, the act of memorizing instructions, with their father/son or teacher/pupil social relationships, and proverbial sayings, with their generalized authoritative voice, reinforces the fundamentally sociocentric orientation of Proverbs and likely inhibits the development of an introspective turn in wisdom literature. Even in the later texts of Sirach and 4QInstruction, the situation is much the same. Qohelet's development of an introspective and retrospective voice may well draw on a different trajectory, perhaps related to that of the didactic introspective psalmic style illustrated in Psalm 73, discussed in chapter 1.

Motivating and Equipping Moral Agents in Deuteronomy

Deuteronomy is a book to be reckoned with for many reasons, not the least of which is its role in shaping issues of moral agency. Its influence on the moral imaginary of early Judaism was profound, becoming, as Juha Pakkala recently described it, "the core document of Second Temple Judaism."[36] Presenting itself as Moses's farewell speech to the Israelites before his death and their entry into the promised land, Deuteronomy has a strongly hortatory framework. But within Moses's speech, its covenantal model of Israel's relationship to Yhwh is strongly shaped by the model of ancient Near Eastern suzerain/vassal treaties. This model introduces a number of distinctive elements into its framing of moral agency, including core assumptions about the nature of the relationship, analysis of potential failure, and strategies for securing the reliable exercise of good agency. It is also an excellent example of the way in which the model of the nation as moral agent is complexly related to individual moral agency, in that the nation's obedience and fidelity depend on the distributed acts of agency performed by each and every Israelite. Given the political framing of the relationship between the nation and God, however, the dire political fate of the nation raised fundamental questions about the people's ultimate capacity for moral agency, an issue with which Second Temple Judaism struggled in various ways.

How to evaluate the role of Deuteronomy in shaping a model of moral agency depends in part on establishing its original *Sitz im Leben* as well as its reception and adaptation in subsequent times. Debates over Deuteronomy's origins have been one of the constants in biblical studies, ever since the groundbreaking work of W.M.L. de Wette,[37] with proposals ranging from premonarchic to postexilic. Moreover, it is evident that Deuteronomy is a complex document that has a complicated literary history, though the contradictory proposals for reconstructing that history are likely indications that it will never be conclusively recovered in any detail. Currently, the majority of scholars appear to think that Deuteronomy is significantly a product of Judean scribes working in the Neo-Assyrian period, with evidence of redactional work in the early postexilic period. An articulate minority of scholars, however, have argued that Deuteronomy, though incorporating some earlier materials, is essentially the product of the exilic or early postexilic periods.[38] Since my interest is in the *type* of moral relationship established through the rhetoric of the book, resolving the issue of the date is not essential, though I am largely persuaded by those who argue for the Neo-Assyrian context.

For my purposes, I am not concerned to analyze the moral content of the core of Deuteronomy, the body of laws in chapters 12–26. My interests are rather in the motivation for obedience and the ways in which such motivation is related to the problem of shaping moral agency. Although occasional references to motivations for commitment to the laws are scattered within chapters 12–26, by and large the issues of motivation and agency are concentrated in the hortatory framing of the book in chapters 1–11 and 27–30. These chapters lay out the moral basis for commitment to the laws *as a whole*, and they do so by highlighting the moral foundations that govern the relationship between the people and God. While I think it likely that some form of the Mosaic framing of the presentation of the laws was part of the literary form of the book before the end of the monarchy, it is evident that aspects of this framing are aware of and attempt to address the events of 586 BCE.[39] Throughout this framing material a tension exists between the absolute necessity for the exercise of moral agency and the recognition of its fragility. As with much other biblical literature, the problems and possibilities of moral agency are framed largely in social categories (the "I-You" relationship) rather than as issues of internal monitoring (the "I-Me" relationship). The notable innovation, however, stemming from the post-586 BCE additions, is the adaptation of the model of divine-human co-agency into the realm of moral agency before God.

Ever since George Mendenhall's research in the 1950s, scholars have recognized the impact of the ancient Near Eastern vassal treaty model in shaping Deuteronomy.[40] The specific points of connection between the Assyrian traditions and Deuteronomy are to be found in chapters 13 and 28, not in the hortatory material. Nevertheless, as John Collins has observed, "the drafters of Deuteronomy conceived of the kind of loyalty demanded by Yhwh by analogy with the loyalty demanded by the Assyrian king," a precis of which is embodied in the Shema in Deuteronomy 6:4–7, and, indeed, throughout the hortatory material.[41] The moral relationship constructed by this model is essentially a feudal one. As Avishai Margalit describes it, feudalism is a primary example of a "thick relationship," one that is deeply personal, as opposed to a "thin relationship" that is less personal and more transactional.[42] The feudal relation is one "based on belonging" but also on "protection for services."[43] The moral values that govern feudal relationships, including those of Deuteronomy, are authority, reciprocity, and loyalty.[44] Although the assumptions and expectations associated with this type of moral relationship are made most explicit in political discourse, they are also broadly constitutive of a wide range of hierarchical social relationships in the ancient Near East. Thus it is helpful to set this model in broader context.

Authority. Social dominance hierarchy is deeply rooted in human societies, although in certain social contexts the countervailing impulse to limit bullying and abuse results in more egalitarian forms of social organization, as is often characteristic of small, isolated hunter/gatherer bands.[45] Settled groups in larger societies, however, especially those that are in frequent contact with outsider groups, are more typically hierarchical, as was the case in the agrarian ancient Near East. In hierarchical relationships a lower-ranking individual shows deference, respect, and obedience to a higher-ranking individual, whose acknowledged status helps ensure social harmony and cooperation, as well as providing other benefits for members of the group.[46] What makes authority a *moral* foundation is the sense that a particular hierarchy is deeply legitimate and fundamentally oriented to the good of the group. It is perceived as supporting security and order and placing a check on arbitrary uses of power within the group. The authority of ancient Near Eastern kings and other ranking males is often presented in just such a fashion. Kulamuwa of Sam'al authorizes his kingship precisely in terms of his provision of security and prosperity for the *mushkabim*, a term that may refer to the poor.[47] Similarly, security, justice, and prosperity are the benefits conferred by the king in Psalm 72. Even in the village context, Job presents a similar justification for his social rank in Job 29. This social authority is grounded in an implicit metaphorical extension of the parent-child relationship to the leader-group relationship, as is made explicit in Kulamuwa's claim that "I was to some a father; and to some I was a mother; and to some I was a brother" (*COS* 2.30:148), or in Job's statement that "I was a father to the needy" (Job 29:16a). In the pastoral ancient Near East, the shepherd/sheep metaphor also belongs to this set of associations. As Moshe Weinfeld and Frank Cross have argued, the political and diplomatic vocabulary and conceptual apparatus of the ancient Near East were grounded in such kinship categories and derived much of their power from those basic bonds.[48] If authority is recognized as legitimate, then the appropriate response to it is respect, obedience, and submissiveness. Rejection of authority expresses itself in disrespect, disobedience, and rebellion.

That Deuteronomy frames the role of Yhwh in terms of authority is evident simply from the repetition of words such as "command" (*'āmar*, some thirty-nine times in chapters 1–11, referring both to God and to Moses) and the various lexemes for "obey," "keep," "observe," "do." Narratively, God is presented as exercising a leadership function in bringing the people out of Egypt and to their new land, providing for them along the way, protecting them from enemies, and instituting a social order to live by, thus representing divine authority as beneficial. The failures of the people are represented largely as failures in relation to authority—that is, disobedience and rebellion. The people's behavior is characterized by such expressions as "you refused," "flouted the command," "behaved insolently," "would not listen," "acted stubbornly," and the like. Authority asserts itself in the face of such opposition largely through the threat of punishment, as one sees in the warnings so prominent in Deuteronomy and the extensive list of curses for violation of the covenant (e.g., Deut 6:15; 7:10; 8:19–20; 9:13–14; 11:28; 28:14–68).

The moral foundation of authority is usually buttressed by other coordinated foundations. Since Deuteronomy is concerned with the authority of a deity, one might assume there would be a strong appeal to sanctity. But while the sanctity of Yhwh is certainly assumed, sanctity plays only a modest supporting role in Deuteronomy's hortatory rhetoric, in contrast to Ezekiel, who tightly binds divine authority to sanctity.[49] Instead Deuteronomy mines the resources of reciprocity and also loyalty to fill out its motivational picture, as one would expect, given its indebtedness to the model of the suzerain/vassal treaty and thus to the kinship models on which it significantly draws.[50]

Reciprocity. Authority on its own does not necessarily tap into strong positive emotions. In *The Righteous Mind*, Jonathan Haidt identifies the characteristic moral emotions keyed to authority as "respect" and "fear" and the relevant virtues as "obedience" and "deference." But because authority, at least as it manifests itself in feudal relationships, involves the provision of important social goods, it can pair easily with reciprocity, which brings with it a different palate of moral emotions, most notably "gratitude" and "guilt."[51] Thus the hortatory material of Deuteronomy is replete with reminders of what Yhwh has already graciously and without obligation done to benefit Israel and what Yhwh is prepared to do in the future. These include election of the ancestors and Yhwh's availability to the people (4:7–8, 35–36; 9:5; 10:15), deliverance from slavery, the gift of land to occupy, victory over enemies (5:6–7; 6:10, 18–25; 7:1–2, 8; 8:7–10; 9:1–3; 11:2–6, 10, 22–25), future prosperity in recognition of obedience (6:3–4; 8:1, 13–15; 10:22; 11:14–15), and wondrous acts both past and future, including provision in the wilderness (7:18–21; 8:2–4). The people have done nothing to "deserve" this benefaction. It is a gift. What is the appropriate response? One cannot "repay" the lavish gift; but one is expected to respond with what *is* in one's power to give, and as Yhwh makes clear, what is desired is obedience to the laws and statutes—that is, recognition of God's authority. Failure in reciprocity is selfishness, characterized by forgetfulness ("take care that you do not forget Yhwh your God," 9:11), fueled by complacency ("when you have eaten and are satisfied and built fine houses to live in . . . beware that your heart not become arrogant and you forget Yhwh your God," 8:11–14), resulting in misattribution ("Do not say to yourself, 'My own power and the strength of my own hand have gotten me this wealth,'" 8:17). Precisely because the moral foundation of reciprocity is so deeply ingrained in human relations, such failures constitute repugnant behavior, as the audience knows.

The logic underlying the account of Yhwh's graciousness and the conferred benefits—and the logic's concomitant expectation of something rendered in return—is what is known in evolutionary biology as the logic of reciprocal altruism.[52] Although reciprocal altruism has been documented in many species, humans are an extraordinarily cooperative species, in large part because we have an exceptional ability to keep track of who has done favors for us and who has not reciprocated when we have done favors for them. Recent studies have also demonstrated the way in which gratitude both reinforces the likelihood of further prosocial behavior on the part of the benefactor and motivates prosocial behavior on the part of the recipient, both toward the benefactor and even toward third parties (cf. Deut 10:17–19).[53] Some social psychologists differentiate between gratitude on the one hand and obligation and indebtedness on the other.[54] By closely associating authority and reciprocity foundations, Deuteronomy blurs the distinction so that the motivation for obedience is simultaneously gratitude for benefits graciously conferred and the obligation of deference to authority.

Loyalty. One might discuss the hortatory sections of Deuteronomy simply in terms of authority and reciprocity. But the significant presence of strong, emotionally charged words and scenarios suggests that loyalty is also relevant to the moral recipe of this portion of Deuteronomy.[55] In traditional societies, and especially in feudal relationships, loyalty is strongly personal. Indeed, feudal loyalty lays claim to priority even over kin and ethnic loyalty. Margalit cites the medieval *Book of Fiefs*: "Vassals must help their lord against everyone—against their brothers, against their sons, against their fathers."[56] Similarly, in Deuteronomy 13:7–19 loyalty to Yhwh explicitly supersedes loyalty to brother, son, daughter, wife, friend, or fellow Israelite. Moreover, in Deuteronomy it is loyalty to Yhwh that is the basis for ethnic differentiation, since the inhabitants of Canaan are to be shunned or even exterminated because of the danger they pose to exclusive loyalty to Yhwh (Deut 7:1–5).

As often noted, Deuteronomy is characterized by an emphasis on love, both the love by Yhwh for the people and the love that the people are commanded to show in return (4:37; 5:10; 6:5; 7:9, 13; 10:12, 15, 18–19; 11:13). While it is generally agreed that the context for the rhetoric of love is the political culture of ancient Near Eastern treaties,[57] it would be a mistake to minimize the affective content, as Jacqueline Lapsley has argued.[58] This is love as affective solidarity, originally grounded in the family and kin group. Political culture appropriated this powerful mechanism by symbolically extending it to relationships of political allies. It is no accident that royal families also practiced intermarriage, thus literally forming kin bonds between different political entities. This is powerful "social glue." The novel appropriation of the covenant model to structure the God-people relationship in ancient Israel, nowhere more fully developed than in Deuteronomy, is a strategy for tapping into strong emotional bases. Although it offers many advantages, one of the most powerful is the way in which it recasts veneration of other gods in terms of betrayal. For most ancient peoples, including many Israelites, the veneration of various gods was simply prudential and advantageous behavior (e.g., 2 Kgs 17:24–33; Jer 44:15–19; Hos 2:7). But once the relation to Yhwh has been cast in terms of the exclusive loyalty owed to a sovereign on the model of political treaties like Esarhaddon's vassal treaties, then such practices become repugnant treachery.

Agency. Deuteronomy's foregrounding of authority, reciprocity, and loyalty elevates the role of agency in distinctive ways. One can begin to see how by contrasting the role of agency in Deuteronomy and Proverbs. Many scholars have noted the similarities between aspects of the language, categories, and values of Deuteronomy and wisdom texts. Certainly the scribes responsible for Deuteronomy were formed by and drew on their grounding in the sapiential tradition and brought elements of that tradition into the service of their moral vision.[59] But the differences in the way the moral relationships are cast in Deuteronomy and in Proverbs are significant. Above all, the moral relationship in Deuteronomy is a thick one, whereas in Proverbs it is thin, or at least thinner. In Proverbs, the father, God, and Wisdom are all authoritative figures, but the relationships are not filled out with histories or with strong emotional content. In Deuteronomy, those features are central. In Proverbs, the successful student ultimately internalizes the teachings, so that his formation results in his, too, becoming a "father" (Prov 4:3), stabilizing his agency as part of his identity. The formation of proper agency is deeply tied up with the replication of the social order, which it represents as the manifestation of reality (Wisdom) itself. The student is directed to "see" patterns of the act-consequence relationship that he then can confirm for himself. This prioritizing of the cognitive element also provides a profound stability to successfully formed agency.[60] By contrast, Deuteronomy represents the central moral relationship as historically contingent. In fact, the contingent nature of the relationship characterizes it at every moment. The moral relationship in Deuteronomy is both powerful and fragile. Whereas Proverbs aims to form a subject who is habituated to good agency and whose failures are subject to correction by the community, Deuteronomy frames agency as a series of repeated choices, any one of which is potentially capable of destroying the relationship. Consequently, a certain tension, even an anxiety, attends to the problem of agency in Deuteronomy. There, too, the emotions, both positive and negative ones, have a more prominent role to play. Finally, Proverbs focuses on the formation of the individual in the context of replicating the social order. Deuteronomy, though it often addresses the people as individuals and is concerned with individual behavior, is ultimately concerned with the formation of the nation as a moral agent. The complex political context of national policy is not the same as the context of individual decisionmaking; yet this difference is strategically obscured because of the way in which national agency is represented as distributed individual agency in Deuteronomy.

What, then, are Deuteronomy's strategies for forming successful moral agency? First is solemnizing and ritualizing the act of commitment. Just as certain rituals may be used to strengthen biological and marital kinship relations (e.g., naming ceremonies, coming of age rituals, betrothal and wedding ceremonies), so the implicit extension of the kinship model to political relations depends even more on ritual formalization. A solemn oath of fealty is often sworn in the presence of deities as witnesses and guarantors, as in the Near Eastern vassal treaties (e.g., VTE i.13–40). In Deuteronomy, the people are vividly reminded of their participation in the awful and solemn events at Horeb when Yhwh "declared to you the covenant that he commanded you to observe" (4:13). A second solemn ceremony is prescribed for enactment when they have crossed the Jordan (27:1–26), as well as a periodic public reading of "this Teaching" every seventh year at Sukkot (31:10–13).

Second, and closely related, is fear. In Deuteronomy, the seriousness of the covenant relation is grounded in the awe and fear the people experience at the "mighty voice" that came "out of the fire and cloud" (Deut 4:9–14; 5:2–5, 19–24). Moreover, punishment for violation is a frequent motif of the rhetoric of Deuteronomy (4:3, 25–28; 6:15; 7:10; 8:20; 9:7–21; 11:6, 17).[61] The covenant curses may be a formal part of the covenant document, as in VTE vi.414–viii.668. Or, as in Deuteronomy 27–28, they may be employed in ritual reinforcement of the obligation undertaken.

Third, in ways that are somewhat similar to the Hittite covenant tradition, Deuteronomy constructs agency that supports authority, reciprocity, and loyalty by attempting to heighten the emotions that motivate the relationships. In keeping with the implicit folk theory of moral failure found in many biblical texts, Deuteronomy identifies three areas of vulnerability. The most prominent in Deuteronomy is cognitive—the problem of forgetting (4:9, 23; 6:12; 8:11, 13, 17, 19; cf. 7:17, 21). This "forgetting" is, of course, not simple lapse of memory but describes rather a refusal to acknowledge the nature of the relationship. Thus it is closely linked to the second area of moral failure, the stubborn will and the reluctance to embrace heteronomy, most vividly described as being "stiff-necked" (9:6, 13, 23, 27; 10:16). The third has to do with desire, sometimes related to words for seduction (4:19; 11:16) or entrapment (7:16, 25), and the attractions of other cultures (7:4) or visible images (9:12, 16). All three dimensions of moral failure are intertwined and reinforce one another.

For Deuteronomy, the remedy for these problems is a cognitive/affective one that puts responsibility on the agent. Scholars have often noted the central role of memory in Deuteronomy.[62] The preferred term, however, is not *zākar* but *šāmar*, "to guard, keep," suggesting a kind of hypervigilant attention. What is to be remembered is above all the founding events (e.g., "take utmost care and watch yourselves scrupulously, so that you do not forget the things that you saw with your own eyes and so that they do not fade from your mind," 4:9; NJPS) and the catalogue of benefits conferred by God (e.g., 4:32–34, 37–38; 6:10–11, 20–23; 7:8, 13–15, 21–24; 8:3–4, 7–9, 15–16; 9:1–3; 11:2–4, 9–15). These events form the deeply emotional basis for the gratitude, loyalty, and respect that make only one choice imaginable: the choice for obedience. The techniques for remaining in this state of vivid presence are exhaustive, including eternalized reminders, internalized reminders, use of the body as a reminder, reminders keyed to every activity of the day, teaching one's children, and so forth. Constant emotional arousal of profound gratitude ensures proper agency (4:9, 13–14; 6:6–9, 20–25; 8:2–6, 10; 11:18–21).

Fourth, a striking part of Deuteronomy's strategy is vivid recitation of past moral failures and the creation of scenarios of potential failure in the future. In its present form the book opens with an extended narration of the people's moral failure at Kadesh-barnea, when they refused to enter the land out of fear (1:22–45), a rebellion that resulted in the condemnation of virtually the entire generation of those who had left Egypt. That narrative is bookended by a similarly extended recounting of the moral failure at Horeb when the people made the golden calf (9:6–29). In various other places past, potential, and future failures are lifted up (4:25–28; 6:10–19; 7:1–5; 8:11–20). Although it might seem counterintuitive to bolster agency by repeatedly drawing attention to past and potential failure, such a strategy works by stirring up anxiety that then stimulates vigilance. This rhetoric makes vivid why scrupulous "keeping watch over" oneself (4:9) is required. To be sure, there is as yet no cultivation of an introspective conscience in Deuteronomy in any psychological sense, though its rhetoric of self-monitoring begins to move in that direction, a shift that will be taken further in many Second Temple texts. In keeping with the general social or "I-You" orientation of the rhetoric, Deuteronomy mostly frames the scenarios of disobedience in terms of specific events and the actions of the people in those past or potential situations. But in the extended description of the apostasy of the people at Horeb, the rhetoric shifts to suggest that the people are intrinsically given to willful disobedience, being "stiff-necked" and persistently defiant (e.g., 9:6, 13, 24). The moral problem is thus not simply what one might do but who one is by disposition. Again, Deuteronomy does not develop this claim extensively, though in a very important passage it presents a model for moral self-repair that becomes highly influential in the Second Temple period. "Circumcise the foreskin of your heart, and do not stiffen your neck any more" (10:16). The striking metaphor of circumcision of the heart may actually originate with Jeremiah and have been incorporated into Deuteronomy from that text as part of the reworking of Deuteronomy in the exilic and early postexilic periods.[63] It is noteworthy in that in this formulation it is not just that one must monitor one's will and behavior (as in the instruction not to stiffen the neck) but must turn attention to the organ that plays a key role in disposition and agency (the heart) and intervene to improve its functioning.

Theoretically, Deuteronomy's strategies for constant vigilance would seem to be effective, though in practice it would be difficult to sustain the degree of emotional arousal that the book envisions. Even if Deuteronomy's utopian memory practices had been instituted, they would have risked becoming routine and rote. Indeed, the final layers of redaction in Deuteronomy have to grapple with the reality of moral failure. And yet, it appears that this failure does not significantly alter Deuteronomy's approach to agency. Deuteronomy 4:25–31 envisions the future from Moses's perspective, a future in which the people commit disloyalty and undergo destruction, exile, and service to idols. In effect, this experience serves as a traumatic memory practice, causing the people to turn again to Yhwh, who redeems the people as in the foundational past.[64] The ability to renew a broken relationship is one of the inherent resiliencies of thick relations based on models of kinship and/or shared history, so that failure may be incorporated into the model itself. The destruction of Judah in 586 BCE, however, would have appeared from the Deuteronomic perspective as a massive failure of moral agency, one that could cast into question the adequacy of the model of moral agency upon which it is based.[65] Indeed, there is evidence within Deuteronomy for just such a recognition of a limit to human moral agency that makes self-repair impossible. In the postexilic addition in 30:1–10, as in 4:25–31, the trauma of exile serves to restore the proper emotions and dispositions that lead to obedience and fidelity, so that Yhwh once again enacts a redemption and restoration (30:1–5). The innovation is in verse 6, in which Yhwh circumcises the hearts of the people, a deliberate alteration of 10:16, in which the people are themselves to perform this repair. But what is the relation of 30:6 to 30:1–2, which seems to envision a prior "turning" of the people to Yhwh? Most scholars assume that the alteration of the heart in verse 6 is an additional gift by Yhwh to make future failure less likely.

More radically, Marc Brettler argues that the syntax of the passage allows one to understand that it is divine action itself that makes possible the human turning to Yhwh in verses 1–2.[66] Syntactically, the question has to do with where the protasis ends and the apodosis begins. Most scholars take the protasis to consist of verses 1–2, with the apodosis beginning in verse 3 (e.g., "When all these things befall you . . . and you take them to heart . . . and you return to the Lord your God . . . , then the Lord your God will restore your fortunes"; NJPS). It is also syntactically possible, Brettler argues, that the apodosis begins in verse 1. Thus the logic of the passage would be governed by the theological perspective of verse 6.

> [The passage] would be saying that once the blessing and curse are fulfilled (1a), the following will happen: you will return (vv. 2–3); Yhwh will return

> and will return you to the land (vv. 3–5), he will then circumcise your hearts (v. 6) and punish your enemies (v. 7); you will indeed return (v. 8), and Yhwh will bless you (v. 9).[67]

If the syntax is construed in this manner, then the presupposition would be much the same as in the narratives in which God engages in dual or co-agency with Samson to cause him to desire Philistine women, or with Abimelech to cause him not to have sex with Sarah, or with Pharaoh to cause him to refuse to let the Israelites go. But for the first time this model of agency would be applied to the repentance of the people as a whole, a relationship that otherwise assumes only the model of autonomous free agency. That is not to say that there was any conscious or intentional construction of an analogy with those narrative texts of co-agency. Cultural models are often present subliminally and brought into play as circumstances require without anyone being aware of the innovation.

As Brettler demonstrates, certain later Second Temple texts, including Baruch 2:27–35 and 4QDibHam[a] (4Q504) 18:13–18, interpret the text as describing divine rather than human initiative. Baruch refers to the mercy that God has shown Israel and alludes to the words of God as cited by Moses in Deuteronomy 30:

> If you do not obey me, this very great multitude will be reduced to a small number among the nations where I shall banish them. For I know that they will not obey me—because they are a stiffnecked people—but in the land of their captivity they will repent, acknowledging that I am the Lord their God. I shall give them a heart and ears that hear . . . , and they will turn from their stubbornness. (Bar 2:29–33; trans. Brettler)[68]

The shift of agency is even clearer in 4QDibHam[a]. There the liturgist speaks of the people dispersed in exile: "You have again placed it on their hearts to return to You, to obey Your voice. . . . You have poured out Your holy spirit upon us. . . . You have caused us to seek You in our time of tribulation, [that we might po]ur out a prayer when Your chastening was upon us" (18:13–18; *DSSR*).[69]

Because the syntax in Deuteronomy is ambiguous, however, it remains unclear whether the passage *itself* intends to displace the role of the people in turning to Yhwh or if this interpretation was part of a later tendency to displace the source of moral agency from the people themselves to God. In support of Brettler's reading, however, are the roughly contemporary strategies of Jeremiah and Ezekiel. The Deuteronomistic tradents of Jeremiah also understood the people's adherence to the covenant obligations to be sustained by the same kind of teaching and memory practices that one finds in Deuteronomy. But teaching had failed. Now, if a "new covenant" is to be a possibility, it "will not be like the covenant that I [Yhwh] made with their ancestors" (Jer 31:32). Instead, "I will put my teaching into their inner parts, and I will inscribe it upon their hearts. . . . They will no longer teach each one his neighbor and each one his brother saying, 'Know Yhwh,' for all of them will know me, from the least to the greatest" (31:33–34). As in Proverbs, the internalization of teaching is an indication of its indelible presence. In Jeremiah, however, the personal agency of teaching and memorization is displaced by direct divine agency, bypassing the fallible human agency. Ezekiel's imagery is even more stark, as will be discussed below. All of these texts, however, point to the events of the fall of Judah as creating a crisis in the models of moral agency and the need to displace the source of agency onto God. The most sophisticated development of the notion of dual or co-agency will appear in the Hodayot from Qumran. Early Judaism could not do without a theory of moral agency. The covenantal basis of the relationship with Yhwh required it. Faced with apparent evidence of profound failure of human moral agency, they envisioned a secure and unassailable source for moral agency in the divine covenant partner. In no other text was this more radically imagined than in Ezekiel.

The Collapse and Reconstitution of Moral Agency in Ezekiel

In contrast to Deuteronomy, which is framed by an explicitly hortatory address, Ezekiel consists largely of prophetic indictment, followed by prophecies of hope. In investigating the moral values that inform Ezekiel, one must take account of this different rhetorical context. Furthermore, although some Deuteronomic assumptions are present in the book of Ezekiel, his conceptual and moral world is shaped overwhelmingly by priestly traditions, with a particularly close connection to the Holiness Code in Leviticus 17–26.[70]

As with Deuteronomy, Ezekiel also frames his engagement with his audience in terms of the moral value of divine authority, as one sees immediately in the prominence of terms for rebellion in the accusations that open chapter 2: "That nation of rebels, who have rebelled against me . . . defied me . . . brazen of face and stubborn of heart . . . a rebellious breed" (2:3–4). Similar language, coupled with accusations of disobedience to laws and rules, occurs throughout the prophetic indictments (e.g., 5:5–9; 12:1–3, 9, 25; 17:12, 15, 19; 20, passim). The ability of the people to obey the laws and statutes is the goal of their transformation (11:20; 36:27; 37:22–24). In contrast to Deuteronomy, however, Ezekiel pairs authority almost exclusively with sanctity.

It should be borne in mind that not every mention of a deity is an index of a concern with sanctity or holiness per se. Anthropomorphized deities may be incorporated as "superpersons" within various social relations and the moral foundations that organize them, as one sees in Deuteronomy, where authority, reciprocity, and loyalty are all ways of organizing the divine-human relationship. The realm of sanctity has to do with the radical qualitative difference between the divine and all else. Thus, whereas other moral foundations are grounded in social bonds and pragmatic relationships, the logic of sanctity appears to operate differently.

I am not persuaded that comparative moral theories have yet given a persuasive account of the evolutionary basis for human concern with sanctity or holiness. In Moral Foundations Theory, sanctity is discussed primarily in terms of concerns about purity and the emotion of disgust. It traces this focus evolutionarily to the concern to avoid contaminants and disease ("pathogens and parasites"). The things associated with these features are marked as unclean or impure and often elicit physical disgust.[71] The physical residue of the substance is seen as capable of spreading contamination through contact and/or as miasma, necessitating cleansing.[72] This schema also provides a basis for metaphorical or analogical extension to other phenomena, such as certain types of moral or social wrongs, that can be treated as though they left a similar dangerous residue, what Yitzhaq Feder calls the "stain of transgression."[73] While Moral Foundations Theory understands sanctity as in many respects the mirror opposite of impurity, it has not articulated the evolutionary bases for the positive role of the sanctity foundation. It is not possible to address the lacunae in Moral Foundations Theory analysis here, but it seems likely that, just as those things that elicit disgust signify invisible vectors of disease and death, so early humans may have posited forces that sustained life and vitality (e.g., divine blessing). Thus, sanctity and impurity concern the ultimacies of life and death. This dynamic might suggest why the sacred seems to have an ontological status unlike other moral foundations, so that ordinary pragmatic considerations do not apply—a violation of this realm is a threat to existence per se.

The ultimacy of the sacred may help explain the extreme rhetoric and practice that attend the role of sanctity. In the biblical tradition, the justifying motivation for sanctity is tautological: it is the sacred itself (e.g., "so that you may know that I am Yhwh"; "be holy as I am holy").[74] Responses to violations of the sacred are also distinctive. Although provisions for purification for unavoidable, everyday pollutions are readily available, and the dangers and pollution of inadvertent sins can be dispelled by sacrifice, intentional sin as a violation of sanctity has no remedy other than death, *kārēt* (being "cut off"), or "bearing one's sin."[75] The more socially grounded moral concerns, such as reciprocity and loyalty, drawing on different emotional resources, have greater flexibility for repairing even serious violations by means of enactments of repentance and reconciliation. But unauthorized contact with the sacred, even if unintentional and well-meaning, can evoke a response of immediate annihilation, as in the case of Uzza in 2 Samuel 6:6–7 (see also Num 4:18–20; 1 Sam 6:19).[76]

A concern for sanctity is evident in Ezekiel, beginning with the impressive theophany in chapters 1–3 and the definitive contrast between God and the human Ezekiel, pointedly referred to as *ben-'ādām* ("mortal being"). The focus continues with extensive cultic-related themes and vocabulary. The violations for which the people are blamed are overwhelmingly described in terms related to defilement, impurity, and idolatry. The improper shedding of blood is also prominent in the accounts of the people's sins. Key passages include the temple vision of chapters 8–11, which details defilement of the temple itself; the history of disobedience in chapter 20, which presents the sins in almost exclusively cultic terms; chapter 24, which highlights blood and impurity imagery; and, of course, the two allegories of chapters 16 and 23, which combine depraved sexuality, infanticide, and idolatry as means by which holy things were defiled. The restoration of the people and the land is described primarily in terms of cleansing from defilement (36:22–28), and the resolution of the book is expressed through the vision of a new temple and the laws that will ensure it is never again defiled (chaps. 40–48).

Also in contrast to Deuteronomy, Ezekiel explicitly dispenses with the foundations of reciprocity and loyalty and the resources of their rich emotionality. One sees this in Ezekiel's rejection of altruistic motives on the part of God or any emotional bond with the people. God acts only for the sake of his holy name—a sanctity motive (20:9, 14, 22; 36:22; 39:35; 43:7). As Baruch Schwartz puts it, "Ezekiel denies its [divine mercy's] very existence.

Nowhere in his prophetic teaching is Yhwh thought to do anything out of love, longing, compassion, or grace; indeed, the entire vocabulary pertaining to these concepts is missing from Ezekiel."[77] Though a covenant is reestablished, Ezekiel often describes it as imposed punitively and unwillingly on the people who wished rather to "be like the nations" (16:59–62; 20:32–38).[78]

In analyzing Israel's sin from the perspective of sanctity, Ezekiel frequently uses vocabularies of pollution and disgust (e.g., "defile" [*ṭāmēʾ*], "abomination" [*tôʿēbāh*], "loathe" [*qûṭ*]). Alien deities are not referred to as other gods whom people might serve, as in the relational language of Deuteronomy 7:4, but as "shit-fetishes" (*gillûlîm*) and "disgusting things" (*šiqqûṣîm*). His imagery often evokes physical disgust—food cooked over human excrement (4:12), a pot with indelible scum (24:6, 12–13), an infant covered in unwashed birth-blood (16:4), and so forth. Although not all sanctity violations are framed in impurity terms, where they are, the person who violates sanctity is not just a rebel but a degenerate, someone perverted and thus morally disgusting. Sexuality is a common category for characterizing persons as degenerate (in ways that can be deeply problematic), as one sees in Ezekiel's allegories of Jerusalem and Samaria in chapters 16 and 23, with their descriptions of disgusting sexual depravity and the moral disgust of infanticide.

Although anger is a response to violations of all moral foundations,[79] the annihilating rage that Ezekiel depicts in God's response to Israel's sin is both quantitatively and qualitatively different from the depiction of anger that accompanies violations of reciprocity or loyalty bonds and may well be related to the absolute quality of the sanctity foundation. In prophetic rhetoric such as one finds in Hosea and Jeremiah, which draws extensively on the moral values of reciprocity and loyalty, divine anger is often couched in emotional, relational terms and is frequently tied to a larger narrative of potential reconciliation or to a contrast between the faithless many and the faithful prophet (e.g., Hos 2; 4; 6; 11; Jer 4–5; 8; 15). In Ezekiel, however, the emotional model of anger that arises from betrayal is absent. Instead, in accounts that are often extended, focused, and graphic (e.g., 5:7–17; 7:1–27; 16:37–42; 21:1–22; 22:17–22; 23:22–34, 46–49), the rage that is expressed explicitly excludes competing emotions of compassion and pity (e.g., 7:4, 9). "Wrath" (*ḥēmāh*), one of the favored terms for divine anger in the prophets, occurs some thirty-three times in Ezekiel, as opposed to fourteen in Jeremiah and thirteen in Isaiah. Ezekiel frequently uses idioms that liken rage to a liquid that boils over or pours out (thirteen times with *šāpak*).

The utter completeness of the expenditure of God's rage is expressed in the expression *kālā 'āp* ("vent anger," 5:13; 6:12; 7:8; 13:15; 20:8, 22). Most unnervingly, the expression *hēnîaḥ ḥēmāh* ("satisfy wrath," 5:13; 16:42; 21:22; 24:13), unique to Ezekiel, suggests an almost orgasmic quality to the rage, which, once expended, brings quiet and satisfaction to Yhwh. There is, naturally, no narrative of reconciliation. The end result is simply that the people "know that I am Yhwh" (e.g., 7:4; 23:49) and that they experience self-loathing and shame (e.g., 16:61, 63; 20:43).

Agency

In the grouping of authority, reciprocity, and loyalty that one finds in Deuteronomy, it is easy to see how appeals to emotion and memory serve to support the kind of agency that those moral values require. But what sort of agency corresponds to sanctity, and how does one produce it? Since sanctity makes an ultimate claim, good tends to be framed as "like the sacred" and evil as "unlike the sacred." What is pure or clean is associated with the sacred and what is impure or unclean is excluded. Moral agency, where it is deemed possible, is manifested in a form of imitation of the divine, a kind of nonontological divinization. Conversely, in order to denigrate human moral agency, negative anthropologies, such as one finds in the speeches of Elihu and Bildad in Job 4:17–21, 15:14–16, and 25:4–6, combine an ontological opposition between the divine and the human with divine loathing of human pollution and sin.

To pursue the question of agency within a sanctity context, it is useful to look, not first at Ezekiel, but at the conceptually closely linked Holiness Code in Leviticus 17–26. These chapters largely consist of instructions of what to do or not to do in various realms of life—primarily in relation to the cult and to sexuality, but also in certain other areas of communal life. Rationale and justification are sparse, compared with Deuteronomy, and often articulated very simply in terms of not defiling oneself because "I am Yhwh your God." On several occasions, however, the text is explicit that obedience to these stipulations makes the people "holy" as Yhwh is holy (19:1; 20:7, 24–26; 22:31–33), though there is no ontological transformation of the people. In the Holiness Code the people are simply assumed to be capable of following the commandments.

Both the Holiness Code and Ezekiel, however, have to deal with the problem of catastrophically failed moral agency and the possibility of a future beyond moral failure. In Leviticus 26, which may be an exilic or postexilic addition to the Holiness Code,[80] the logic of condemnation is articulated largely in authority and sanctity terms. The disobedience of the people has polluted the land. No cultic expiation for the situation exists; the only possible remedy is expulsion from the land.[81] The possibility of an alternative to the utter destruction of the people and the grounding of a future is not worked out in terms of the sanctity foundation alone but through a combination of the resources of the logic of sanctity and the more relational foundations of reciprocity and loyalty. The severe punishment of expulsion and near extermination leads to an emotion described with a distinctive idiom found only in Leviticus 26:39 and Ezekiel 4:17, 24:23, and 33:10 (and possibly in Ps 106:43), "to be heartsick over iniquity" (NJPS; *yimaqqû / nāmaqqû ba'ăwōnām*). The verb has a concrete meaning of "rot, decay" and seems to suggest a distinctive emotional repugnance in the recognition of a sin against the sanctity of God. The "uncircumcised heart" of the people is "humbled," a socially conciliatory stance, and the people "atone" for their iniquity (Lev 26:41). How atonement is effected is initially unclear but is then related to the absence of the people from the land, which allows for the making up of the violated sabbath years (v. 43).[82] The relational resources of loyalty are also invoked, however, apparently as a motive for this cultic innovation, as the memory of the covenant with the ancestors and the Exodus is recalled (*zākar*).

Ezekiel, however, has radicalized the critique of the people's moral agency. Their depravity and obsessively disordered desires go back to their very origins. This argument is made both in the allegorical histories of chapters 16 and 23 and in the narrative history of chapter 20. As Jacqueline Lapsley has persuasively argued, the people are seen utterly to lack moral agency.[83] Despite Ezekiel's representation of the people as "heartsick," the option for their active participation in a process of atonement, as in Leviticus 26, is excluded. Ezekiel, however, further plumbs the possibilities of the sanctity foundation for a novel resolution. He recasts "divinization" not as an agential imitation of the holiness of God but as an actual transformation. Although the deep moral pollution of the people is beyond the reach of the ordinary institutions of cultic reparation, God unilaterally cleanses the people (36:25).[84] Then the people are recreated. The heart of stone is removed and a heart of flesh is given (36:26).[85] More significant, "a new spirit," which is specifically God's spirit, is placed into the people (36:26–27). Although there are other traditions of divine breath or spirit as the vivifying element in humans and other animals (Gen 2:7; Ps 104:30), Ezekiel uniquely associates the implanting of the spirit with the capacity for obedience to the laws and ordinances (36:27). The new divine element in humans is the source of agency. The other effect of this moral transformation, however, is recognition of the gravity of the previous offenses against sanctity, which expresses itself in the characteristic emotion of the sanctity foundation, moral disgust, here directed inwardly as self-loathing (36:31; 43:7–11).

The traumatic experience of the fall of Judah to the Babylonians, the destruction of the temple, and the exile of significant portions of the leadership classes drew into question the fundamental assumptions of the widespread understanding of the covenant relationship with Yhwh and the moral agency it assumed on the part of the people. While there were some resources for incorporating the failure into a narrative that could anticipate human repentance, divine forgiveness, and reconciliation (e.g., Jer 29:12–14), other, more radical constructions emerge in response. Analyses of moral failure begin to incorporate the possibility that not only the moral will but even the moral equipment of the people are flawed. Although self-repair is occasionally envisioned (Deut 10:16; Jer 4:4), other passages treat the inherent moral flaw of humans as something that requires divine agency to enact a repair or transformation of human moral organs (Deut 30:6; Jer 31:33–34; 32:39–40; Ezek 11:19; 36:25–27). That alternative conceptions that are logically inconsistent with one another should exist side by side is not surprising, nor should one necessarily assume a developmental trajectory that resolves the tensions. Multiple cognitive models are to be expected, especially in cases where new ones are emerging to cope with unprecedented experiences. But the innovative nature of divine intervention to reconstruct a fatally flawed moral nature in humans should not be overlooked. Deuteronomy, Jeremiah, and Ezekiel appear to envision this divine action as resolving the problem, so that the preexilic understanding of the covenant relationship could be resumed as the basis for the future of the people with God. Correspondingly, the assumptions of human moral agency and responsibility for moral failure reassert themselves in postexilic texts, such as the newly developing penitential prayers, the historical analysis of Chronicles, and other texts. But alongside these texts are others that assume that the capacity for moral agency requires a repeated or continual divine action, as already noted in Baruch and 4QDibHam. The shift in Deuteronomy, Jeremiah, and Ezekiel develops, of course, to address a problem in the model of the nation as a moral agent. But significantly, in the Second Temple period the models constructed to deal with the problem of national moral agency are coopted to explore the dynamics of individual moral agency. The consequences of this redirection of cultural resources are profound. The developing trajectory of personal prayers and psalms increasingly focuses on the condition of human sinfulness and moral incapacity and the necessity of divine assistance. Not only is this a shift in moral anthropology, but it also begins to construct new forms of more introspective selfhood as well as new modes of spirituality.

4 Sin-Consciousness, Self-Alienation, and the Construction of Interiority

Although cultural models are historical artifacts, it is difficult to catch them in the act of coming into being. Generally, such constructs are built up as modifications of existing models and may be motivated by a variety of cultural needs. Their development tends to be irregular rather than linear, and divergent models may flourish alongside one another. That is certainly the case with the models of the moral self, the conceptualizations of agency, and the construction of new spaces of interiority in Second Temple Judaism. As I have attempted to show in the previous chapters, Judean culture in the monarchical period tacitly assumed a robust understanding of moral agency. The loci of moral failure and the construction of good agency that could resist such failure were a concern of many texts, but there was no assumption that humans were constitutionally incapable of such agency or significantly impaired. Nor was significant attention given to the possibility of subindividual agency that might provide the basis for articulating and exploring experiences of inner conflict. With respect to agency more generally, although individual human agency was taken for granted, it was also assumed that Yhwh could influence and direct human decisionmaking in ways that persons might or might not be aware of. Although the mechanisms of such influence were not always of interest to narrators, the notion of "spirit" provided a category for the development of a variety of cultural models that could conceptualize the role of Yhwh's agency interacting with human agency. As for interiority, although ample evidence exists for basic assumptions about a certain inwardness, there was little apparent interest in cultivating these assumptions to create a complex inner realm of experience and reflection.

In the Second Temple period, however, all of these possibilities were developed and given a place alongside the continuation of traditional models of self and agency. By attending to the subtle modifications of inherited tropes and language, intertextual allusions, and novel interpretations of influential texts, it is possible to identify certain trajectories in the development of more complex models of subjectivity in Second Temple Judaism. A significant stream of this development focused on the problematics of human moral agency, an emphasis that was in part a legacy of the impact of the destruction of the kingdom of Judah as it was viewed through the lens of covenant theology. Yet it would be a mistake to see in these Second Temple texts only the growth of an anxious selfhood. While there are texts in which such an anxiety is foregrounded, in many cases the problematic moral self becomes the foil for the development of a spirituality of intimacy with God and an experience of personal transformation. In the most developed cases the transformation approaches something like a divinization or angelification of the speaker. But it is also not the case that all of Second Temple Judaism's interest in developing and exploring subjectivity can be understood as the working out of the surprisingly fruitful spiritual possibilities of a flawed human nature. Ample evidence exists of a widespread interest in subjective experience more generally, as I suggested at the end of chapter 1.

The Construction and Uses of Self-Alienation

Jeremiah, Deuteronomy, and Ezekiel. As discussed at the end of the preceding chapter, the catastrophic events of the early sixth century elicited several novel attempts to preserve the viability of a future for the covenantal relationship with Yhwh in the face of pervasive national failure. The imagery by which this situation is explored pushes past the model of functional moral failure and toward the imagery of intrinsic defect. In doing this, the texts in question make use of but intensify the self-reflexive attention that allows a person to focus on his or her own intentions, emotions, and motivations. They develop a model of what I would term "self-alienation." That is to say, a critical aspect of the self is strongly objectified in a manner that makes it repellent and fearful, yet undeniably and inextricably a part of one's own self. This shift provides one of the important sources of the development of an introspective self in Second Temple Judaism. In Jeremiah, the postexilic additions to Deuteronomy, and Ezekiel, new tropes are introduced that begin to objectify the heart as the locus of profound and intrinsic moral incapacity. These tropes were likely employed initially simply as emphatic rhetorical gestures, not as reflective speculations about anthropology. But tropes have their own momentum, regardless of the intentions of their speakers, and later uses of them may run down paths never foreseen by their inventors. The prophet Jeremiah appears to have been the source of some of these critical new images.[1] In Jeremiah, the problem of moral failure is framed in a variety of ways, but among the most important is the failure of understanding (5:4–5, 13, 21; 6:10; 8:4–8; 9:3; etc.). This is a failure of the rational organ, the heart. Jeremiah's trope hovers between a *functional* failure and a *material* solution. The heart, which should have been capable of receiving instruction (*tôrāh*), has inexplicably proven impervious. As Jeremiah envisions the solution, it involves a physical placing of the teaching into the body (the "interior," *qereb*) and writing or inscribing it onto the heart itself (31:33–34). Although the trope may be inspired by the idiom for memorization, "to write on the tablet of the heart," something more radical than memorization is in play here, since the result obviates the need for the failed process of teaching and learning.[2] The image of physical intervention is novel and draws attention to the heart as an objectified, problematic *thing*.

More striking is the trope found in both Jeremiah and Deuteronomy in which the heart is envisioned as having a foreskin that must be removed or circumcised before the heart can properly function as a moral organ. The conceptual metaphors underlying this image are complex. The heart is analogized to the penis with its foreskin. But the foreskin, which is simply a symbol of something that is removed in order to consummate a covenant in Genesis 17:11–14, is here treated as an objective impediment to the covenant and to obedience. The facilitating conceptual link is presumably the use of the term "uncircumcised" to identify ethnic outsiders who do not recognize Yhwh or know the requirements of the covenant and who, in their uncircumcised state, are incapable of obedience.[3] In this image, the heart that a person (i.e., the nation) is born with is intrinsically defective and incapable of covenant obedience. Only through a surgical act that changes the physical organ is one empowered to be obedient. Initially, in Jeremiah 4:4 and Deuteronomy 10:16 this transformation is referred to as something that a person can do for himself, in keeping with the assumptions about free moral agency that form the grounding perspective of First Temple moral discourse. In the wake of the disaster of 586, however, the redactional addition to Deuteronomy rejects this possibility. In Deuteronomy 30:6 the circumcision of the heart is no longer something the people can accomplish for themselves. Instead, it is a transformation that Yhwh effects for the people.

While both of these texts objectify and problematize the heart, they do not fully develop a dynamic of self-alienation or the introspective possibilities that are opened up by it. In Ezekiel, however, the heart is figured through an outrageous, physically impossible image. The heart of the people has in fact been a heart of stone, one that would be incapable of acting as a heart. The heart of stone serves as Ezekiel's condensed image of the utter moral incapacity of the people that he presents in many passages throughout the book.[4] For the people to become an effective moral agent this heart has to be removed and a heart of flesh, a proper heart, put in its place (11:19, 36:26). In being made into an objectified, problematic focus of concentration, the defective heart is no longer simply the representation of the "Me" that is the person (or the nation as person). It is in some sense a now-alienated aspect of the self, an intractable but inescapably problematic part of the person.

This rhetorical gesture by itself does not create interiority, of course. Indeed, Ezekiel's concerns are not primarily anthropological; they are theocentric. What he wants of persons is that "they will know that I am Yhwh." The main effect of the transformation is that the people are now capable of covenant obedience and will no longer defile the holy places. But there is one element of their transformation that is of significance for an account of the origins of interiority. That is the emotion that Ezekiel attributes to the reconstructed nation/person—the sense of moral disgust focused on their own prior actions. What makes this a significant innovation?

In his work on the genealogy of repentance, David Lambert argues that repentance, as it is classically formulated in Jewish and Christian tradition, is an expression of a fully developed interiorized subjectivity that does not make its appearance within Judaism until the Hellenistic period at the earliest.[5] Classical repentance involves introspective self-examination, remorse, and resolution to transform one's behavior. It is not only an act of introspection but also one of agency, since forgiveness by God is seen as consequent upon the act of repentance. The biblical phenomena that scholars have typically referred to as acts of repentance, Lambert argues, are not expressions of interiorized psychological states but social phenomena, that is, social enactments of self-diminution that serve to restore a relationship in which the generous and compassionate disposition of the superior (God) can be turned toward the inferior party (person, nation).[6] These social performances are agential in that the confessions and changes of behavior are transactions that effect desired results; but the texts pay no attention to possible interior mental states and do not depict inner self-reflection as part of the process. What makes Ezekiel's account so significant is that it does describe a developed act of introspection, and yet the act is not agential in that it does not serve to accomplish any outcome. It is, I would suggest, the earliest depiction of a form of introspection that does not lead directly to the classical western model that associates introspection with inner depths and autonomous agency, but to an alternative model developed in numerous later Second Temple texts in which introspective subjectivity is associated precisely with a displacement of agency, as Yhwh gives the person the gift of knowledge, including moral knowledge of the self. This model will be perfected in the Qumran Hodayot.

In Ezekiel's account Yhwh acts for his own sake in reconstructing the nation as a moral agent. The people's response has no effective force. Their response is the result, not the cause, of Yhwh's action. Indeed, the act of introspection occurs not only after the transformation of the people but also after their restoration. In the scenario Ezekiel describes, after they receive their hearts of flesh and are restored, the people first perform an act of remembering (36:31). They remember their evil ways and their actions that were the opposite of good, and consequently they "loathe themselves" (*qûṭ*). Literally, they feel nausea in their own presence.[7] The description of this act of remembering and the emotional response to it are a self-reflexive and self-reflective action that is unparalleled in earlier literature. It precedes and is connected with the social sense of being "ashamed and humiliated" (v. 32), but it is represented as a distinct element.[8] Undoubtedly, the model of social shame, in which one is diminished in the eyes of another, plays an important role in shaping the interior emotional drama that Ezekiel describes. Indeed, what introspection does is to move the function of the social other into one's own psychic space and, through the subject/self differentiation, to see and judge oneself as though from the perspective of another.

Adapting Ezekiel's Tropes for Personal Piety: Psalm 51 and the Construction of Interiority

The earliest appropriation of Ezekiel's imagery that is extant is in Psalm 51.[9] What had been a way of talking about the transformation of the nation through the re-creation of heart and spirit in Ezekiel 36 is here appropriated for an individual psalm of petition, articulated by a voice that speaks in the first-person singular. Although the specific appropriation of Ezekiel occurs in verses 12–14, the psalm shares with Ezekiel a general orientation to the moral framework of sanctity/disgust, reflected in the vocabulary of "blotting out," "washing," "cleansing," and "purging" in verses 3–4, 9–11, as well as the representation of the "crushed" heart and spirit as a sacrifice presented to God in verse 19.[10]

New potentials are created whenever a trope from one discourse is inserted into another genre or type of discourse with different patterns of thought and social purposes. This is one of the ways in which conceptual blending takes place, a mode of creativity that is simultaneously ubiquitous, culturally powerful, and generally unnoticed.[11] Both Ezekiel and Psalm 51 share the framing of sin as a congenital and inescapable condition. In contrast to Ezekiel, however, the speaker in Psalm 51 has an awareness of this condition *before* the transformation occurs, not merely as a result of it. It is unlikely that the author of Psalm 51 was conscious of this deviation from Ezekiel's model. Rather, it was a by-product of using Ezekiel's images in the speech-act of petition, which identifies a problem that the petitioner cannot resolve but that requires divine assistance. In earlier lament psalmody these threats were generally external in origin (e.g., attacks by enemies, affliction), though they could include the anger of God at some transgression by the speaker. But the focus was generally outwardly directed. Even in a psalm such as Psalm 38:5–9, which includes an extended account of distress related to sin, the speaker's awareness of the problem is traced to divine punishment, an external source (38:2). The central problem in Psalm 51, however, is not so much the punishment resulting from sin but distress at the sin itself. Moreover, even though verses 3–6 seem to speak of specific transgressions, verse 7 makes it clear that the fundamental problem is the congenital nature of sin ("Indeed, I was born with iniquity, with sin my mother conceived me"). The issue is not sinful acts but a sinful condition.[12] The nature and locus of the sinful condition, as well as its remedy, are identified primarily through the allusions to priestly traditions and to Ezekiel. Although metaphors for washing away sins as one might wash away ordinary dirt can be found in Isaiah 1:15–16, 4:2–4, and Jeremiah 2:22, 4:14, the uncleanness in Psalm 51 is specifically associated with ritual defilement that requires ritual purification (vv. 4, 9).[13] The hyssop referred to in Psalm 51:9 is associated with cleansing rituals, both those involving the blood of sacrificed animals (Lev 14:4, 6, 49, 51–52) and the water from the ritual of the red heifer (Num 19:6, 18).[14] Although Ezekiel 36:25 uses a different expression

("I will sprinkle you with clean water"), in both passages cleansing from sin and impurity by God precedes the more fundamental transformation.

The allusions to Ezekiel are taken up again in verse 12. The combination of *lēb*, *rûaḥ*, *ḥādaš*, and *qereb* establishes clearly the allusion to Ezekiel 36:26–27, though again with interpretive innovations to suit the purposes of the psalmist. That the psalmist asks God to "create" (*bārā'*) rather than to "give" the heart (*nātan*, as in Ezek 36:26) indicates that the psalmist interprets the act as one of new creation (cf. Ezek 37:1–14). The psalmist does not pick up the materiality of the trope in Ezekiel (i.e., the contrast between stone and flesh) but rather continues the purity motif in asking for a "pure heart" (*lēb ṭahôr*). Instead of using "new" in an adjectival fashion as Ezekiel does, the psalmist reframes it as a verb ("make anew") as a parallel to "create," again suggesting the model of a new creation. Having done that, there is an opportunity to use a different adjective to characterize the spirit. In Ezekiel the emphasis is on the replacement of the defective human spirit with God's own spirit ("new spirit," "my spirit," Ezek 36:26, 27). Instead, in Psalm 51:12 the newly created spirit is qualitatively described as "firm" or "steadfast" (*nākôn*, v. 12), "willing" (*nĕdîbāh*, v. 14) and "contrite" (*nišbārāh*, v. 19). Where Ezekiel was concerned with the transformed people being able to obey God's laws (36:27b), the psalmist frames the transformation in more pietistic terms, focused on the disposition of the worshiper.[15] The psalmist's contrite spirit is itself the sacrifice offered by his willing spirit (vv. 14, 19). The more ontological emphasis in Ezekiel is reworked into a moralizing interpretation. The psalmist does not neglect Ezekiel's emphasis on the divine spirit, however. In verse 13 the psalmist does not simply refer to "your spirit" but to "your holy spirit." The locution "holy spirit" is extremely rare, and it is possible that this is an allusion to and interpretation of Isaiah 63:10–11, probably the earliest reference to God's "holy spirit" as a means of God's presence with the people ("the one who put in its [Israel's] midst [*qirbô*] his holy spirit," 63:11b).[16] The noun *qereb* would serve as a semantic link between Isaiah 63:11 and Ezekiel 36:27 and facilitate the notion of the holy spirit not so much as the ontological presence of God within the person but rather of the mode of God's nearness to the person. Thus the psalmist prays, using a spatial metaphor, "Do not cast me out from your presence, and your holy spirit do not take away from me" (Ps 51:13). This is obviously not the only way in which Ezekiel's radical passage might be appropriated, and in chapter 6 I will show how the Hodayot explored the more ontological significance of the verses.

My primary interest here, however, is to assess the effect—almost certainly unconscious—of the appropriation of Ezekiel's trope of divine re-creation of the human heart and spirit into the different genre of personal psalmody. In earlier psalms terms such as heart, spirit, or soul often function as synecdoches for the speaker's "I" (e.g., Pss 10:17; 13:6; 16:9) or are addressed in an apostrophe that figures a basic "I-Me" differentiation (e.g., Ps 42:12). By appropriating Ezekiel's imagery of the fundamentally defective heart and spirit into petitionary prayer, the psalmist constructs something different. In Ezekiel the divine voice naturally speaks in objectified terms of the problem of the human heart. The psalm requires the shifting of perspective to that of the praying subject, who then speaks in an objectifying manner of his *own* heart and spirit, which are cast as alienated aspects of himself that must be re-created. In contrast to earlier psalmody, where the problem was external, the gaze in Psalm 51 turns not outward but inward. To be sure, there is no extensive analysis of the defects of the problematic heart and spirit. But there is a desire that new ones be constituted in place of the obviously defective old ones. The rhetorical construction of the space between the speaking voice and its distress at its own self is the construction of a space of interiority.

The subsequent addition of a superscription that correlates this psalm with an event in David's life ("when Nathan the prophet came to him after he had come to Bathsheba") is part of later Second Temple Judaism's increasing interest in mental states of characters represented in narrative, as I briefly discussed in chapter 1. In 2 Samuel 12:5 David says only, "I have sinned against Yhwh." Psalm 51 supplies a complex script that not only gives the reader access to David's disposition at that time but also constructs a complex psychology for him. As David was seen as an exemplary figure, so he becomes a model to be imitated. Changes in cognitive models, including models of the self, often proceed by small and subtle changes that both reflect new cultural interests and create momentum for further developments. By tracking the traces that such changes leave in the literary record we can obtain at least some information about changes in the way people understood themselves.

The Body as Ground of Sin and Transformation: Barkhi Nafshi (4Q436 1; par. 4Q435 2 i 1–5)

The bodily psychology of ancient Israel, discussed in chapter 1, was rich with expressions that identified various parts of the body with issues of moral concern, such as "stiff neck," "hardness of heart," "haughty eyes," "lying tongue." Typically, such expressions occur in hortatory or accusatory contexts and use the characteristic body part as a way of addressing the moral disposition of the person as a whole. The phrases usually occur in isolation or in parallel pairs, with only a few instances of passages containing a concentration of body language (e.g., Isa 59:1–4) or a short sequence of illustrative body parts (e.g., Prov 4:23–27; 6:12–19). But there is little focus on the organs per se. In a remarkable composition in the collection of prayers known as Barkhi Nafshi (4Q434–438), however, one can see how the importation of such body language into a first-person prayer of thanksgiving opens up new ways of experiencing the body, the alien agency of sin, and the transforming agency of God.[17] The prayer exhibits a kind of poetic playfulness in the ways in which it constructs a veritable catalogue of the body, employing a number of intertextual allusions. But in doing so it creates something like a novel spiritual exercise. By transferring references to the moral body from one discursive context to another, in this case from prophetic and hortatory contexts into the language of first-person thanksgiving, the social distance that had been constituted by the admonitions of the prophet or of Moses to the people as they pointed out problems with the moral organs is recast as the subjective distance between the "I" and its "Me."

In the portion of the composition that begins in 4Q436 1 i 4, the speaker considers a sequence of his body parts in turn, with a particular focus on an action taken upon each of them by God. While this is not self-alienation in the sense that Psalm 51 enacts it, there is a space of differentiation that constitutes the moral body as a field of self-directed focus. The nature of the reference to the parts of the body is thus unlike those in psalms in which the parts of the body are a synecdoche for the "I" of the speaker or registers of the experience of the person as a whole (e.g., Pss 40:3–4; 42:1; 69:4).

In the first part of the passage (ll. i 4–9) the organs of heart, kidneys, mouth and tongue, foot and hand are presented as morally neutral. In contrast to a psalm like Psalm 119, where the speaker foregrounds his own agency and only occasionally speaks of God's actions aiding him (e.g., vv. 18, 36–37), in the prayer in Barkhi Nafshi virtually all moral agency is transferred to God. Lines 4–7 form a tightly constructed unit focused on the heart and kidneys. An inclusio using the expression *ḥāzaq ʿal* ("prevailed upon") and complemented with infinitives describing the result of God's forceful action form the envelope of the stanza:

(1 i 4) *wtḥzq ʿl lb* (5) [*ndkh*]
llkt bdrkykh

. . .

(6b) *wtḥzq ʿly*
lrdwp ʾḥry drkyk[*h*
(7a) *lʿśwt kwl rṣw*]*nkh*

(1 i 4) You have prevailed over the heart (5) [of the contrite],
so that he should walk in your ways.

. . .

(6b) and you have prevailed over me,
so that I pursue after you[r] ways,
(7a) [and perform all] your [good plea]sure.

The internal lines of the stanza (between *wtḥzq* and *wtḥzq*) constitute a play on the Jeremianic trope of God's writing torah on the heart in place of ineffective teaching, though there is little verbal overlap with Jeremiah 31:33. Frequently, however, sophisticated allusions substitute synonyms for the words of the intertext. Thus, in place of Jeremiah's "write" (*ktb*) the author uses "engrave" (*ptḥ*), and where Jeremiah dismissed human-to-human learning, the author tropes on Deuteronomy 6:7's use of *šnn* ("impress by repetition") but with God as the effective teacher (cf. 1QH[a] 12:11, "your torah, which you impressed upon my heart"). As in the inclusio, the introductory verb is one that connotes force. Moshe Weinfeld and David Seely note that *pqd* is used with the sense it has in Mishnaic Hebrew, "order, command."[18]

(5) *lby pqdth wklywty šnnth*
bl yškḥw ḥwqykh
(6a) [*ʿl lby pqd*]*th twrtkh*
wklywty ptḥth

(5) You have commanded my heart, and my kidneys you have taught well,
lest they forget your statutes.
(6a) [On my heart] you [have enjoined] your law,
on my kidneys you have engraved it.

Agency for formation, especially in the areas of knowledge and volition, is transferred from the human to God, ensuring its efficacy.

Lines 7–9 take up the body parts of mouth and tongue, foot and hand and repeat some of the preceding verbs but with different nuances. Here the speaker's actions are enabled and directed by God. The one clear intertextual allusion is to the servant song in Isaiah 49:2 (*wayyāśem pî kĕḥereb ḥaddāh*).

(7b) *wtśm py kḥrb ḥdh*
wlšwny ptḥth ldbry qwdš
wtśm (8) [*ʿlyhmh*] *mwsr*
bl yhgw bpʿwlwt ʾdm
bšḥt śptyw

(7b) And you have made my mouth like a sharp sword,
and my tongue you have set loose to (utter) holy words.
And you have set (8) [upon them] a bridle,
that they not meditate upon the deeds of mankind,
upon the destruction (emerging from) his lips.

Thus the mouth and tongue are simultaneously empowered by God and also restrained with a bridle or band. There is perhaps an echo of Psalm 73:23b (*ʾāḥaztâ bĕyad-yĕmînî*) or Psalm 139:10 (*gām-śām yādĕkā tanḥēnî, wĕtōʾḥăzēnî yĕmînĕkā*), though the author prefers to use the theme word *ḥzq* here, albeit with a different nuance than in lines 4–6.:

(8) *rgly ḥzqth* (9) [. . .]*h*
wbydkh hḥzqth bymyny
wtšlḥny byš[*r*

(8) My foot you have strengthened, (9) [. . .]
and with your hand you have caught hold of my right hand,
and you have sent me forth in the straigh[t . . .]

Although the attribution of agency to God is assumed elsewhere in Israelite literature, as discussed in chapter 2 above, the language developed in Barkhi Nafshi creates something new. It focuses attention in a disciplined and extended fashion upon the speaker's bodily centers of intention, speech, and action and perceives there the active presence of God, thus creating a kind of conscious intimacy with God quite unparalleled in other texts concerning moral pedagogy. The speaker's task is not to perform the actions upon himself (e.g., Deut 6:7–9; Prov 3:3) but to testify to what God has done within him.

The second half of the passage, lines i 10–ii 4, treats the body not as morally neutral but as inherently morally defective, so that God's agency takes the form of repair of the moral organs themselves.[19] Although the passage is broken in various places, the editors' restorations are cogent.

(10) *[lb h'bn g]rth mmny*
wtśm lb ṭhwr thtyw
yṣr r' g'r[th mn klywty]
(11) [. . .]
(ii 1) *[wrwḥ qwd]š śmth blbby*
znwt 'ynym hsyrwth mmny
wtbṭ '[t kwl (2) *drkykh*
']wrp qšh šlḥth mmny
wtśmw 'nwh
z'p 'p hsyrwth [mmny
wtśm (3) *ly rwḥ 'r]wk 'pym*
gbh lb wrwm 'ynym
htn . . th mmny
[rwḥ šqr (4) *'bdt . . .]h*
wlb [nd]kh ntth ly

(10) [the heart of stone] you have [re]buked out of me,
and have set a pure heart in its place.
The evil inclination [you] have rebuked [out of my kidneys][. . .]
(11) *vacat*
(ii 1) [and the ho]ly spirit you have set in my heart.
Lechery of the eyes you have removed from me,
and they (lit. it) gazed upon [all] (2) [your ways.
The s]tiffness of neck you have expelled from me,
and you have made it into humility.
A wrathful nose you have removed [from me,
and have set] (3) [in me a spirit of lo]ng suffering.
Haughtiness of heart and arrogance of eyes
you have for[got]ten to reckon to me.
[A spirit of deceit (4) you have destroyed]
and a [bro]ken heart you have given to me.
(4Q436 1 i–ii 4; par. 4Q435 2 i 1–5 underlined)[20]

That the sequence begins with gratitude for the replacement of the "heart of stone" (restored) by a "pure heart" suggests that the imaginative starting place for this sequence is Psalm 51's engagement with Ezekiel 11:19 and 36:25–27.[21] This verse is paralleled by a similarly worded line that associates the "evil inclination" (*yṣr r'*) with some other bodily organ, now lost in a lacuna. The editors are likely right that the missing term is "kidneys," since heart and kidneys are paired in previous lines. Thus the evil inclination is not only reified as a spiritual force but also given a specific moral organ that it affects. Even more significant, the verb that identifies God's action upon the heart of stone and the evil inclination is "rebuke" (*gʿr*), a term that is used for the exorcism of evil spirits, suggesting that the speaker's agency was previously controlled by an alien will.[22] Compare, also, references to "expel" (*šlḥ*) and "destroy" (*ʾbd*) in ii 2, 4. Although some of the moral problems repaired are familiar defects of the will or desire ("lustful eyes," "stiff neck," "wrathful anger"), the reference to the "lying spirit" is an allusion to 1 Kings 22:22, in which a spirit-being enters into Ahab's prophets. Similarly, the positive reference to the "holy spirit" (if the restoration is correct) is likely an allusion to Isaiah 63:11, referring to God's presence with people by means of the holy spirit.

While the line between metaphorical language and metaphysical assumption can be difficult to judge, in many ways it scarcely matters whether the author is speaking metaphorically or literally. Cognitive metaphors also describe reality. The self is represented as a complex psychic body whose key organs are not under its own control and whose transformation into a desired moral state requires forceful action by God on these organs. Moreover, its body is depicted as a permeable site that can be invaded by hostile demonic spirits but can also be cleansed of those and be made host to God's own holy spirit. The way in which such a prayer constructs the body as a scene for the actions of God against evil changes the nature of the speaker's subjectivity. He becomes an observer of a drama that is being enacted upon and within his body, a drama that is the very constitution of his moral self. The mighty acts of God are performed not only within history but within the self, and the transformation of the self is now incorporated into the praise of those acts.

The Alien Within: 11QPsa 24:3–17 (Syriac Psalm III) and 19:1–18 (Plea for Deliverance)

Both Psalm 51 and Barkhi Nafshi develop the "I-Me" relationship as one of differentiation between the "I" as knowing subject that yearns for righteousness and a proper relationship with God and the "Me" as a body that is the site of resistance to such a relationship. In Psalm 51 there is no suggestion of anything other than a human defect of the heart/spirit. The verbs in Barkhi Nafshi hint at a resistance in which the alienated aspect of the self is metaphorically configured as demonlike in that it has to be rebuked from the body. In Syriac Psalm III and the Plea for Deliverance the alien-other aspect of sin becomes more pronounced. The self is depicted more as victimized and under threat.

Syriac Psalm III has many of the characteristics of a traditional petition for relief. Its request for God's aid in understanding laws and statutes and its anxiety over sin are characteristic of many Second Temple prayers. The request that the sins of youth and transgressions not be remembered is similar to Psalm 25:7. But it contains a distinctive image of sin that conceptualizes it as an alien force within the person. In contrast to Psalm 51, the alien element is not the malfunctioning heart or spirit but sin itself. This image depicts sin not simply as something one does but as an inimical entity located with the person. The tropes figure sin as disease and as a "parasitic plant."[23]

> (11) *ḥṭ'h n'wry hrḥq mnny*
> *wpš'y 'l yzkrw ly*
> (12) *ṭhrny yhwh mng' r'*
> *w'l ywsp lšwb 'ly*
> *ybš* (13) *šwršyw mmny*
> *w'l ynṣw '[l]yw by*

> (11) The sins of my youth cast far from me,
> and let my transgressions not be remembered against me.
> (12) Purify me, O Lord, from (the) evil affliction,
> and let it not return again to me.
> Dry up (13) its roots from me,
> and let its le[av]es not flourish within me.
> (11QPs[a] 24:11–13a; trans. Brand)

Although "affliction" (*ng'*) can sometimes designate a disease or pain that might be construed as the result of or punishment for sin (cf. 2 Sam 7:14; Isa 53:8; Ps 89:33), that does not appear to be its significance here. Miryam Brand is correct in my opinion in taking it as a way of describing the condition of sinfulness or of the propensity to sin, as the following image of the plant refers back to the affliction. That striking image represents the condition of sinfulness as an objectified, alien entity within a person that has a hostile power and vitality of its own. And yet, it is *one's own* sinfulness. In Deuteronomy 29:17 a similar image of a poisonous weed is used of the wicked who are other than the speaker and his audience (cf. also Sir 3:28). Here, however, the image is appropriated to describe the speaker's own self and perhaps the condition of humankind in general. Moreover, the speaker is himself powerless against it. His agency consists only in recognizing it, being distressed by it, and beseeching God to destroy it. I do not think it is incidental that, once again, a trope that was initially developed to characterize the relationship between social others is reconfigured to describe an anxiety about the self. Anxious subjectivity is the internalization of concern that what had been a clearly defined social differentiation between good and bad persons is now reconfigured as a differentiation between good desires and bad impulses within the self. Social dynamics become psychological dynamics.

This recontextualization of a traditional image constructs a new cognitive and imaginative space in which it is possible to envision the paradoxical nature of sin both as an autonomous alien and as rooted and flourishing within a person. By placing this image within the genre of petitionary prayer, the speaker's self comes to be represented as a context, a scene inhabited by an aspect of itself that causes distress. The speaking subject becomes an observer of this interior scene, a subject position that is critical for the development of introspection.

Other prayers of supplication develop the category of the interior alien in ways similar to the tropes found in Barkhi Nafshi. The composition known as the Plea for Deliverance is actually a complex prayer that contains elements of thanksgiving for previous salvation as well as a petition for present deliverance. In the relevant lines (11QPs[a] 19:13–16) the speaker asks for purification from sins (*ṭhrny m'wwny*) and for positive qualities ("a spirit of faithfulness and knowledge," *rwḥ 'mwnh wd't*, l. 14). He continues, "Let not a satan rule over me, nor an impure spirit; let pain and evil inclination not have control over me" (*'l tšlṭ by śṭn wrwḥ ṭm'h mk'wb wyṣr r' 'l yršw b'ṣmy*, ll. 15–16). What is striking here is the combination of both internal and external forces as alien wills that threatened the speaker's desire for righteousness. Since the positive qualities of "a spirit of faithfulness and knowledge" appear to refer to dispositions, there is some debate as to whether the "impure spirit" is also an internal disposition or an external evil spirit.[24] While it is not possible to be certain, the parallelism with "a satan" inclines me to think that the impure spirit is also demonic. And yet, as has often been noted, the reference to a satan here is based on an exegetical allusion to Psalm 119:133 ("and let not any iniquity [*'āwen*] rule over me"). Presumably the interpretation identifies iniquity as the effect of the power of the satan and so substitutes the cause for the effect in the Plea for Deliverance. If so, then the question as to whether the "impure spirit" is internal disposition or external power may impose a false distinction. A related ambiguity is evident in the following clause. Pain is typically the effect of either demonic attack[25] or sin, and perhaps it stands here metonymically for one or both of them. The evil inclination is a human disposition, constructed as a reification of the phrase in Genesis 6:5 and 8:21 concerning "the inclination of the thoughts" of humankind. As noted already in connection with Barkhi Nafshi, it can sometimes be depicted in ways that draw on the imagery of the demonic. What is common to all four elements is that they are depicted as agential forces that "rule over" or "have control over" the speaker as competing hostile wills. The blurring of the boundaries between external alien entities and internal ones is not surprising.[26] After all, when demons become active in causing moral as opposed to physical destruction, they operate precisely on the thoughts and on the moral inclination of a person (e.g., Jub 12:20–21). In the Plea for Deliverance, as in Barkhi Nafshi, what the speaking subject fears is that intimate aspects of himself—his own intentions and his own thoughts—may in fact be taken over and controlled either by an external force that operates within him or by an alienated aspect of himself that evades his control and from which he desires to be free. Whether external or internal in origin, these forces are objectified as the "not me" that operates "within me." The speaker experiences himself as internally divided and must pay attention to the multiplicity of his conflicting impulses, aligning with some and rejecting others. He becomes an observer of his interior landscape.

Yeṣer and Related Terms as Alienated Aspects of the Self in Hortatory and Discursive Texts

As the Plea for Deliverance and Barkhi Nafshi indicate, significant developments occur during the Second Temple period in the understanding of the term "inclination" (*yēṣer*). The occurrence of that word in Genesis 6:5 and 8:21 does not designate an objectified entity but is simply a summary term for an observable tendency that characterizes human plans and actions. The Plea for Deliverance is likely one of the earliest attestations of its reinterpretation as a feature of anthropology, though in Second Temple literature the term never achieves the privileged status that it has in later Rabbinic Judaism.[27] Its role as an objectified and problematic feature of anthropology is also evident in the Damascus Document (CD 2:16), where the syntax of Genesis ("the inclination of the thoughts of its [i.e., humankind's] mind was only evil, all the time," *yēṣer maḥšĕbōt libbô raq ra' kol-hayyôm*, Gen 6:5; cf. 8:21) is recast as "the thoughts of a guilty inclination" (*mḥšbwt yṣr 'šmh*). In shifting the term "inclination" from its position as *nomen regens* in the phrase to *nomen rectum*, what had been simply a descriptive term comes to identify a force internal to the human being that has to be intentionally resisted. In CD 2:16–18 the "guilty inclination" is paralleled by "lustful eyes" and associated with "stubbornness of heart," two phrases familiar from prophetic and Deuteronomic rhetoric. In the passage in CD, however, the key term for innate moral impairment is not *yēṣer* but *rāṣôn*, which appears to function as a synonym for *yēṣer*. The generation of the flood is destroyed "because they acted upon their desire" (*b'śwtm 't rṣwnm*, 2:20).[28] That this is not just an incidental desire but something constituent of the human moral condition is suggested by the repeated use of *rāṣôn* in the negative phrase "to choose the desire of one's spirit." Even more telling than the examples of moral failure is the way in which Abraham is described as one who "did not choose the desire of his spirit" (CD 3:2–3). That is to say, it is *not* that Abraham had only good desires but rather that he, too, was characterized by wrongful desire but *chose* not to follow it. The moral life thus involves choosing against one's own desire. To do this requires that one scrutinize and become aware of what one's desire is and then engage in an act of repudiation of what is an intrinsic aspect of one's nature. This model of the human self mandates practices of introspection for the identification and management of inner conflict. It is important to note that Abraham appears to have been completely capable of choosing against his own desire, unlike the speaker in the Plea for Deliverance, who fears being dominated by hostile indwelling forces. The contrast illustrates the way in which different types of speech acts activate different models. In a prayer the speaker seeks divine aid and so minimizes his own agency, except via the prayer request itself. In hortatory literature the addressee's agency is emphasized. This contrast reminds one that cultural models for framing certain topics tend to be diverse and generally should not be thought of as self-consistent "beliefs." The underlying concern may be the same, but the genre of speech will frame the issue according to its own goals and values.

In one sense the passage in the Damascus Document simply describes something that is a universal human phenomenon—the ability of self-reflexive humans to monitor their emotions and desires and to practice self-inhibition.[29] But, as discussed above, this automatic process is not always and everywhere named and made a topic of cultural reflection. Only where it is framed in such a way does the common human capacity for self-monitoring become an element of a cultural introspective self. The book of Proverbs, for example, is also deeply concerned with the differentiation between good and destructive desires and the inhibition of bad desires (as illustrated in the various erotic motifs to be found in Prov 6–8).[30] But it does not objectify problematic desire itself or locate it as an inherent aspect of the human constitution. It does not configure the process of choosing as a form of self-alienation and the perfecting of a good self as accomplished thorough the rejection of those alienated elements within oneself. Thus one sees in the Damascus Document a different and more introspective construction of the self.

The structure of the self that the Damascus Document alludes to in its hortatory section is represented more vividly in the later work of 4 Ezra.[31] In 4 Ezra the term "evil heart" is apparently also derived from Genesis 6:5 and 8:21 and functions similarly to that of the evil inclination.[32] Like it, the evil heart is either an inherent feature of human nature or one that is so common as to be virtually so (4 Ezra 3:21–22, 25–26; 7:63–72). Though the imagery used in 4 Ezra varies,[33] a trope similar to the plant image in 11QPs[a] 24 occurs in 4 Ezra 4:30, which speaks of an evil seed. "For a grain of evil seed was sown in Adam's heart from the beginning, and how much the fruit of ungodliness it has produced until now, and will produce until the time of threshing comes!" (trans. Stone). The pathos of this condition is the pathos of introspective awareness. Although 4 Ezra is not systematic in its presentation, it asserts that the evil heart is something that both Adam and his descendants are "burdened with," which is to say that it is inherent.[34] Thus even though the Torah is also placed within the heart (3:22), the heart's flawed nature (also referred to as "the evil root") makes obedience impossible for all but a very few. "For an evil heart . . . has brought us into corruption and the ways of death, and has shown us the paths of perdition and removed us far from life—and that not just a few of us but almost all who have been created!" (7:48; trans. Stone).[35] But the heart is also the organ of consciousness,[36] and so Ezra articulates the anguish of a consciousness that perceives both its moral responsibility and its inability to fulfill this responsibility, the split between a subject-heart that desires righteousness and a self-heart that is incapable of it.

> O earth, what have you brought forth if the mind is made out of the dust like the other created things! . . . But now the mind grows with us, and therefore we are tormented, because we perish and know it. . . . For all who

> have been born are involved in iniquities and are full of sins and burdened with transgressions. (7:62–68; trans. Stone)[37]

Although there are social dimensions to Ezra's distress (after all, it is the relentless judgment of God that makes the situation acute), the emotional focus of this passage is on the interior drama of consciousness and the subject/self division.

While I would argue that the trope of the split between subject and self as I have traced it is largely a construction of Second Temple Judaism, it is important to remember that it is never simply a fixed belief. Instead, it is a flexible cultural tool that can be modulated in a variety of ways to address a variety of social contexts and needs. Although it could be used to explore the anguish of the generation after the destruction of Jerusalem by the Romans in 70 CE, who pondered why human efforts at righteousness had proved insufficient, in other contexts it could be used to construct unprecedented forms of subjectivity in which the self is constituted through access to transcendent knowledge. But how could a claim to transcendent knowledge be experientially verified? Through knowledge of the person's own self. Whereas only a few select seers, such as Enoch, were granted direct access to heavenly secrets through ascents to heaven, revelatory disclosures about the esoteric meaning of the nature of the self both constructed and then verified a sense that the addressee had access to the mysteries of God. This development of the trope is most clearly exhibited in the dualistic models of the self in Qumran literature.

Dualism and the Construction of an Interior Landscape

As the impulse to sin became reified in various texts of the Second Temple period, the very attempt to describe and address it constructed something of a binary oppositional dynamic. In petitionary prayers the speaker's subjectivity recoils from this aspect of itself, whether it is identified as an inherent but defective organ or function (e.g., heart, spirit, *yēṣer*) or whether it is a demonic spirit that has become active in him. Because he cannot himself overcome the feared alien entity, he invokes God, thus setting up another vector of opposition between God and the sinful force. In only a few texts, however, is this oppositional binary dynamic conceptualized as a dualistic opposition and incorporated into a larger theological program.[38] Nevertheless, these texts are particularly generative, because they demonstrate how models of one's own internal experience can be developed as analogues of larger social or metaphysical levels of reality—or vice versa.[39]

The most fully developed example of such a model is, of course, the Two Spirits Teaching from the Cave 1 version of the Community Rule (1QS). But two other fragmentary sectarian texts from Qumran appear also to reflect such ideas. All three use notions of demons or evil spirits, and all three have an implicit or explicit model of psychic interiority. 4Q444, which is officially titled "Incantation" but might be better considered as an apotropaic prayer,[40] contains the following passage:

> (1) And as for me, because of my fearing God, with his true knowledge he opened my mouth; and from his holy spirit [. . .] (2) truth to a[l]l [the]se. They became spirits of controversy in my (bodily) structure (*mbnyty*), statute[s of God] (3) [. . . in]nards of flesh (*tkmy bśr*). And a spirit of knowledge and understanding, truth and righteousness, God placed in [my] he[art . . .] (4) [. . .]*wh* and strengthen yourself by the statutes of God, and in order to fight against the spirits of wickedness, and not [. . .]. (Frgs 1–4i+5 1–4)

The identification of "spirits of controversy" foregrounds a dualistic model of the self, but the precise meaning of *tĕkāmîm* is uncertain. It is clearly a bodily term, attested only at Qumran. Brand gives a learned discussion of the semantics and concludes that it is a "general expression referring to the innards of the body, particularly when the body is 'infested' with sinfulness or affliction."[41] The passage thus appears to be describing the individual's body as a place in which spirits are located and in which they are fought against. Although these wicked spirits are likely demonic ones, the passage does not indicate whether they are independent spirits or are directed by a leader, such as Mastema in Jubilees or Belial in various texts from Qumran. God's agency is referred to in line 1, which seems to attribute the author's ability to understand and to speak about his situation to his piety. It is less clear whether "the spirit of knowledge and understanding" is understood as a spirit-agent corresponding to the "spirits of wickedness" or rather as a character trait, especially since the internalized statutes of God serve the same function. God is said to place this positive spirit into the speaker (śm *'l bl*[*bby* . . .]), so that it is spoken of as objectlike. But in many texts there is asymmetry in the way in which evil spirits may be personified, whereas positive spirits appear more as extensions of God's charismatic qualities, even if they are treated as objectlike (e.g., Plea for Deliverance, 11QPs[a] 19:13–17). What is relevant here, however, is that the speaker conceives of the interior of his body as a space where this struggle takes place. His mind contemplates and describes an interior drama, creating an implicit triangular structure in which the observing mind describes the inner conflict that is configured by two opposing internalized forces. This structure contrasts with compositions like Psalm 51 and Barkhi Nafshi, where the observing "I" is contrasted simply with the observed and problematic "Me." It also contrasts with the Syriac Psalm III and Plea for Deliverance, where the observing "I," with which subjectivity is invested, is contrasted with a focused alien other. In the dualistic texts the situation is more complex. Following Kenneth Burke's dramatistic terms, it is more "scenic."[42] The observing self, in which primary subjectivity is located, watches what is, in some sense, a staged drama of moral desire and impulse. Both sets of protagonists (the "spirit of truth and understanding" and the "spirits of wickedness") appear to be objectified over against the observing self. A rhetorical and thus psychological space is opened up in which knowledge of what is going on is distinguished from involvement with it, in contrast to the dynamic of Psalm 51 and related texts. But the text is too broken to make many more nuanced observations.

A similar model is articulated in a fragmentary part of the Songs of the Sage (4Q511 48–49+51 ii 1b–6a):

> (1) . . . [. . .]*t* his knowledge he put [in my] hear[t . . .] (2) the praises of his righteousness, and [. . .]*'h* and by his mouth he frightens [all the spirits] (3) of the bastards to subdue [. . .]*ṭy* impurity. For in the innards of (4) my flesh is the foundation of *d*[. . . and in] my body are battles. The statutes of (5) God are in my heart, and I prof[it] for all the wonders of man. The works of (6) guilt I condemn . . . . (trans. Brand)[43]

Here, too, it is likely that the speaker's ability to understand his situation is the result of divinely given knowledge (l. 1), and thus subjectivity is invested primarily in knowledge rather than in a reaction of fear toward the spirits. The indebtedness to the demonology of 1 Enoch is evident in the allusion to the "bastards," that is, the offspring of the watchers and human women (1 En 6–16), though the place of the struggle is inside the body of the speaker, as in 4Q444.[44] That the "statutes of God" are also given a location in the heart may owe a debt to the Jeremianic tradition of Torah written on the heart, though there is little similarity of wording. In a striking manner the problem of obedience and resistance to obedience, which is a staple of Israelite moral discourse in Proverbs, Deuteronomy, and prophetic writings, has been recast as an intrapsychic problem. Rather than envisioning the subindividual agencies as parts of the body (e.g., the various organs named in Barkhi Nafshi), here the body becomes the scene, and the agents are envisioned as external forces that have invaded the body or been placed there by God. The subjectivity of the individual is constructed by the knowledge that allows him to understand the truth of his situation, a knowledge that also comes from God. This understanding, which manifests itself in his speech and praise, becomes the form that his agency takes. What he testifies to, however, is his experience of his own moral struggle and what it means. The various dualistic structures shift the locus of subjectivity. In contrast to the binary models (e.g., Ps 51, Barkhi Nafshi, Plea for Deliverance, Syriac Psalm III) in which the speaking subject is directly involved in a fearful relationship with evil within or without, the dualistic models create a secondary level of separation between the perceiving "I" and its complex "Me." Though these models are not without their emotional components, they tend to reconstitute the nature of subjectivity in knowledge and understanding rather than in emotional terms.

The Two Spirits Teaching

The most sophisticated speculation on the structure and dynamics of the human self and its significance that makes use of this dualistic model is the Two Spirits Teaching found in 1QS 3:13–4:26.[45] This extraordinary document introduces itself as an instruction. In this way it differs from most of the texts I have examined in this chapter, which are primarily first-person-singular prayer texts. In petitionary and thanksgiving prayer the knowledge of the self is articulated in relation to the need to resolve a danger or a fear. In the Second Temple prayers I have considered the danger may be located within the speaker rather than in an external agent. Or, if the agent is a demonic force, the locus of its activity is the mind and will of the speaker, a corrupting domination of the psyche. Given the nature of the speech-act of prayer, however, highly developed speculative discussion has little place. By contrast, the Two Spirits Teaching introduces itself as a comprehensive teaching for "all the children of light" designed to teach them "the genealogy [*twldwt*] of all human beings [*kwl bny 'yš*] with respect to all the types of their spirits, with respect to the signs of their deeds in their generations, and with respect the visitation of their chastisements as well as the times of their reward."[46]

In the case of a psalm of petition or thanksgiving the purpose and function in drawing attention to the interior defect or act of demonic aggression is clear, since it is the problem from which one seeks relief. But a teaching may or may not explicitly identify the purpose it serves or what the knowledge it presents will do for the addressee. In the case of the Two Spirits Teaching the reason for presenting the information is not explicitly stated and so has to be deduced from the rhetoric and logic of the Teaching itself. One influential analysis is that of Hermann Lichtenberger, who argues that the Two Spirits Teaching attempts to account for why the elect righteous nevertheless sin.[47] This topic is introduced in 3:21–24 and becomes the focus of the concluding sections in 4:15–26. In that concluding portion a discussion of the dynamics of opposition between the two spirits themselves (4:15–18a) chiastically parallels a discussion of how that opposition manifests itself within the cognitive/volitional dimensions of human beings (4:23b–26).[48] These two sections bracket a discussion of the eschatological intervention by God that will resolve the problem of sin by the elect. Lichtenberger's reading certainly identifies a major theme of the Two Spirits Teaching, one that comes into prominence especially if one attempts to grasp how the Two Spirits Teaching functions within the larger context of the Serek ha-Yahad. This is the approach that I, too, adopted in *The Self as Symbolic Space* in analyzing how presenting knowledge of the operation of the two spirits in the cosmos and within human beings might have been important for motivating sectarians to be willing to submit to the disciplines of the community.[49]

I now think, however, that such a reading mistakes an important subtheme of the document for its actual and more comprehensive purpose. The explanation for why the righteous sin is only part of the more fundamental purpose of the text, which reveals the process by which God created humankind in the likeness and image of God. This theme is first hinted at in the heading ("the genealogy of all humankind"), which appears to be an interpretive gloss on Gen 5:1 ("This is the document of the genealogy of *'ādām*. When God created *'ādām*, he made him in the likeness of God"). It is also articulated in corresponding statements at the beginning and end of the body of the composition. Immediately after the introductory reference to God's absolute predetermination of all things in 3:15–17, the teaching proper begins: "He created humankind to rule all the world" (3:17), an evident allusion to Genesis 1:26–27. In Genesis that passage is also the locus of the references to "image and likeness." But in 1QS 3:17 there is no reference to the image and likeness of God. Instead the following statement says that God "assigned two spirits for him in which to walk until the appointed time of his visitation." The eschatological transformation of humankind, described in the final part of the composition (4:23), is what results in their possessing "all the glory of Adam," a further allusion to Genesis 1:26–27. The last line of the Teaching (4:26) refers to the two spirits as an "inheritance" given so that humans might "know good [and evil . . .]," an allusion to Genesis 3:5 ("like God, knowing good and evil"). Thus the argument of the Two Spirits Teaching is designed to show how God created humankind in the divine image.

Understanding the logic and development of the Two Spirits Teaching depends on recognizing how extensively it is engaged with the creation accounts of Genesis, especially Genesis 1, for the purpose of constructing a theological anthropology and also for developing a model of subjectivity and agency based on this anthropology. The exact nature of the relationship of the Two Spirits Teaching to Genesis 1 is difficult to characterize. At least ten terms from Genesis 1:1–2:4a are echoed in the Two Spirits Teaching (*twldwt*, *'wr*, *ḥwšk*, *myn*, *'wtwt*, *br'*, *ṣb'wt*, *ml'*, *mmšlt*, *'dm*), four of which appear in the heading itself in 1QS 3:13–15a.[50] The Teaching, however, is neither an allegorical reading nor a sustained exegetical interpretation of Genesis 1.[51] Virtually all of the terms that echo Genesis are used in a context different from that in the biblical text. It would be more apt to say that the Teaching draws on critical vocabulary and symbolic structures from Genesis 1 to construct a parallel esoteric teaching focused on the role of humankind in God's intentions for the world and how the nature of human selfhood is critical to that role. It is in that sense a revelatory text, even though the Two Spirits Teaching does not situate itself within a narrative of ascent to heaven, such as Enoch experiences when he is taught by the angels, or as an angelic revelation of what is written in the heavenly book of truth, such as Daniel receives. It is an example of revelation through inspired exegesis, if one takes exegesis in a broad sense. In contrast to Enoch, Daniel, or Jubilees, where the content of the revelation is astronomical and cosmological, historical and legal, the Two Spirits Teaching is a revelation about the nature and destiny of humankind and how that nature and destiny can be read in the very experience of the moral self and its struggles. Moreover, the teaching does not provide information so that the addressee can *do* something but simply so that he can *know*. The radically predestinarian claim in 3:15–17 frames all that follows as a disclosure of aspects of the *mḥšbt kbwdw*, God's glorious plan, which has predetermined the *mḥšbt* ("design, plan") of all that will come into existence. To know the design of the self, how it comes into being, and what its destiny will be is to know fundamental aspects of God's glorious predetermined plan. In contrast to the other texts examined in this chapter, here the very structure of the self is explicitly *meaningful*. In the Two Spirits Teaching the self truly becomes "symbolic space." Moreover, in this text knowledge is the form that agency takes, since it is through knowledge that the elect subject participates in the unfolding of the divine plan. It is a subjectivity of terrible sublimity.

The key to the Two Spirits Teaching is its engagement with Genesis 1:26–27 and God's expressed intention, "Let us make humankind [*'ādām*] in our image, according to our likeness." In Genesis 1:26–27 the image of God is what fits humankind for the purpose God has created them, namely, to rule over (*wĕyirdû*) "the whole earth" (*bĕkol-hā'āreṣ*). In the Two Spirits Teaching the first reference to the purpose of humankind is also to the function of rule: "He created humankind [*'nwš*] to rule the world [*mmšlt tbl*]." Allusions to biblical texts in Second Temple literature often engage in the substitution of synonymous words, as if teasing the reader to make the connection. In Genesis the word *mmšlt* is used only in relation to the role of the two great luminaries in Genesis 1:16. But Psalm 8's rendering of the creation tradition uses not only *mšl* to describe human dominion over the earth (v. 6) but also other vocabulary that is significant to the Two Spirits Teaching (*'nwš*, *pqd*, v. 5). The adept reader recognizes that Psalm 8 is required to bridge the link of association. But where in the Teaching is the reference to the image of God? The omission of such a reference in lines 17–18 is actually key to understanding the teaching itself. In the Two Spirits Teaching the image of God is not manifest in humankind until the eschatological purification when "to them [i.e., the chosen] will belong all the glory of Adam" (4:23). The phrase "the glory of Adam" is itself the product of an exegetical combination of Genesis 1:26–27, with its references to humankind as being in the "image" and "likeness" (*dĕmût*) of God, and Ezekiel 1:26–28. There Ezekiel describes the Glory of Yhwh and summarizes what he sees as "the appearance of the likeness of the glory of Yhwh" (*mar'ēh dĕmût kĕbôd-yhwh*). This connection between "glory" and "likeness of God" in relation to the creation of humans is an established exegetical trope, one that is already attested in 4QDibHam (4Q504 1:4).[52] In essence, in the Two Spirits Teaching God's creation of humankind is divided between the initial act of creation and its completion at the time of the eschatological visitation. What stands in between is the education of the elect through learning to discern "good and evil" (1QS 4:26; cf. Gen 2:9, 17; 3:5). Although the Two Spirits Teaching is primarily oriented to Genesis 1 in its discourse, Genesis 3:5 plays a critical role. There the claim is made that "to know good and evil" is to become "like God/gods." While that status is treated ambivalently or even negatively in Genesis 2–3, it is recontextualized in the Two Spirits Teaching so that it has a positive connotation.[53] This godlike capacity is essential before humankind can embody the "glory" or "likeness" of God and so carry out its task to rule the world.

The strikingly novel aspect of the Teaching, its model of "spirits" as constitutive of human selfhood and experience (3:14, 17), does not appear to be derived from Genesis 1, which only uses the word *rûaḥ* in relation to the *rûaḥ ʾĕlōhîm* in 1:2. My assumption is that certain antecedent forms of spirit dualism, similar to that reflected in 4QVisions of Amram, are adapted and developed by the author of the Two Spirits Teaching in a speculative fashion by reading them in relation to Genesis 1. Both the light/darkness opposition and the rulership over all humankind by the two spirits are already present in 4QVisions of Amram (4Q544 1, 11–15; 2, 12–16).[54] In the Two Spirits Teaching the dualistic nature of the relationship of the spirits is developed in 1QS 3:18–4:1. References in 3:19 to "a spring of light" (*mʿyn ʾwr*) and "a well of darkness" (*mqwr ḥwšk*) connect the two spirits to the cosmological division between light and darkness in Genesis 1:4 and likely also to the division of the "waters from the waters" in Genesis 1:6, though in Genesis no negativity attaches to darkness itself. This is in no sense an exegesis of Genesis 1:4 and 6 but rather a more associative interpretive practice that uses terms, tropes, and structures from Genesis, alongside other sources of revelatory knowledge (e.g., Amram's vision), as a means of uncovering and unlocking aspects of the mystery that is the predetermined plan of God.

The repeated references to "walking" in the "ways" of the spirits of truth and deceit (3:18, 20–21; 4:2, 6, 11, 15, 18, 24) locate this discourse firmly within the pedagogical tradition of ancient Israel, as it is found in Proverbs and in various prophets and psalmic texts (Deut 8:6; 10:12; Isa 30:21; Jer 6:16; Ps 1:1; 86:11; Prov 2:20; 4:26). In contrast to the volitional ethic assumed in those texts, however, humans are predetermined to belong either to the "children of righteousness" or to the "children of perversity" (3:20–21). This fundamental dichotomy will be complicated by the claim in 4:15–26 that the two spirits actually operate within each human being, though the two claims are not incompatible. As 4:15–16 clarifies, the two classes are distinguishable according to whether the person's "inheritance" in each spirit is "great or small."[55] The Teaching has no interest in those persons who have a preponderance of the spirit of perversity. They figure only as among those whose fates will be determined "according to the spirit within [him at the appointed time . . . of the] visitation" (4:26). The Teaching is addressed to the "children of light" (3:13) who do need to understand the hard pedagogy of sin. This is the burden of 3:21–25, which explains the dynamic by which the "angel of darkness" and his "rule of hatred" cause the sin of the children of righteousness, a state of affairs aptly characterized as "the mysteries of God" (3:23).

Column 4 narrows the focus of the teaching from the cosmic dimensions of the "genealogy" or "origin" of human nature to its manifestation in behavior and subjective experience. This part of the teaching is introduced by a heading that has perplexed scholars. "These are their ways in the world" (4:2) clearly refers to both spirits. But the following infinitive clauses are all of a positive nature ("to enlighten the heart of man, to make level before him all the ways of true righteousness, and to instill in his heart reverence for the precepts of God"; trans. Knibb).[56] Thus many have assumed that the introduction refers only to the functions of the Spirit of Light, since the list of the effects of this spirit in line 3 otherwise begins abruptly. I would agree, however, with Siegfried Wibbing and Hermann Lichtenberger that the heading actually refers to the "ways in the world" of both spirits.[57] The function of enlightenment (*lhbyn*) anticipates and forms an inclusio with the concluding affirmation that God "has given them [i.e., the two spirits] as an inheritance to humankind that they may know good [and evil]" (4:26). While it is true that the "children of perversity" will learn nothing, both spirits are essential for the moral pedagogy of the "children of righteousness." Though it may seem paradoxical that experience of the spirit of perversity could have a positive value, the knowledge of both spirits is indeed what "makes level before him all the ways of true righteousness" and "instills in his heart reverence for the precepts of God" (4:2–3). Not to have knowledge and to be able to distinguish between good and evil would be to forgo the very possibility of moral agency.[58] Such an interpretation is actually in keeping with certain other interpretations of Genesis 2–3 in Second Temple sources, as I will explore in the following chapter.

This claim becomes clearer if one considers the triangular subjectivity that the dualistic discourse creates. As an instruction, the Teaching addresses the "I," the active agent component of self-awareness, of its reader or hearer. The "I" is the self in its capacity to perceive and know. By identifying the addressee as one of the "children of light," the Teaching has given him a subject position in the discourse. The Teaching then tells the reader or hearer about his "Me," the object component of self-awareness and self-identification, as well as about the nature of other human beings in the world. He learns why he sins, even though he belongs to the righteous. His "Me" is thus constituted by both experiences, the positive and the negative, as will be developed in detail in the remainder of the column. But his identification with the two aspects of himself and his experience is not equivalent. Like God, his "I" "loves the one" whereas "the other, he loathes" (3:26–4:1), and his destiny will only be complete when God purifies him of evil and removes the spirit of perversity from his flesh. By knowing about the "ways in the world" of both spirits the addressee will indeed find that his mind has "reverence for the precepts of God" and that the "paths of true righteousness" are clear. This teaching says little to nothing about moral improvement, however. Because the reality it describes is predetermined, the form that agency takes is knowledge and, through knowledge, a passionate identification with God and God's truth. This knowledge of both good and evil makes the children of light "like God," as Genesis 3:5 says, and thus equips them to rule the world.

The section in 4:2–14 is often compared to various "two ways" discourses and to virtue and vice lists, though the incorporation of such language into a predestinarian metaphysic changes the function of such lists. Nevertheless, it is clear that the two lists represent the manifestations of the two spirits in human dispositions and behavior.[59] References to "walking" in these ways (4:6, 11) tie the language back to the initial discussion of the function of the two spirits (3:18, 20, 21). The heterogeneity of the items in the list, however, suggests that the items are the specification of "all the kinds of spirits" (*kwl myny rwḥwt*, 3:14) mentioned in the introduction to the Two Spirits Teaching. The first list even utilizes the term "spirit" ("a spirit of humility . . . a spirit of his knowledge . . .," 4:3, 4), though in a somewhat sporadic fashion. These references are clearly to spirit as a characterological phenomenon, not a spirit-being. The introduction had promised to teach about the spirits "with respect to the signs of their deeds." The term echoes Genesis 1:14, where the luminaries serve as signs for "the festivals, the days, and the years," signs that priestly scribes studied and interpreted in order to understand the calendrical structure of time. Similarly, in the context of the Two Spirits Teaching, one learns about the "signs" (3:14) or "counsels" (4:6) of the two spirits in their specific manifestations for the purpose of recognizing and understanding them. They are a semiotic mapping in human behavior of a transcendent reality.[60] The specificity of these lists also enables the addressee to read himself as a place where the effects of the spirit are made manifest. Thus they fill in the general dualistic division of the "Me" that was introduced earlier. The account of the respective "visitations" picks up the remaining topic foreshadowed in the introduction and undergirds the motivation for identification with the spirit of truth. It also provides for a transition to the eschatological discussion in the section that follows.

The final section in 4:15–26 takes up many of the themes and terms already discussed in 3:13–4:1, though important new terms and tropes are also introduced, and it is in this final section that the subjective experience of the individual comes most into focus. As Peter von der Osten-Saken has observed, key statements from 4:15–18 are taken up chiastically in 4:23–26. But where the topic in 4:15–18 is the relation of the spirits to each other, in 4:23–26 the focus is on the relation of the spirits within the hearts of human beings.[61] In between these treatments is the discussion of the eschatological resolution of the role of perversity in the world and the purification of the flesh and deeds of the elect. If the primary purpose of the Teaching were simply the assurance of a happy ending, then one would expect the eschatological discussion to conclude the passage. That it does not and that the final subsection is introduced by a temporal resetting ("until now," 4:23) indicates that the primary concern of the teaching is that the addressee should understand his present condition, albeit in light of his final destiny.

In contrast to Genesis 1, which organizes its binary structures through the trope of "separation" *(Hiphil., bdl,*; 1:4, 6, 7, 14; cf. 9), the dualistic structure of the Two Spirits Teaching is organized according to the tropes of enmity (*'ybt 'wlm*, 1QS 4:17), mutual abomination (*tw'bh*, 4:17), and struggle (*ryb*, 4:18). If this were all, then the eschatological resolution of the destruction of the spirit of perversity (*šmd*, 4:19) would seem to locate the "plot" of the Two Spirits Teaching in line with other apocalyptic texts in which alien evil is destroyed. What gives an additional complexity to the Two Spirits dualism is the concept of "inheritance" (*wynḥyln*, 4:26). Ordinarily, "inheritance" is a positive term, denoting the land or land-equivalent that a person or group receives either as a gift from God or as patrimony (Num 34:17, 29; Deut 12:10; Jos 13:32; Isa 49:8; Jer 3:18; Ezek 46:18), indicating a special relationship between the parties, though the term is occasionally used in a neutral sense. In Job, it has an extended sense as the fate God decrees as appropriate for the righteous or wicked (Job 20:29; 27:13; 31:2). Initially the references to humankind having an inheritance in both spirits (4:15, 16) would seem simply to be a way of asserting their predetermined entanglement in good and evil from which God will deliver the elect at the eschaton (4:20–22). But the return to the theme of inheritance in the final line of the teaching (4:24–26) shows that more is at stake. The inheritance in both spirits is explicitly said to be given by God and has a pedagogical as well as a forensic purpose. "He has given them as an inheritance to humans in order that they may know good [and evil]." As noted above, this allusion to Genesis 3:5 refers to the claim that to know good and evil is essential to becoming "like God."[62] But how does God's knowledge of good and evil manifest itself? According to 3:26–4:1, though God created both, God's moral clarity is expressed in his disposition toward each: "God loves the one for all the [ti]mes of eternity, and in all its actions he delights forever; as for the other, he abominates its counsel and all its ways he hates forever." What then of humans? Picking up the terms "hate" and "abominates" from 4:1, the text explains the complexity of human dispositions: "According to a person's inheritance in truth and righteousness, so he hates perversity; and according to his inheritance in the lot of deceit he acts wickedly by it and so he abominates truth" (4:25). The nonelect act blindly, unaware of the nature and source of their dispositions. But the person who is addressed by this teaching now has a perspective that transcends the mere force of his dispositions. He knows that he is implicated in both so that he may know both good and evil. He must also delight in good and abominate evil.

It remains unclear how this knowledge might be related to praxis that would enable a person to alter the balance of the spirits, as the disciplines of the community seem to assume is possible (1QS 5:20–24). The forensic function of the inheritance (so that God "might [ca]st the lots for all the living according to his spirit within [him . . . at the appointed time] of the visitation") might seem to suggest that the knowledge given is for the purpose of spiritual discipline, though it is also possible that the only agency the elect have is in understanding the dynamics of their conflicting impulses and dispositions. But even that knowledge allows for identification with the good and emotionally distancing oneself from evil, a transformation of the "I-Me" relationship that is unavailable to the wicked. That the elect cannot complete their own transformation is made clear through the images of eschatological purification that are modeled on Ezekiel's account of God's purification of morally incapacitated Israel in 36:25–27, where purification and the gift of the spirit and a new heart transform the people. So here, the spirit of perversity is removed "from the innards of his flesh" (4:20–21; cf. Ezek 36:26), the elect are "purified by the spirit of holiness" (4:22; cf. Ezek 36:27), and God "sprinkles upon him the spirit of truth like the waters of purification" (4:22; cf. Ezek 36:25). The result of this transformation is not simply obedience to the laws, as in Ezekiel, but transcendent knowledge, "so that the upright may understand the knowledge of the Most High, and the perfect of way may have insight into the wisdom of the children of heaven" (4:22). The implication would be that humankind is transformed into a godlike being through godlike knowledge, an implication that is made explicit in the following line: "to them shall belong all the glory of Adam" (4:23). Just as Ezekiel saw the "likeness of the glory" in his vision, so the elect will finally manifest the "likeness of God," which was God's intention in creating humankind (Gen 1:26).

Agency in Predestinarian Contexts

In cultures in which agency is primarily associated with volition, the notion of agency in a predestinarian context can appear problematic. Predestinarian discourses are often generated through a desire to emphasize divine sovereignty, though they are loath to dispense with moral accountability. Thus most predestinarian accounts reflect some form of compatibilism in which human moral agency and accountability are preserved. Jonathan Klawans's study of fate and free will in Second Temple Judaism examines several ways in which these tensions were managed.[63] He does not, however, treat those accounts in which knowledge rather than will is the form that agency takes. In such cases compatibilism does not fully capture the nature of agency. In order to explore this issue I wish to engage a somewhat unusual conversation partner, the speculative fiction writer Ted Chiang. His writing often takes up philosophical questions, and in "Story of Your Life" he examines the relationship between free will and knowledge of a predetermined future.[64] The story is told from the perspective of a woman who is just about to make love and conceive a child. As the story unfolds we realize that she already knows the future of the child's life, including the fact that her daughter will be killed in a rock-climbing accident at age twenty-five. She refers to various events in her daughter's life by saying versions of "I remember that you will. . . ." Despite knowing the tragedy that will cut her daughter's life short, when her husband asks her,

"Do you want to make a baby?" she smiles and answers "Yes." In short, she wills what is fated.

The woman in the story is a linguist who is called upon by the government to study the language of aliens who have set up communications stations on the earth. The process is difficult. Both the spoken and written language of the creatures they call "heptapods" lack sequential structure, even to the extent that "there was no preferred order for the clauses in a conditional statement, in defiance of a human language 'universal.'"[65] Physicists are also perplexed that concepts that seem intuitive to humans appear difficult for heptapods and concepts that are difficult for humans appear intuitive for heptapods. The differences derive from the fundamentally different ways in which humans experience the world (causally, sequentially, in temporal order) and the ways in which heptapods experience the world (simultaneously, atemporally). A physicist explains the difference by the example of Fermat's Principle of Least Time, an account of how light travels through air and water.

> Okay, here's the path a ray of light takes when crossing from air to water. The light ray travels in a straight line until it hits the water; the water has a different index of refraction, so the light changes direction. . . . Now here's an interesting property about the path the light takes. The path is the fastest possible route between these two points.[66]

All alternative routes can be shown to be less fast. When the linguist appears disturbed by the account of Fermat's Principle, the physicist acknowledges its apparent oddity.

> You're used to thinking of refraction in terms of cause and effect: reaching the water's surface is the cause, and the change in direction is the effect. But Fermat's Principle sounds weird because it describes light's behavior in goal-oriented terms. . . . The thing is, while the common formulation of physical laws is causal, a variational principle like Fermat's is purposive, almost teleological.[67]

It is as though the light has to know its destination before it begins its course. Nor is this situation unique to the refraction of light. Indeed, the physicist says "almost every physical law could be stated as a variational principle" similar to Fermat's Principle.[68] This insight leads the linguist to her breakthrough in understanding the heptapod language and worldview. "Humans had developed a sequential mode of awareness, while heptapods had developed a simultaneous mode of awareness. We experienced events in an order, and perceived their relationship as cause and effect. They experienced all events at once, and perceived a purpose underlying them all."[69]

The linguist ponders the thought experiments that philosophers conduct concerning free will and foreknowledge, the question of whether free will excludes knowledge of the future. If one knew the future, would that not change how one acted and thus change the future? And if that were so, then the future could not be fixed and foreknown. "Volition was an intrinsic part of consciousness. Or was it? What if the experience of knowing the future changed a person? What if it evoked a sense of urgency, a sense of obligation to act precisely as she knew she would?"[70] She realizes that

> the heptapods are neither free nor bound as we understand those concepts; they don't act according to their will, nor are they helpless automatons. What distinguishes the heptapods' mode of awareness is not just that their actions coincide with history's events; it is also that their motives coincide with history's purposes. They act to create the future, to enact chronology.[71]

They *perform* in a temporal frame the reality that already exists atemporally. And in that performance is deep satisfaction.

To return to the Two Spirits Teaching, the typical Israelite account of human existence and moral agency is causal, sequential, and grasped through a principle of moral freedom. The Two Spirits Teaching presents the history of human existence from a perspective more like that of the heptapods. The "glorious plan" of God (*mḥšbt kbwdw*) is one in which everything exists atemporally and before creation. With the act of creation and the creation of time itself, then, the plan of God functions as a teleology governing history. The Two Spirits Teaching is a revelation of that teleology to persons who stand in the midst of history and who had previously only understood their situation in terms of free agency, moral success or failure, the playing out of acts and consequences in reward and punishment. Now they see it differently. Knowledge of the plan of God does not remove them from the work of moral agency or from the distress of sin. But it shifts the nature of their participation. "It is not just that their actions coincide with history's events [cf. 1QS 3.15–16]; it is also that their motives coincide with history's purposes." Knowing God's glorious plan, they enact it. They can examine their deeds ("zeal for the precepts of righteousness," "slackness in the service of righteousness") and grasp their significance. They can experience their hatred of perversity and their (less frequent) loathing of truth

(4:24–25) and understand why they have these dispositions. Their moral selves are no longer grasped primarily through the experience of the agency of choice but through the experience of knowledge. For the present the elect have only an incomplete and still distorted knowledge, since they are not free from the spirit of perversity. The centrality of knowledge both as a quality of subjectivity and as the essential quality of divinity is underscored in the way eschatological transformation is defined as purification for the purpose of acquiring "understanding in the knowledge of the Most High and . . . insight into the wisdom of the children of heaven" (4:22). In perfected knowledge the elect experience something like divinization. The revelatory quality of the Two Spirits Teaching constructs a subjectivity for the addressee that is a foretaste of that transformation.

The texts examined in this chapter illustrate one of the trajectories by which models of the self and agency develop in Second Temple Judaism. Stimulated initially by the need to grasp the significance of the fall of Judah to the Babylonians within the frameworks of moral agency as it had traditionally been understood, the culture moved to consider the likelihood that there was some structural impediment that had prevented the people from exercising good moral agency. If that were the case, then it appeared increasingly likely that the people could not overcome the problem through their own efforts. Imagery developed by which it was possible to envision God as effecting the change for the people. In these texts the source of moral agency shifted from the people themselves to God. Through this innovative response the people were able to incorporate the gravity of their failure and yet to receive back the possibility of exercising moral agency in the future.

Severe collective traumas often leave reverberating effects on cultures that can last for many generations, and it is plausible that some of the increased sin-consciousness in individual prayers and psalms is in fact the transfer of the collective sense of guilt to the realm of personal piety. One should not think of this new emphasis simply as cultural scar tissue. Instead, it becomes a creative site for the development of forms of piety and spiritual experience in which the encounter of the divine and the human is one of deep intimacy in body and spirit. These newly developing modes of praying and thinking established templates by which persons might also experience themselves differently, attending more to differentiations between subject and self and so developing a greater sense of what we have come to call the interior life. In the most theologically sophisticated expressions, such as one finds in the literature of the Yahad, these new ways of thinking about the self and God became vehicles not only for speculation about the nature and destiny of humankind, but also for profound ways of attending to one's own moral life—the evil as well as the good—not as the experience of an autonomous but weak will but rather as the process by which God was transforming the person into the glorious likeness of God. As the Two Spirits Teaching indicates, creation traditions become increasingly drawn into reflections on the nature of the self and its agency, as well as into forms of spiritual practice that connect such ideas to the experience of the individual, as I will explore in the next chapter.

5 Rational Agency and the Birth of the Human: Genesis 2–3 and Its Early Interpretation

For modern readers, especially those raised in Christian cultural traditions, it is difficult to overcome the sense of priority and privilege that attaches to the narrative of the garden of Eden. Even for biblical scholars accustomed to deconstructing the Bible, the effect has to be reckoned with. Although historical-critical scholarship used to argue that the text was a composition from the early monarchy, in fact the narrative is likely to belong, not to the beginning, but to the later stages of biblical literary composition.[1] Most of the canonical biblical texts seem oblivious to its existence. It appears only to have begun to exert cultural influence in the middle Second Temple period, specifically in the Hellenistic era. Even then, what Second Temple writers perceived as its significance is generally not what historical-critical and literary exegetes would identify as its narrative meaning.

As for date and provenance, my working assumption, in agreement with what I think is more or less the current consensus, is to take this text as a product of early postexilic wisdom circles. The narrative is, to be sure, unlike the traditional wisdom genres of instruction and proverb collection. But it is characterized by a significant number of both wisdom words and tropes.[2] During the early Second Temple period the scribal activity that biblical scholars have typically characterized as "wisdom" underwent a rapid expansion, encompassing new forms and topics. Although traditional proverb collections and instructions continued to be composed, as the works of Qohelet, 4QInstruction, and Ben Sira attest, wisdom themes and vocabulary emerge in a variety of other genres, including didactic psalmody, mythic narrative, court tales, apocalyptic literature, and other novel forms of literature. Not surprisingly, the Second Temple landscape of sapiential literature includes not only what we think of as traditional wisdom values and the development of a distinctly sapiential piety but also a stronger presence of the skeptical tradition that was likely always a part of wisdom. Moreover, this literary production needs to be seen as part of the forms of scribal inquiry throughout the ancient world that were concerned with the origins of knowledge and the means of access to it.[3] I would locate Genesis 2–3 within the context of this more speculative intellectual literature. It is a sly, wry, and sophisticated literary troping on mythic narrative that provides an account of the odd nature of human beings, focusing in particular on the acquisition of the rational cognitive capacity for deliberative judgment ("knowing good and bad").[4] In introducing the discussion of moral agency as it is implicitly understood in Israelite literature, I noted that three interacting elements are always present: will, desire, and knowledge. The narrative in Genesis 2–3 models an initial creation of human beings who are equipped with will and with desire. Its plot describes how knowledge was obtained and humans became fully equipped moral agents. Whether the narrative considers this to be a good thing or not will be considered more fully below.

As has often been noted, the syntax of the opening verses of the narrative follows the traditions of other creation texts, beginning with a temporal subordinate clause that establishes the context, placing the critical moment of creation in the main clause. The construction is sometimes referred to as the "when . . . then" style and is attested in the Babylonian Enuma Elish, the Worm and the Toothache incantation, as well as in Genesis 1:1–3 and 2:4–7, and Proverbs 8:22–31, among other texts. Thus the creation of the human is the focal point of the creation account: "*Then* Yhwh God formed the human from the dust of the earth and puffed the breath of life into his nostrils, and the human became a living being" (2:7). The being formed through that initial shaping and animation is not, of course, identical to humans as they are known to the author and readers of the story, and the point of the narrative is to give an account of how human beings came to be the way they actually are. Although the narrative incorporates a number of specific etiologies for such things as marriage, sexual reproduction, pain in childbirth, gender relations, field agriculture, and legless snakes, it is primarily concerned with providing an explanation of the distinctive human cognitive capacity to make deliberative judgments. A series of puns and related wordplays signal patterns of relationship within the world that are key to its order.

The initial episode of creation in verse 7 succinctly delineates the dual components of humans. The physical formation of the *'ādām* from the dust of the *'ădāmāh* indicates the essential relationship between the human body and the soil. But what of the divine breath that is puffed into the nostrils, animating the physical object? Although *nišmat ḥayyîm* and *nepeš ḥayyāh* are not counted among the puns of Genesis 2, assonance and repetition closely connect the two phrases. As I discussed in chapter 1, the widespread understanding that basic human sentience and agency are derived from the divine breath/spirit is present in this passage. But as in other ancient Near Eastern myths that associate some life essence of a divine being (e.g., blood, semen, spirit) as constituent of human life, there is no other qualitative effect.[5] No divinization is involved. The breath itself does not make humans "like God/gods." It merely animates them.

The second episode deals with the garden that forms the home for the newly created human and culminates with the identification of the two trees that play such an important role in the narrative: "the tree of life in the middle of the garden, and the tree of the knowledge of good and bad" (v. 9b). While the tree of life is a trope that appears in Hebrew wisdom literature (Prov 3:18; 11:30; 13:12; 15:4) and has certain analogues in other ancient Near Eastern literature,[6] the tree of knowledge is not otherwise attested and appears to be an innovation on the part of the author of Genesis 2–3. In Proverbs the figure of the tree of life is particularly associated with the flourishing that attends the person who is formed by wisdom (11:30; 15:4), and in Proverbs 3:13–18 the tree is a metaphor of wisdom itself.[7] If the tree of life already incorporates dimensions of wisdom and knowledge, why would the author of Genesis 2–3 disaggregate the tree of life into two components and place the tree of knowledge at the center of the story? The full significance of this decision only becomes apparent with the unfolding of the narrative, but whereas Proverbs suggests a natural and positive unity between life and wisdom, Genesis 2–3 will emphasize that in terms of human origins, coming into possession of the one excludes the other. To be sure, the referents in Proverbs and in Genesis 2–3 are not exactly the same. In Proverbs the "life" that is associated with wisdom is not immortality but a condition of flourishing and resiliency.[8] This vitality is ultimately derived from the life-giving power of God, but it is a part of the ordinary mortal life of the righteous and wise. In Genesis 2–3 the concern at the end of the narrative will be to prevent the human from eating from the tree of life and so "living forever" (3:22), a quality that is distinctive to divine beings. Similarly, whereas Proverbs uses the more comprehensive term *ḥokmāh*, Genesis 2–3 uses the phrase "the knowing of good and bad" (*hadda'at ṭôb wāra'*, 2:9). Some have argued that the phrase should be taken as a merism, designating omniscience, since that quality would seem like a godlike parallel to immortality, the other quality reserved for divine beings alone.[9] While there may be some trace of a tradition that the first human possessed access to divine knowledge in texts such as Ezekiel 28 and Job 15:7–8, and while such a notion does seem to be present in some Second Temple speculations about Adamic glory (e.g., 4QDibHam[a] [4Q504] 1:4–5), it does not appear to be the significance of the phrase in Genesis 2–3, as the logic of the story will demonstrate.

One gets a better sense of the phrase from its other occurrences in biblical and extrabiblical literature. As often noted, both the terms *ṭôb* and *ra'* are very broad in range, encompassing both the moral and the nonmoral realms of value. The full phrase "knowing good and bad" occurs several times in the context of age-related competency. Deuteronomy 1:39 refers to "your children who do not yet know good from bad," distinguishing them from the older generation. In the Qumran Rule of the Congregation a young man must be "fully twenty years old, when he knows [good] from bad," in order to marry and have sexual relations and also to join the holy congregation and "to testify concerning the statutes of the law" (1QSa 1:9–11). Similarly, Barzillai refers to his age-related loss by saying, "I am eighty years old today; how can I know good from bad?" (2 Sam 19:36). Such knowledge is associated with the mature judgment required for participation in social decisions. The clearest sense of the meaning of the phrase comes from 1 Kings 3:9, where Solomon prays that God will "give your servant a listening mind in order to judge your people, to be able to perceive the difference between good and bad; for who can judge this vast people of yours?" The quality of "knowing good from bad" is the quality of perceptive and discerning judgment, an aspect of deliberative rationality.

The flow of narrative is interrupted by a digression on the geography of the rivers that have their source in Eden (Gen 2:10–14), requiring a resumptive repetition in verse 15 concerning the placement of the human in Eden. Then comes the critical command from God. The human may eat from any of the trees in the garden, "but from the tree of the knowledge of good and bad you may not eat, for on the day you eat of it, you will surely die!" No reason is given, but as Susan Niditch astutely notes, "in the lore of all cultures interdictions such as Genesis 2:17 ('But of the tree . . .') exist to be disobeyed by the tales' protagonists. That is what makes the story."[10] As with the tale of Pandora's box, both the prohibition and its violation are essential in order to account for how the world came to be the way we know it. The death threat that accompanies the prohibition should also not be overinterpreted or puzzled over in light of the fact that the first couple does not in fact die. The threat is a rhetorical gesture. As Erhard Gerstenberger argues, it is "a wonderful example of how divine threats are to function. . . . Threat of destruction is not a legal sanction, calling for a lawsuit, but a signal of warning, alerting people to the horrible consequences which are inherent in misconduct."[11] It is of significance that no explanation is given for the prohibition but only a drastic threat. The being to whom it is addressed is not yet a mature moral agent. A simple "No!" can be fully understood even by small children and social animals who grasp that violation of the prohibition entails a disagreeable consequence, even if they are not able to understand why the prohibition is made. As David Clines has observed, the depiction of the humans in Genesis 2–3 is very much like that of the *petî* in Proverbs, impressionable, gullible, and lacking in discernment.[12]

In its effort to give an account of the place of human nature in relation to the other beings in the world, the story must construct two boundaries in its map of the world: the animal/human boundary and the human/divine boundary. Animals will emerge as beings who possess neither deliberative judgment nor immortality; humans are beings who possess deliberative judgment but not immortality; and divine beings possess both. Animals are first introduced in Genesis 2:18–20 in response to God's perception that "it is not good for *hā'ādām* to be alone." The intention is to form "a helper corresponding to him." The details of the text appear to assert the fundamental commonality between humans and animals. Not only are they made from the same substance (*'ădāmāh*), but God also seems to anticipate that the human might find his companion among them. That is the purpose of the naming. If *hā'ādām* gives a name to an animal that establishes some sort of linguistic relationship with his own name, then that will be the sought-for companion. Some interpreters argue that because there is no explicit mention of God's breathing the breath of life into the animals, they are already qualitatively different from *hā'ādām*. But in a form of storytelling in which repetition figures prominently, not every detail is necessarily repeated.[13] There is no reason to think that God animated the animals through any different method than the way in which the human was animated, and the cultural understanding of "the breath of life" in ancient Israel included animals as well as humans (e.g., Gen 6:17; 7:15, 22; Ps 104:29–30).[14] Moreover, the assumption of a *created* difference between humans and the other animals would undercut the very point of the narrative. The critical act that will make humans "like gods" is precisely what will differentiate them from the other animals. The fact that *hā'ādām* does not find the companion corresponding to him among the other animals in no way renders them lesser. Rather, the story is providing an etiology for sexual difference and sexual reproduction.[15] The "helper corresponding to" *hā'ādām* models a different and more intimate form of "same" than being made from the same dust of the earth. The helper-corresponding-to-him is a "bi-form" of his very body, made from it as "bone of bone, flesh of flesh" (2:21–23). This type of correspondence goes beyond that possible for one species of animal with another, and so it is marked by the linguistic pun *'îš* ("man") and *'iššāh* ("woman"). This commonality allows them to embrace and become "one flesh," referring either to the joining of bodies in coitus or to the flesh of the child that results from coitus, or to both. But at this point in the narrative there are only two types of beings in the world: divine beings and animals, including the human.

Although the other puns in the narrative have been transparent, the third pun that plays on *'ărûmîm* ("naked," 2:25) and *'ārûm* ("clever, shrewd," 3:1) is not, and its very opacity marks it as the key to the narrative. To increase narrative interest, however, the full disclosure of its significance is deferred to the critical moment in the story. One need not puzzle over how the snake became so clever. The snake's cleverness is an element of its role as a trickster figure, and its role is as much a narrative necessity as is the prohibition. Concerning such figures Niditch observes that the trickster is "a character having the capacity to transform situations and overturn the status quo," having "less power than the great gods but enough mischief and nerve to shake up the cosmos and alter it forever."[16] Somewhat like Prometheus, who gave fire to humans, the snake directs the woman's attention to a possibility that will change everything.

The conversation between the snake and the woman is the critical episode of the story. The snake's disingenuous question prompts the woman to reiterate and even exaggerate the divine prohibition (3:3). She has grasped the significance of "No!" The snake dismisses the divine threat and supplies what was missing from the prohibition in 2:17—the reason for it. "God knows that when you eat of it, your eyes will be opened and you will become like divine beings, knowing good and bad" (3:5), a state of affairs confirmed by God in 3:22. The significance of 3:6 is debated. It describes the woman's seeing the fruit and taking it. One might object that the woman already seems to have the power to choose between good and bad because she chooses to eat the fruit, though the power of such choice should be the consequence of the act. I do not think, however, that the scene is in any way the result of clumsy or self-contradictory storytelling. Rather, the story is making a subtle distinction. When the focus of the narrative shifts from the snake's words to the woman's perspective, what the narrator's words describe is simply the moment of desire. And desire is not the same as discriminating judgment. The sentence emphasizes the involvement of the senses and uses the vocabulary of appetite and attraction. The first two clauses incorporate the description of all of the trees from 2:9, as the third adds the description of the forbidden tree given by the snake: "Then the woman *saw* that the tree was *good to eat*, and that it was *pleasurable to look at*, and that it was *desirable for making wise*, and she took some of its fruit and she ate" (3:6a). The desire for wisdom is described in language that suggests it is not truly a rational choice but is folded into a more enveloping experience of desire that operates on a prerational level. It is no accident that the crucial symbolic object in the story is a food rather than, for example, a talisman of some sort. Food is a basic object of desire, grounded in the physical nature of all animals. Desire is thus a quality intrinsic to our prehuman state and capable of mobilizing the will over against a prohibition. In this narrative it is desire that serves as the mechanism by which decisive change is set in motion.

Consequently, it is important to reflect on the structure of desire. Typically, desire is described in terms of lack. But the condition of lack is not properly a negative one, and thus it serves well in a narrative about the transformation of a being from one status to another. Desire is always desire *for* some thing, and so it is a form by which persons transcend themselves. As Anne Carson has suggested in her study of desire in early Greek poetry, desire helps to create one's sense of oneself as a self, because desire teaches one about the nature of boundaries. In her words, "the experience of eros [or desire] as lack alerts a person to the boundaries of himself, of other people, of things in general. It is the edge separating my tongue from the taste for which it longs."[17] Carson notes that in the play of desire a curious shift of perspective occurs. I want this object to be mine because even though I never knew I lacked it before I saw it, this thing or person now appears as a *necessary* part of myself. I am incomplete without it, and so I draw it to myself.[18] This is the brilliant artistry of Genesis 2–3. The author knows that human beings are in fact characterized by the capacity for discriminating judgment, the quality represented by the tree of knowledge. That is a necessary part of what it means to be a human being. But the story takes the reader back to the moment when this capacity to make judgments, represented symbolically by the desirable fruit, was both outside of the human and yet seen and longed for, felt for the first time as a necessary part of who humans are.

And the result of desire fulfilled? "And their eyes were opened, and they saw that they were naked" (3:6b–7). At this remove, it is difficult to know if the story intended this line to be humorous, though I think it likely. This perception hardly seems like wisdom of the gods. And yet it is a brilliant and densely packed symbol. Frequently, the image has been associated with awakened sexuality. That is not entirely incorrect, since the fig-leaf coverings the woman and the man make for themselves serve to cover the genitals. But the recognition of sexual difference is not the main issue here. After all, sexual difference was what the man had exclaimed so happily about when he first saw the newly created woman in Genesis 2:23. Something else is primarily at stake here. Perhaps one can get at it by considering the contexts in which the concept of "nakedness" can and cannot meaningfully be used. It is a concept that can appropriately be used only of human beings. One cannot properly say of a trout or a lion or a deer that it is "naked." The concept of nakedness is one of the sharpest boundaries between the animal and the human. Animals make many things: shelters, tools, perhaps even weapons. But no animal makes clothes. Or, as Genesis might say, an animal is naked but not ashamed. Thus as the woman and the man confuse the boundary between themselves and the divine, that action simultaneously establishes the definitive boundary between themselves and animals. If humans have become "like gods," the consequence is that they are no longer like animals.[19]

In what respect, though, is this "eye-opening" knowledge related to a new type of cognition, which was hinted at through the punning association between nakedness and cleverness in 2:25 and 3:1? The philosopher Baird Callicott makes the astute observation that what the woman and the man see is *themselves*. They become *self*-aware, *self*-conscious; and this self-consciousness is the prerequisite for the experience of shame. Thus the woman and the man make clothes to cover themselves. That quality of reflexive self-awareness is also relevant to what distinguishes humans from the other animals.[20] Although recent studies in animal and human cognition acknowledge a greater degree of complex cognitive capacity, subjectivity, and self-consciousness among animals than earlier models recognized,[21] the fact of a dramatic cognitive difference between humans and other animals is undeniable. Modern analysis would locate this difference in the capacity of humans for symbolic thinking. Such symbolic capacity is certainly essential to the highly developed sense of self and self-in-relation that characterizes human existence. The ancient narrative, however, locates the difference in deliberative judgment.

One still must consider how such self-awareness or self-consciousness is related to the capacity to "know good and bad." All decisions regarding "good" and "bad" have to be made, of course, with reference to some center of value (good for whom? good for what? bad for whom? bad for what?). Presumably the now self-aware and self-conscious humans will make such decisions with respect to their own deliberative judgments about what is good or bad for themselves. In that respect they have indeed become "like gods." They are fully equipped as moral agents, having the capacity for will, desire, and knowledge of good and bad. But is this necessarily a bad thing in and of itself? That God is upset by this turn of events is evident, as God reiterates the prohibition on eating from the tree when confronting the humans (3:11, 17). Though some would argue that the consequences announced in 3:14–19 should not be understood as punishments, it is not clear why leglessness, enmity between snakes and humans, pain in childbirth, male privilege in sexual matters,[22] and field agriculture on degraded land are the inevitable outcomes of the acts in question.[23] These are better understood as punishments, though of course they also function as etiologies for aspects of the known world.

Nevertheless, God never explicitly indicates that humans having this capacity is intrinsically dangerous. The only expressed concern is that humans, having "become like one of us, knowing good and bad," might also eat from the tree of life and so "live forever" (3:22), the other distinguishing characteristic of divine beings. Thus the concern appears to be about the disturbance to the natural order of beings as created. Instead of there being only animals and divine beings, now a hybrid has appeared.[24] Typologically, Genesis 2–3 is in important respects a mirror image of Genesis 6:1–4 and its elaboration in the Enochic traditions of 1 Enoch 6–16. In those texts it is *divine desire* for the human that causes a confusion between categories that had been strictly separated. In 1 Enoch the resulting hybrids, the giants and the evil spirits released at their death, are characterized by insatiable hunger, a desire that wreaks havoc on the earth (1 En 7:3; 15:8–11). The breaching of boundaries is a powerful and dangerous act, but it may have either a positive or a negative valence. The same is true for hybrid creatures, which are common in the ancient Near Eastern religious imagination.[25]

If Genesis 2–3 is read on its own, then the new reasoning capacity of humans is a contained breach of world order and might be judged as morally neutral or even positive in its potentiality, since it makes possible moral agency.[26] But if Genesis 2–3 is read as part of a continuing "non-P" account of the primeval events that explains the formation of the world as later humans experience it, then one can follow the reflections on moral agency further in the subsequent chapters, attending to points of verbal connection with Genesis 2–3. In Genesis 4, when Cain is angry at the neglect of his offering, Yhwh reminds Cain of his ability to choose his course of action ("If you do right . . . if you do not do right," 4:7aα). The rest of verse 7 is difficult and contested but seems to personify sin as an aggressive animal or demon.[27] Imitating the language of the woman and the man's relationship from 3:16bβ, God warns that "its desire is toward you, but you can master it." The sin is objectified and externalized as an alien figure with its own aggressive desire, and yet it represents Cain's own desire to do violence. As the previous chapter discussed, several other Second Temple texts similarly objectify sin and represent it as an alien hostile will. Whereas many of those texts present the person as helpless against this hostile force, even using the language of sin or an evil spirit "ruling over" the individual (e.g., Plea for Deliverance [11QPs[a] 19:15]; Aramaic Levi Document 3:9), here Cain's own moral capacity is affirmed. He can master it. His failure to do so locates the perspective of the text squarely within the heart of ancient Israelite understanding of capable moral agency. Nevertheless, Cain's failure sets an ominous tone for the narrative.

The second echo of Genesis 2–3 in the non-P narrative concerns the figure of Noah. In the genealogy in Genesis 5 Lamech explains the name of his son Noah by saying, "Out of the ground that the Lord has cursed, this one shall bring us relief from our work and from the toil of our hands" (5:29; NRSV), echoing 3:17b.[28] That Noah is subsequently said to have "found favor" with God (6:8) indicates that good moral agency is not impossible; but the context paints a far more dismal picture, as the rest of humanity is found to be wicked.[29] The critical verse for the view of the non-P narrative on the eventual result of humans having obtained the autonomous capacity to "know good and bad" is 6:5. "Yhwh saw how great was the evil of humankind [*rāʿat hāʾādām*] on the earth; every inclination of the thoughts of their mind [*yēṣer maḥšĕbōt libbô*] was nothing but evil [*raq ra'*] all the time." Here the interpreter must negotiate the nuance of *ra'*. If one reads it in the milder sense of "bad, defective," then the judgment merely points toward the essential defectiveness of the hybrid creature who is not capable of handling the godlike capacity it has obtained. But the totality of the judgment and the drastic remedy proposed suggest that the problem is not only defective functioning but also the content of what the human mind devised. The human is not only poor in functioning but fundamentally "bent" (*yēṣer*) toward evil. The flood, however, does not solve the problem by preserving only the line of the righteous Noah. Although Yhwh resolves not to destroy the earth and all living creatures on account of humanity, it remains the case that "the inclination of the human mind is only bad/evil from its youth" (8:21). Taken as a whole, the non-P exploration of the origin and nature of human moral agency is profoundly negative.

If, as many scholars argue, the non-P narrative was produced in the early Persian period, then it is likely that it reflects some of the disillusionment about moral agency that characterizes other post-586 texts. Unlike Deuteronomy, Jeremiah, and Ezekiel, however, it offers no way of imagining a solution to the problem of the human heart. In that respect the non-P narrative appears to be somewhat similar to the view articulated many centuries later in 4 Ezra. In that text, of course, Ezra blames God for creating humankind with an "evil heart," which condemns the vast majority of humanity to sin and its consequences. At the same time Ezra recognizes that Adam is also at fault. But God affirms that Ezra himself, like Noah, is able to be righteous and will be saved, along with a small number of other righteous persons, in the eschatological judgment (e.g., 7:45–60). Unlike 4 Ezra, however, the non-P primeval history has no eschatological horizon, and so human existence becomes a narrative more characterized by moral failure than moral success.[30] For a number of Second Temple authors, however, this negative view of the human condition was problematic. They found creative ways in which to inflect and even subvert its perspective.

Moral Agency in Second Temple Interpretations of the Primeval History

Narrative Retellings of Genesis

Although modern scholarship disentangles a P and a non-P strand in the primeval history, traditional readings of the text tend not to do so and thus can exploit the ambiguities that the polyphonic text constructed of human nature not only in the primeval history but also in the larger body of scripture. Second Temple Jewish and early Christian interpretation reflect a range of perspectives on the significance of the narrative for moral agency. Many scholars have noted the comparative neglect of Genesis 2–3 in Second Temple literature as compared with the influence of Genesis 6:1–4 and its elaboration in 1 Enoch and related traditions about the Watchers and the Giants.[31] Nevertheless, there are a significant number of interpretive treatments of Genesis 2–3, though not all of them are particularly interested in the implications of the narrative for moral agency. Among the narrative retellings of Genesis, Pseudo-Philo largely replaces the narratives of Genesis 1–5 with genealogies, adding only a few narrative notes pertaining to Genesis 4 and 5. Though the text is interested in how the earth's inhabitants came to do evil and corrupt the earth, it appears to lay the blame on Lamech for his exemplary violence, and on his sons Jubal—for his invention of musical instruments and their role in seduction—and Tubal-Cain, whose metalworking techniques facilitated idolatry (Ps-Philo 2:7–10), thus accounting for the three major sins that particularly concerned Second Temple Judaism.

Jubilees does include the episode of the snake persuading the woman to eat from the prohibited tree, but the focus of the outcome of the story is more on explaining how animals lost the ability to speak and why humans cover their nudity (Jub 3:17–31). Quite possibly, the Genesis Apocryphon may not even have included an account of Genesis 1–4, though debate over the number of missing columns makes it difficult to be certain. Only in the Life of Adam and Eve does one find a developed and mythologized narrative account in which the devil is the evil antagonist who plots the ruin of the human couple. Although the narrative focuses on the fact of disobedience and the consequences that follow from it, there is no interest in the actual cognitive or moral effects of "knowing good and evil." The moral damage that comes from the fruit is not due to its intrinsic qualities but rather to the action of the devil who "sprinkled his evil poison on the fruit which he gave me to eat which is his covetousness. For covetousness is the origin of every sin" (Life of Adam and Eve [ApMos] 19:3; trans. Johnson).[32]

The only re-narration of Genesis 1–3 that seems to focus on the implications of the narrative as an etiology of bad moral agency is the very fragmentary text from Qumran, 4QParaphrase of Genesis and Exodus (4Q422). The relevant lines are as follows:

(6) [. . . the heavens and all] their hosts he made by [his] word [
(7) [. . . which]h he had done. And [his] holy spirit [
(8) [. . .] living [creat]ures and the creeping things [
(9) [. . . sowing see]d he set him in charge to eat the fru[it . . .]
(10) [. . .] that he shoul[d n]ot eat from the tree of know[ledge of good and evil
(11) [. . .] he imposed upon him, but they forgot [. . .]
(12) [. . .].[. .] in evil inclination and to deed[s of wickedness . . .]

(trans. Feldman, adapted)[33]

Lines 6–8 summarize Genesis 1. Unfortunately, it is not clear what the role of God's holy spirit is. With line 9 a transition from Genesis 1 to 2 occurs, apparently blending the reference to the human diet in Genesis 1:29 with the garden tradition and the permission to eat the fruit of the garden in 2:16. The motif of dominion (1:26, 28, with the common Second Temple preference for *mšl* rather than *rdh*) replaces the command to "work and tend" the garden (2:15). The prohibition against eating from the tree of knowledge is explicit, though using *lblty*, drawing on the syntax of 3:17. Line 11 seems to refer again to the prohibition and its violation, which is characterized as "forgetting" (*škḥ*). The most striking innovation in the account, however, is the apparent association of this violation with the evil inclination and "deed[s of wickedness]," an interpretive paraphrase of Genesis 6:5, reflecting the reification of the term *yēṣer*. Given the impossibility of distinguishing *waw* and *yod* in the scribe's hand, however, one can read the text as either *bywṣr* or *bwyṣr*. Feldman interprets the letters as the preposition *b-* plus a *qutl* pattern of the biblical noun *yēṣer*. He notes, however, that given the scribe's tendency to run some words together, one could read *bô yēṣer*, "in him [i.e., Adam] was the evil inclination."[34] This reading appears to me contextually more suitable, as it provides a reason why the human "forgot" the command. In either case the eating from the tree appears to be associated with the evil inclination. What was implied but not explicit in the narrative sequence of the non-P account about the inability of humans to appropriately use their new capacity appears to be construed in 4Q422 as a now-constitutive moral flaw (the *yēṣer raʿ*) that may manifest itself already in Adam. Not enough of the text is preserved to know whether the use of the verb *wayyîṣer* ("and he formed") in Genesis 2:7 provided a verbal connection to Genesis 6:5.

Sapiential Engagement with Genesis 1–3: Sirach

Ben Sira, who understood the capacity for moral agency to be essential for covenantal participation, constructs an account in Sirach 16:24–17:14 that merges Genesis 1 and 2–3, drawing on its vocabulary but eliding any reference to the violation of a prohibition. Shane Berg describes Ben Sira's method as follows: "He has deftly taken key words and phrases and woven them subtly into his renarration. The end result is that in Ben Sira's skillful wordsmanship the plot of Genesis 2 has been suppressed and some of its most important vocabulary has been taken over and redeployed in the service of Ben Sira's emphasis on obedience to the law" (Sir 16:24–17:14).[35] Similar strategies are employed in other Second Temple texts to various ends.

The opening of the passage in 16:24 frames it as an instruction ("Listen to me, my son . . ."), with Ben Sira presenting himself in language evocative of personified wisdom herself ("I will pour out my spirit," 16:25; cf. Prov 1:23). A succinct summary of Genesis 1 is provided in 16:26–30, echoing key vocabulary but often subtly shifting the perspective or referent of phrases ("at the first God created," "filled it with his blessings," "every kind of living creature"). The most striking change is the inclusion of mortality for all living creatures as a part of the design of creation ("its surface he covered with every kind of living creature, which must return into it again," 16:30; NABR). In 17:1–7 he combines Genesis 1 with Genesis 2–3:

(1) The Lord created human beings from the earth,
  and makes them return to earth again.
(2) A limited number of days he gave them,
  but granted them authority over everything on earth.
(3) He endowed them with strength like his own,
  and made them in his image.
(4) He put fear of them in all flesh,
  and gave them dominion over beasts and birds.[36]
(6) Discernment, tongues, and eyes,
  ears, and a mind for thinking he gave them.
(7) With knowledge and understanding he filled them;
  good and evil he showed them.

(NABR)

Moreover, the following verses associate such knowledge with fear of God, which enables perception of "the grandeur of [God's] works," so that humankind might praise "his holy name" (vv. 8–10). This motif is strikingly similar to the response of the angels at creation in the Hymn to the Creator (11QPs[a] 26:12, "When all his angels saw, they rejoiced in song—for he had shown them what they knew not"). The final consequence of the gift of knowledge is the "law of life, an everlasting covenant" (vv. 11–14).

As for the passage's interpretation of creation, not only is death simply treated as a natural entailment of human beings created from the earth (Gen 2:7, 3:19), but there is no mention of a prohibition and thus no occasion for a trespass. Instead, two things are highlighted. Alluding to Genesis 1:26–28 and 9:2, Ben Sira emphasizes the royal dignity of humankind. As part of the endowment of the human with qualities befitting its dominion, God provides what Alexander Di Lella summarizes as "intellectual-moral" qualities (discernment, mind) and "sensory-physical" ones (tongues, eyes, ears).[37] In the wisdom tradition, however, tongues, eyes, and ears are all primary agencies through which one exercises wisdom or folly. Thus they also belong to the moral equipment of humanity.[38] The reference to filling humans with knowledge and understanding in verse 7a recalls the way in which various gifted biblical characters are said to be "filled with the spirit" (see the discussion in chapter 2), and there is little doubt that these characteristics are part of what it means to be made in the image of God. The final line flatly contradicts Genesis 2:17 and 3:11. Instead of prohibiting access to knowledge of good and evil, God shows it to the humans. As Samuel Adams rightly observes, in Ben Sira's sapiential reading of Genesis 1–3 "the ability to distinguish good and evil is an essential and God-given attribute. Moral discernment is a positive gift rather than a forbidden fruit."[39] Thus Ben Sira corrects the tradition.[40]

Ben Sira recognizes, of course, that humans do not always choose rightly and so sin. His most polemical treatment of the issue occurs in Sirach 15:11–17, where he rebukes those who would blame God for their actions. It is not clear who his opponents might be. The position he critiques ("Do not say, 'It was the Lord's doing that I fell away,'" 11a [NRSV]) bears some similarity to the complaint of Ezra in the much later 4 Ezra that God apparently created humans with an evil heart, causing them to sin. Ben Sira may be caricaturing some forms of moral determinism such as one finds in the slightly later literature from Qumran, though it is possible that he simply constructs a pseudoquotation as a straw man. His insistence on moral freedom in this passage is squarely in the Deuteronomic tradition. In 17:30–32, however, following a discussion of divine mercy toward the repentant, Ben

Sira focuses on human limitations as a reason for sin, apparently as a rationale or motivating factor in divine mercy (cf. Ps 103:14, discussed below). He continues with a negative assessment of human capacity. The passage is textually problematic, but it appears that verse 30b contrasts human and divine nature ("for not immortal is any human being," trans. Skehan). The logic of the passage is a *qal vaḥomer* argument based on the "chain of being," similar to the arguments used in the very negative anthropologies of Eliphaz in Job 4:17–19 and 15:14–16; and of Bildad in 25:4–6. Ben Sira observes that even the sun may be eclipsed (17:31a) and the host of heaven held accountable (17:32a).[41] He further says that "flesh and blood devise evil" (*kai pomeron enthumythnsetai sarx kai aima*, 17:31b), perhaps evoking Genesis 6:5, and that "all humans are dust and ashes" (*kai anthropoi pantes gy kai spodos*, 17:32b), a phrase he also uses in 10:9 for human material frailty (cf. Gen 18:27; Job 30:19; 42:6). This passage is the closest that Ben Sira comes to suggesting an innate moral frailty rather than simply a physical one (cf. 10:9–11; 18:7–14). It seems likely that the idea insinuates itself into Ben Sira's presentation through his use of the rhetorical device and thus should not be overemphasized within the context of his thought, though it has currency elsewhere.

Dust and Decay in Ben Sira's Predecessors

Ben Sira's allusion to this trope of human moral evil as a problem of ontology, as one finds it in Job 4:17–19, 15:14–16, and 25:4–6, serves to set in high relief the fact that Genesis resolutely avoids this implication of moral frailty grounded in human materiality. It is certainly possible that Genesis associates the creation of humans from the "dust of the ground" with mortality. The formulation in Genesis 3:19 ("until you return to the ground, for from it you were taken. For dust you are and to dust you will return") is in itself no assertion of death as punishment but rather an argument grounded in ontology. Syntactically, it is simply an explication of the phrase "all the days of your life" in verse 17. For the author of the non-P primeval history, problems only emerge as animated dust *acquires* a godlike quality and then apparently is incapable of using it well. The problem emerges as this creature ascends the chain of being. The logic is different in Eliphaz and Bildad's formulations. Although Eliphaz does not allude to Genesis 2:7 and 3:19, he does use the trope of the body as formed from clay and dust ("those who dwell in houses of clay, whose foundation is in the dust," Job 4:19) and associates the process of dissolution with human death (v. 21). Bildad does not use the image of the body as clay but does allude to the decay of the body in death through his metaphor of the human as metonymically "worm" (*rimmāh*, Job 25:6a) and "maggot" (*tôlēʿāh*, Job 25:6b). The association of what decays and crumbles with what is morally abhorrent is a common symbolic association in many cultures, as one can see in the history of the word "corrupt" in English, which had the archaic meaning "putrid, rotten or rotting; infected or defiled by that which causes decay," as well as the meaning "debased in character; infected with evil; depraved; perverted; evil, wicked."[42] The notion that physical corruptibility is an index of moral corruptibility is, however, extremely rare in the Hebrew Bible. Except for Eliphaz and Bildad's statements the only other occurrence of the association is in Psalm 90:3–12, which emphasizes the ontological difference between God and humans. There, too, God's wrath at humans and awareness of human iniquities and hidden sins (v. 8) are associated with God's action of returning humankind (*ʾĕnôš*) to dust (*dakkāʾ*, v. 3a). It is possible that verse 3b is an allusion to Genesis 3:19 ("and you said, 'Return, mortal/children of Adam'" [*bĕnê-ʾādām*]). The interpretation of dust in Genesis 2:7 and 3:19 as an etiology for human moral depravity is explicit and central to the anthropology of the Hodayot, as I will discuss in the following chapter. It is possible that one other Second Temple text, 4QDibre HaMeʾorot, discussed below, may reflect a milder version of this interpretation.

Sapiential Engagements with Genesis 1–3: 4QInstruction, 4QMeditation on Genesis A and C

Like Ben Sira, 4QInstruction associates the garden of Eden with positive access to wisdom. The passage in question (4Q423 1) is less a retelling of Genesis than it is an appropriation of selected imagery in order to characterize the context of the one who seeks wisdom.[43] Like Ben Sira, the passage is cast as an instruction, with the recipient referred to as "you."

(1) [. . .] and every fruit of produce,
 and every pleasant tree desirable to make wise;
 is it not a pl[easant] garden,
(2) [desirable] to [ma]ke one exceedingly wise?
 And he has given you authority to tend it and to keep it.
 vacat g[arden . . .]
(3) [. . . the earth] shall sprout forth thorns and thistles to you,
 and its strength it will not yield to you [. . . .]
(4) [. . .] in your being unfaithful *vacat*.

(trans. Wold, adapted)[44]

In this passage the garden itself models the search for wisdom. The comparison of wisdom to a fruit tree from which one should eat is also present in Proverbs' comparison of wisdom to the tree of life (Prov 3:18; cf. 8:19) and in Ben Sira's poem on wisdom (Sir 24:17–21). The term "pleasant" (*nʿm*), which is commonly associated with wisdom and the wise (Prov 2:10, 3:17, 15:26; 16:24; 24:25), is here paired with "desirable to make wise" (*nḥmd lhśkyl*) from Genesis 3:6 to characterize not just one tree but every tree in the garden of wisdom. The seeker of wisdom is compared to Adam, as the text combines the gift of dominion from Genesis 1:26, 28 (with *mšl* for *rdh*) with the verbs for tending and keeping the garden from Genesis 2:15. Far from interpreting the narrative of the garden as one in which God prohibited access to knowledge, cultivating and eating from the trees that make one wise is the purpose of the one placed there. The thorns and thistles, which in Genesis 3:18 characterize the cursed earth that resists the man's cultivation after expulsion from the garden, here are the result of the gardener's failing to pursue his task of tending the garden of wisdom. As Benjamin Wold notes, the same motif is developed in the Hodayot, where the Teacher describes the edenic garden as a space accessible to the elect but off limits to "stranger" (1QH[a] 16:12–14). When the teacher tends the garden, it flourishes, but if he neglects it, thorns and thistles grow up (16:23–26).[45]

Since there is no indication of textual influence in either direction between Ben Sira and 4QInstruction, it is more likely that both are witnesses to a broader sapiential interpretation that contests the narrative argument of Genesis 2–3, even as it clearly draws on the wording of Genesis 2–3 and combines it with aspects of the more elevated anthropology of Genesis 1. Support for this notion of a sapiential tradition that contests Genesis 2–3 may perhaps be found in two highly fragmentary texts entitled 4QMeditation on Creation A and C (4Q303 and 4Q305). In 4Q303 8–11 the text appears to allude to Genesis 2–3:

> (8)]*r* and insight of good and evil, to[
> (9)] {a man/Adam} takes from it because [
> (10) and] he made for him a helper fit [for him
> (11) He gave her] to him for a wife, because from him [she was taken. . . .
> (*DSSR*, adapted)

The text uses *śkl* instead of *dʿt* to introduce the phrase "good and evil," apparently alluding to the woman's use of *lĕhaśkîl* in Genesis 3:6. But the sequence of lines suggests that this access to the "insight of good and evil" is already given to the man/Adam, even before the creation of his wife. Likewise, although only three lines of 4Q305 are preserved, they suggest a similar reading of the creation tradition:

> (1) and he created in it animals[. . .
> (2) He gave to man/Adam knowled[ge . . .
> (3) and evil[. . .] to know[. . .
>
> (*DSSR*, adapted)

Traditions that emphasize the glory of Adam and his access to knowledge and to the moral capacity it makes possible often have to reckon with the difference between that glorious stage of humanity and the present conditions in which access to wisdom is difficult and wickedness flourishes. Although it is not possible to know how 4QMeditation on Creation A and C dealt with this issue, considerable scholarly debate has occurred over the way in which 4QInstruction accounts for human ignorance and moral incapacity.

The passage around which the debate takes place is 4Q417 1 i. The first part of the passage is addressed to the "one who would understand," the *mēbîn*, and admonishes him to "meditate upon the mystery of existence" (*rz nhyh*, l. 6). As Matthew Goff summarizes, the expression refers to "a comprehensive divine scheme that orchestrates the cosmos, from creation to judgment, presented to the addressee as knowledge that can be ascertained through the study of supernatural revelation."[46] Within the context of 4QInstruction the kind of wisdom the *mēbîn* seeks is not simply deliberative rationality and prudential wisdom but also includes comprehensive understanding of reality as it is expressed in the unfolding of history and the principles that govern it. The mystery of existence also bears a strong typological resemblance to wisdom as the foundation and rationality of the cosmos (cf. Prov 3:18; Job 28:25–27) and to the "glorious plan" of God in the Two Spirits Teaching (1QS 3:13), in which all things are already determined. In 4QInstruction the mystery of existence is also closely related to the term "truth" (*'mt*), which appears to be the fundamental principle by which God orders all aspects of creation (4Q417 1 i 6–9).[47]

The command to meditate on the mystery of existence is itself connected with a variant of the phrase from Genesis concerning knowing good and evil, once again underscoring the divine intention that people should have such knowledge:

> (6) [Day and] night meditate on the mystery of existence, seeking continually. And then you will know truth and deceit; wisdom (7) [and foll]y you

> will understand. Know [their] deeds in all their ways together with their visitation for all the eternal times and the everlasting visitation. (8) And then you will know (how to distinguish) between [goo]d and [evil, according to their] deeds. For the God of knowledge is the foundation of truth, and by the mystery of existence (9) he has spread out its (truth's) foundation and its deeds." (my trans.)

It is noteworthy that knowing good and evil, which was presented as a quality or status in Genesis 2–3, is here understood as the ability to make a cognitive discernment ("know [how to distinguish] between [goo]d and [evil . . .]") that is the result of strenuous intellectual effort. In lines 9–13 the claim is made that God has expounded (*prš*) all of these mysteries to humankind, presumably in the mystery of existence that the addressee is exhorted to contemplate. Thus for 4QInstruction, if we are "each his own Adam" (2 Bar 54:19), it is as an Adam who was intended to have the knowledge of good and evil but who was also expected to work at tending and keeping the garden of knowledge.

Although lines 14–16 are difficult to interpret, a contrast is made between the "children of perdition" (*bny šwt*) and "those who keep his word" for whom a "book of remembrance" is written before God. In some manner the "vision of meditation" (*ḥzwn hhgwt*)[48] is associated with this book of remembrance,[49] and access to the "meditation" becomes the focal point of the critical lines. Cana Werman has argued that the phrase should be understood not as revelation but as "the intellectual effort of looking and studying" or "cognitive insight."[50] Since the *mēbîn* is elsewhere admonished to "meditate" on the mystery of existence, I assume that "meditation" and "vision of meditation" are expressions synonymous with the mystery of existence or access to it. The final lines of the passage, however, explain who does and who does not have access to the "vision of meditation" (l. 16) and are clearly linked to an interpretation of Genesis 1–3 through a series of intertextual allusions. The wording of the passage is difficult and has led to different interpretations.

> (16) *wynḥylh l'nwš ʿm ʿm rwḥ k[y']*
> (17) *ktbnyt qdwšym yṣrw wʿwd lw' ntn hgwy lrwḥ b[ś]r ky l' ydʿ*
> (18) *[ṭw]b lrʿ kmšpṭ [r]wḥw*

John Collins has made a persuasive case that the term *'nwš* is a synonym for Adam and that the phrase *ktbnyt qdwšym* ("according to the pattern of the holy ones," i.e., angels) in line 17 is a paraphrase for *bĕṣelem 'ĕlōhîm* ("in the image of divine beings") in Genesis 1:27.[51] Considerable disagreement exists, however, concerning how to translate *ʿm ʿm rwḥ*, since the letters *ʿm* might signify either the preposition *ʿim* ("with") or the noun *ʿam* ("people").[52] One possibility is to translate "a people with spirit" as a descriptive gloss on *ʾnwš* ("humankind," "Adam") and to see this group as contrasting with the *rwḥ bśr* ("spirit of flesh") in line 17.[53] Collins suggested that the text might refer to a double creation of two types of humans, one a creation of "spiritual" humans, based on Genesis 1:26–27, and the other of "fleshly" humans, based on Genesis 2:7, with "flesh" as the equivalent of the "dust" of that verse.[54] Others have argued against the notion of a double creation, preferring the interpretation that all humankind was created "with spirit" but that one segment has lost access to "the vision of meditation."[55] An alternative reading, suggested by Armin Lange[56] and taken up by Arjen Bakker,[57] is to take *ʿm ʿm rwḥ* as "with a spirit people" or "with a nation of spirit," referring to the angels. Although *ʿm* is not ordinarily used of angels, the Sabbath Songs do refer to the angels as *ʿm bynwt* ("a people of knowledge," 4Q400 1 i 6). Thus, as Bakker translates, "And He has assigned it [i.e., the vision of meditation] to mankind as a portion together with a nation of spirit [i.e., the angels], because He had fashioned him according to the structure of the holy ones."[58] In this interpretation the line explains that humankind is granted access to heavenly knowledge in a manner similar to the angels, the reason being because humans are made according to the pattern of heavenly beings (Gen 1:27). Since the access of the angels to knowledge of God's mysteries is a commonly recurring theme in Qumran and related literature, this is an attractive interpretation.

How, then, should one understand the reference to the "fleshly spirit" and its lack of access to the "meditation"? The problem with the "fleshly spirit" is that "it does not know[goo]d from evil according to the judgment of its spirit." Yet according to lines 6–8 it is only by meditating on the mystery of existence that even the *mēbîn* comes to have this knowledge. Thus it is quite possible that, as Jean-Sébastian Rey suggests,[59] the "fleshly spirit" simply refers here to those who do not undertake the hard work of seeking knowledge. Flesh, then, can represent that aspect of humanity that comes from the earth and that represents its frailty and lack of cognitive acuity, as opposed to the spirit component that comes from God. If this is the case, then the issue in 4QInstruction is analogous to the dilemma already visible in Proverbs. Although all persons are capable of becoming wise, some resist formation and become fools and wicked. They allow their "fleshly spirit" to dominate them. If that is the case, then they will find that they are subject to the punishments inscribed for "the sons of perdition" (l. 15).[60] However one resolves the difficulties of 4Q417 1, it does seem clear that 4QInstruction assumes that seeking the knowledge of good and evil is not only appropriate but a moral expectation grounded in God's intentions in creation. In that regard it is similar to Ben Sira in its subversive rereading of Genesis 2–3.

Liturgical Engagements with Genesis 1–3: 4QDibre HaMe'orot

4QDibre HaMe'orot is a liturgical cycle of communal prayers designed to be recited over the days of a week, concluding with a Sabbath prayer.[61] The first prayer begins with a summary of the creation traditions, and a general historical structure can be identified across the sequence, from creation through the exodus and wilderness experiences, the time in the land, and the exile. The praying community locates itself, existentially, as a penitential community in the aftermath of the exile, in keeping with the normative power of the exile in the spiritual imagination of the Second Temple period.[62] The Mosaic covenant traditions are particularly prominent in the text. In addition to the quasihistorical structure, the text develops its perspectives through sophisticated intertextual exegesis. Thus it is a particularly significant text for grasping how creation traditions concerning human nature may be integrated into a comprehensive religious perspective.

Like the sapiential texts discussed above, 4QDibHam[a] 1:4–14 treats the gift of understanding and moral capacity as divinely intended, not the result of the violation of a prohibition. Unfortunately, the lines in the first column are broken, so some uncertainty remains. It does not appear, however, that the text includes the motif of the tree and the specific prohibition against eating, as one finds in 4QParaphrase of Genesis and Exodus (4Q422).

(4) [. . .] you fashioned [Adam,] our [fa]ther, in the likeness of [your] glory;
(5) [the breath of life] you [br]eathed into his nostrils, [and filled him] with understanding and knowledge. [. . .]
(6) [. . .] Y[ou]set him to rule [over the gar]den of Eden that you had planted. [. . .]
(7) [. . .] and to walk about in a glorious land [. . .]
(8) [. . .] he guarded it. You enjoined him not to turn as[ide . . .]
(9) [. . .] flesh is he, and to dust h[e . . .]

(10) [. . .] his [. . .] *vacat* And you know [. . .]
(11) [. . .] for the generations of eternity [. . .]
(12) [. . .] the living God, and your hand [. . .]
(13) [. . .] humankind in the ways of [. . .]
(14) [. . . to fill the] earth [with vi]olence and to she[d innocent blood.

(*DSSR*, adapted)

In this rereading of Genesis 1–6 the key text is Genesis 2:7, interpreted in light of Genesis 1:26–28. As in Genesis 2:7, God "forms" (*yṣrth*) the human, but forms him "in the likeness of [your] glory" (*bdmwt kbwd*[*kh*). Although "likeness" is drawn directly from Genesis 1:26, the reference to "glory" is an interpretation of "image" (*ṣlm*) by means of Ezekiel 1:28. That text refers to the appearance of God in the vision as "the appearance of the likeness of the glory of Yhwh" (*mar'ēh dĕmût kĕbôd-yhwh*).[63] In this context the gift of the breath of life conveys not only animation but also "understanding and knowledge," a view similar to Job 32:8. It does not appear, however, that this understanding is knowledge of hidden things or divine mysteries, as in 4QInstruction, but rather the moral cognition required for the human task in the world. In the following line the human is not said to "work and tend" the garden (Gen 2:15)[64] but to "rule" it, an allusion to Genesis 1:26, with the characteristic use of *māšal* in place of *rādāh*. Instead of the prohibition of Genesis 2–3 "not to eat" (*lō tō'kēl*, Gen 2:17; *lĕbiltî 'ăkol-mimmennû*, Gen 3:11), 4QDibHam[a] has an admonition, "you enjoined him not to turn as[ide . . .]" (*wtqm 'lyw lblty s*[*wr*], 1:7).[65] Although the text is broken, only a few words are missing, and it is difficult to see how to reconstruct an explicit reference to the tree of knowledge. Indeed, it would be odd to have such a prohibition, since God has already endowed the human with "understanding and knowledge." Thus it seems likely that, as with Ben Sira, that episode is elided. God does, however, treat Adam not only as someone already capable of moral responsibility and with the full moral dignity of rulership but also as someone capable of disobedience, who is warned against it. It seems plausible that the admonition was followed by a brief, summary reference to such moral failure in lines 8–9.[66]

How is the reference to mortality in line 9 ("flesh is he, and to dust h[e . . .]") to be understood? It is not a threat like the warning of death in Genesis 2:17b, since it is an indicative statement. Nor does it seem likely that there is space for the assertion to function as an envelope for the curse of agricultural hard work, as in Genesis 3:19. More likely, the reference to "flesh" and "dust" alludes to the source of moral weakness present in Adam.[67]

As discussed above, such an association of dust and flesh with moral limitation can be identified in Ben Sira and in 4QInstruction, as well as, in a more radical form, in Job. In the Hodayot dust and flesh are linked with extreme moral abjection.[68] That extreme view is certainly not present here, given the significance of the Mosaic covenant in 4QDibHam. A tantalizing hint exists, however, that the text may well draw on the milder versions of this association of moral weakness with human materiality. Line 10 says, "and you know[. . ." (*w'th yd'th*), a phrase that Maurice Baillet and Esther Chazon have suggested is an allusion to Psalm 103:14 (*hû' yāda'*).[69] In Psalm 103:14 the reference to creation from dust ("for he knows how we are formed [*yiṣrēnû*]; he is mindful that we are dust [*'āpār*]") explains the basis for God's compassion toward the people who have sinned. There "dust" clearly connotes weakness, though not specifically moral weakness, since verses 15–16 use the familiar trope of human frailty as like the grass or the flowers that dry up quickly in the hot wind. Whatever Psalm 103:14 originally intended, its use of *yiṣrēnû* would have made it easy to understand this phrase not as "how we are formed" but as "our inclination" in light of Genesis 6:5 and the increasing reification of *yēṣer* as an "evil inclination" (cf. the discussion of 4Q422 above). Psalm 103:14 provided an exegetical basis for locating this flaw already in the very nature of the human as one created from dust, even if animated by divine breath/spirit. If so, then here, too, Adam's materiality may be implicated as the source of moral failure. Despite several badly broken lines, it is clear that the narrative in 4QDibHam[a] continues with an account of the flood, making reference to "humanity" (*h'dm*, l. 10; cf. Gen 6:5) and an allusion to the P narrative's justification for the flood in Genesis 6:11b, "the earth was filled with violence" (*wattimālē' hā'āreṣ ḥāmās*).[70]

Despite the broken nature of the text, 4QDibHam constructs a nuanced view of moral anthropology. Although it would be an overstatement to speak of a flesh and spirit dualism, a tension exists between evident moral capacity constructed for Adam through the divine breath and the inherent weakness apparently associated with his dust/flesh. The cycle of prayers in 4QDibHam traces much of the narrative of Israel from the historical books, so that one can see how this initial problematic moral formation of humans unfolds in Israel's history. The account is deeply indebted to the Deuteronomic emphasis on the Mosaic covenant (e.g., 11:16; 15:10; 16:10, 19; 18:9; 19:9), which emphasizes moral agency. References to moral failure, divine punishment, and Israel's pleas frequently echo the language of Deuteronomy and the penitential prayers of the early postexilic period.

Repentance and return are an essential part of the moral logic of this stance. But in contrast to many of the penitential scenarios that simply assume intact moral agency (e.g., Jer 29:10–14; Dan 9; Ezra 9), 4QDibHam takes its cue from the postexilic additions to Deuteronomy in Deuteronomy 30:1–10, shifting the agency for repentance and return to God's initiative. In 5:11 the people pray, "Circumcise the foreskin of [our heart]," echoing Deuteronomy 30:6. In 18:12–15 the text explicitly interprets Deuteronomy 30:1–2 in terms of divine grace shown to the people in exile and divine initiative that enables human agency. "You have shown mercy to your people Israel in all the lands to which you have banished them, causing their heart again to return and to listen to your voice [according] to all that you commanded by Moses your servant" (cf. 19:9–10).[71] Thus agency for the spiritual and psychological change is deflected from the people onto God. The text conceptualizes the instrument of this divine initiative by drawing on Isaiah 44:3, which speaks of the renewal of the people through God's act of "pouring my spirit upon your offspring." Here, however, "my spirit" is identified as God's "holy spirit," and the renewal is explicitly the capacity to "seek you in the time of our distress" (cf. Isa 26:16). A confession of sin follows in lines 18–20. Lines 21–22, which appear to refer to the present situation of divinely enabled repentance, make clear that this assistance does not amount to an extinguishing of the people's agency. Drawing on and transforming phrases from Isaiah 42:23–24 and 48:17, the prayer asserts that "You have [not] forced us like slaves for our own benefit to leave [our] path for the pa[th that we should walk] upon, [even though] we did not heed [your commandments]" ([*wlw'*] *h'bdtnw lhw'yl mdrky*[*nw*] *bd*[*rk 'šr nlk*] *bh* [*w*]*lw' hqšbnw '*[*l mṣwwtykh*]). Nevertheless, the text reverses the call for human agency of Ezekiel 18:31 ("Cast away from yourselves all your transgressions") and asserts instead that "[You have cast aw]ay fro[m] us all o[ur] transgressions, and you have [cl]eansed us from our sin for your own sake" ([*wtšly*]*k m*[*'*]*lynw kwl pš'yn*[*w*] *wt*[*ṭ*]*hrnw mḥṭtnw*, 19:3–4). How one understands the working of divine moral agency within or alongside of human moral agency is a subject that will be taken up in more detail in the following chapter, where the Hodayot are discussed.

To draw the lines of argument together, 4QDibHam is articulating a subtle but thoughtful perspective on human moral agency. Its reading of the creation accounts combines a high view of human moral endowment through God's equipping humanity with "insight and knowledge" with a sense that the dust-flesh of human material nature prevents the proper functioning of moral agency. Thus 4QDibHam is able to give an ontology for the moral failures that the Deuteronomic and related traditions recognized but never attempted to account for. As a postexilic text grappling with the massive moral failure that resulted in the destruction of the kingdom and the exile of the people, it also begins to explicate Deuteronomy's terse affirmation that God would intervene to repair the moral equipment of the people and so enable repentance and restoration. Although the text is careful to distinguish God's enabling of the moral agency of the people from any form of moral compulsion, it recognizes that God's agency has done for the people what they were at that point incapable of initiating themselves. Enabled by God's holy spirit, the speakers of the text perform acts of acknowledgment of sin, repentance, and praise of God that befits a morally responsive people.

The narrative of humanity's creation in Genesis 2–3 was a subversive and provocative challenge to the centrality of fully functioning moral agency in sapiential, Deuteronomic, and prophetic discourses in ancient Israel. As part of the non-P primeval history, it articulated a decidedly negative human agency for which it envisioned no solution. Not surprisingly, the text was itself resisted and subverted in much of the literature that engaged it in the middle Second Temple period. I am inclined to think of Genesis 2–3 as a kind of "strong poem" in Harold Bloom's terms:

> A strong poem, which alone can become canonical for more than a single generation, can be defined as a text that must engender strong misreadings, both as other poems and as literary criticism. . . . When a strong misreading has demonstrated its fecundity by producing other strong misreadings across several generations, we can and must accept its canonical status.[72]

Bloom's category of strong misreading encompasses contradiction, subversion, deflection, and various forms of recontextualization that struggle against the "strong poem." There is no doubt that Genesis 2–3 was recognized as just such a text that provoked an *agon*. The reassertion of God's intent to create humanity with the moral agency necessary to distinguish between good and evil was essential to those who, like Ben Sira, defended the classic understanding of moral agency and the covenantal tradition. At the same time the doubts about human moral capacity that became part of the cultural reformulation in the Second Temple period led to a parallel strong misreading of Genesis 2–3, one that began to associate the formation of humanity from the dust with an inherent moral flaw that could then be linked to the developing notions of the *yēṣer* and the contrast between flesh and spirit. These recastings of the Genesis tropes also contested the older narrative in that they consistently envisioned some form of redemption from moral incapacity, typically by means of an appeal to divine spirit. One of the most sophisticated of the strong misreadings is to be found in the Hodayot, the subject of the final chapter.

6 The Hodayot of the Maskil and the Subjectivity of the Masochistic Sublime

For a study on self and agency, no text is more significant than the Hodayot from Qumran. If for no other reason, it would be important as the largest collection of first-person-singular poetic prayers extant from Second Temple Judaism. What makes it so extraordinary, however, is the daring and virtuosity by which it constructs a radically novel model of subjectivity, drawing on but transforming the various developments that I have traced in preceding chapters. At the heart of its understanding of the human self is a radical interpretation of God's creation of human beings in Genesis 2. It develops this model through sophisticated intertextual exegesis of a variety of other texts, notably Job and Ezekiel, coordinating them into a powerful narrative of the self and its role in the plan of God. The Hodayot draw on and develop the use of first-person reflections on the experience of the self to construct an experience of intimacy with the divine involving a transformation so profound that it approaches divinization. What is in some ways most remarkable is that it does not simply develop its introspective dynamic by destabilizing the "I-Me" relationship, a technique that can be identified in many other first-person prayers. After all, it is fairly easy for the self as subject to call into question aspects of the self as object. What is remarkable, both from a technical and from a substantive perspective, is that the Hodayot also destabilize the knowing subject itself. That phenomenon is difficult to represent in a literary text. Nevertheless, constructing a plausible "I" voice that calls its very capacity and reliability into question and then reestablishes itself within the prayer-poem is at the heart of the experience of subjectivity that the Hodayot construct. In this manner the

Hodayot embody one of the most sophisticated spiritual practices developed in Second Temple Judaism.

Not all of the Hodayot reflect this model of subjectivity. Since the 1960s, scholars have typically distinguished a set of compositions in columns 10–17 of 1QH[a] that appear to be composed in the voice of a persecuted teacher, most often identified with the Teacher of Righteousness.[1] These compositions are voiced with a subjectivity that is much less complex and resembles the subjectivity of biblical psalms. The teacher refers to external enemies, bodily pains, relationships with others, and support from God, but only occasionally locates moral dangers as lurking within. The more radical exploration of subjectivity occurs in the two collections of Hodayot that bracket the Teacher psalms, specifically columns 1–9 and 18–27.[2] Although these two collections are typically referred to as Hodayot of the Community, there are good reasons for arguing that the non-Teacher Hodayot are not simply compositions of "ordinary" members of the community but compositions associated with the Maskil, the instructor and liturgical leader of the community.[3] Nevertheless, the Maskil is an exemplary figure who represents the highest manifestation of the subjectivity of all community members.[4] In some roles, such as liturgical leader, he is differentiated from the rest of the community,[5] but in the majority of the hodayot compositions associated with him the subjectivity that is developed is a subjectivity that all of the members would identify with. Although these compositions are not presented as instructions in the way that the Maskil's teaching in the Two Spirits Teaching is, they are themselves very much instructional texts. Thus it is likely that the modeling of selfhood and subjectivity in these compositions was one with which the membership of the community could identify.

The Role of Thanksgiving Prayer in Constructing Subjectivity

Essential to the construction of the distinctive subjectivity of these Hodayot is the generic form of the thanksgiving prayer. Although Hodayot differ significantly in form-critical terms from biblical psalms of thanksgiving, they share the basic generic stance, opening with words of thanksgiving and blessing of God for a gift received. In order to express gratitude it is necessary not only to describe the gift and its benefits but also to describe the condition of neediness and distress from which God delivered the speaker. Such rhetorical gestures are well known from biblical psalmody. In the case of these Hodayot, however, the gift is most frequently described as knowledge, and the distress from which the speaker was delivered is disclosed to be a state of moral putrefaction of which he was unaware until given the gift of knowledge by God. In essence, this is the scenario that Ezekiel had sketched in Ezekiel 36. But Ezekiel was uninterested in exploring the potential of this transformation for the experience of subjectivity. These Hodayot do so, however, with remarkable erudition and creativity.

The Gift

The broken state of many of the compositions makes a complete analysis difficult. Even though each composition is distinctive, there is sufficient similarity among them to establish a set of recurring themes and tropes. It appears that, with rare exceptions, each of the hodayot in the Maskil collections began with the expression "Blessed are you," a benediction that was also used in several places to introduce subsections of the compositions.[6] Thus the fundamental stance of the speaker is that of benefaction. Some description of the gift from God occurs in the opening sentences, though references to the benefaction may also appear later in the psalm. One of the most common of the descriptions has to do with knowledge, which is often described as transmitted from God to the speaker by means of an implanted spirit or spirits. For example, in 4:21 the speaker begins, "[Blessed are you . . .] on account of the hidden things that . . .]." The following subsections are similar: "[Blessed are you . . .] on account of the spirits that you have placed in me" (4:29) and "[Blessed are you . . . that] you have sprinkled your holy spirit upon your servant [and you] have purified [. . .] his heart" (4:38).[7] In column 5:12 the beginning of a composition explicitly linked to the Maskil is preserved. Although the line containing the blessing of God is broken (5:15), the following lines preserve references to "all insight and in[struction] and the mysteries of the plan and the origin[. . .]" (5:17) and assert that "in your wonderful mysteries [you] have instructed [me . . .]" (5:19). Similarly, in column 6:19 the speaker says, "[Blessed are you,] O Lord, who places understanding in the heart of your servant . . . ." A subsection of a psalm that uncharacteristically begins, "[I thank] you, O Lord" (6:34) and speaks of God's forgiveness and judgment continues with "as for me, your servant, you have favored me with the spirit of knowledge" (6:36). In column 7:12 the speaker says, "[Blessed are you . . . who] by the spring of your power gave us insight." In 7:21 a Maskil heading begins with "Bless[ed are you . . .]." Several lines refer to the speaker's commitment to obedience to God's commandments. Then the speaker continues with the line "and as for me, I know, by the understanding that comes from you . . ." (7:25). The subsection in 8:26 is one of the few that blesses God for God's deeds without making explicit reference to the gift of knowledge.

In the second collection in columns 18–27 the pattern is similar. A broken benediction in 17:38 cannot be reconstructed, but is followed in line 41 with the statement that "[. . . according to] his insight he will praise [your name]." In 18:16 a subsection begins, "Blessed are you, O Lord, God of compassion and [abundant] kindness, for you have made known to me these things." A psalm or subsection that begins in 19:6 with the less common expression "I thank you, O my God" continues in the following line with the rhetorical question "what am I that you have [inst]ructed me in the secret counsel of your truth?" (19:6–7). The end of that composition is a section marked with three short benedictions, the first of which reads: "Blessed are you, [O Lord, w]ho has given to your servant insightful knowledge to understand your wondrous works" (19:30). The Maskil hodayah that begins in 20:7 has an uncharacteristic structure, but the body of the composition in 20:14 begins, "And I, the Maskil, I know you, my God, by the spirit that you have placed in me."

In these compositions, knowledge is not merely "knowledge about" some aspect of reality, although the gift of knowledge is sometimes figured as instruction (5:19; 19:6–7) and includes insight into the mighty acts of God, cosmic mysteries, God's judgment, and other such things. In numerous places, however, reference is made to God's placing a spirit (or spirits) into the body or heart of the speaker, a gift that is closely associated with both agency and understanding (4:29; 5:36; 8:20, 29; 20:14–15; 21:34; cf. 6:19).[8] Thus what the speaker thanks God for is fundamentally God's constituting him as a perceiving, understanding subject. The trope is clearly one of creation. It generally echoes the creation accounts of Genesis 2:7, Psalm 104:29–30, and Job 33:4, among others, in which humans receive breath (*nĕšāmāh*) or spirit (*rûaḥ*) from God, and so become animate, agential, and perceiving subjects. The model in the Hodayot is especially similar to the understanding of Genesis 2 in Second Temple texts such as Job 32:8, Sirach 17:6–7, and 4QDibHam[a] 1:4–5, where the gift of breath or spirit was understood as the gift of knowledge. But the wording of these passages in the Hodayot, in particular the use of the verb *nātan* with the preposition *b*-, indicates that the immediate source of the image is Ezekiel 36:27,[9] where

God places God's own spirit into the bodies of the people (*wĕʾet-rûḥî ʾettēn bĕqirbĕqem*). As I will discuss below, the original creation of humans, as recounted in Genesis 2, is actually viewed negatively in the Hodayot. The passage in Ezekiel appealed to the authors of the Hodayot in part because it is an account of the *re-creation* of a people who are morally abject. In the Hodayot, as in Ezekiel, this new creation is associated both with the creation of moral capacity (Ezek 36:27b) and with a disturbing self-knowledge (36:31). In Ezekiel, however, the moral transformation of the people appears to be both sudden and decisive. Insofar as the people are represented as experiencing self-loathing, it is directed retrospectively to their past actions. As will become apparent, in the Hodayot the situation is more complex. Despite the election of the speaker, experienced through the gift of the spirit of understanding from God, this transformation is not so complete as in Ezekiel. The speaker continues to experience anxiety about being subject to the innate incapacities of his mortal condition and prays to God to continue and enhance his transformation (e.g., "your servant is a spirit of flesh," 4:37; "a foundation of shame and a well of impurity, a furnace of iniquity and a structure of sin, a spirit erring and perverted, without understanding, and terrified by righteous judgments," 9:24–25; "I am a sinful man, and one who has wallowed[. . .] wicked guilt," 22:8). Thus when the speaker refers to the condition of humankind in general, he is referring also to himself as he has been and as he still is in some respects.

The claims about the self and its nature in the Hodayot are not simple outpourings of distress but statements based on sophisticated exegesis that radically challenge traditional Israelite understandings of human nature. At the same time these intricately derived insights are incorporated into prayers that construct a powerful experience from these claims. In what follows I want first to examine the complex exegesis through which the claims in these compositions are derived and authenticated. Some readers may wish to skip this technical discussion and move to the following section, which examines the way in which the performative power of the psalms makes its claim about sectarian subjectivity experientially accessible to those who recite or hear them.

The Exegetical Derivation of Negative Anthropologies in the Hodayot of the Maskil

Anthropologies that posit inherent and intractable moral flaws in humankind occur in a number of earlier Second Temple texts. These include elements of the primeval history in Genesis 1–11, certain tropes in the speeches of Eliphaz and Bildad in the book of Job (4:17–19; 15:14–16; 25:4–6), the negative connotation of "flesh" (*bāśār*) in 1Q/4QInstruction and 1Q/4QMysteries, and a variety of texts that begin to develop the concept of an evil inclination (*yēṣer rāʿ*). Dualistic frameworks, as one finds in the Two Spirits Teaching, incorporate a distinctive account of sinful aspects of human nature. None of these texts, however, make negative anthropology so central, so extreme, or so experientially immediate as do the Hodayot. In the Hodayot this perspective is represented in its most developed form in the passages dubbed *Niedrigkeitsdoxologien*, passages that contrast human nothingness with the glory of God (e.g., 5:30–34; 9:23–25; 20:27–31).[10] But the negative anthropology is actually widely diffused throughout the two collections of Maskil compositions in the Hodayot.[11]

The negative anthropology in the Hodayot is overwhelmingly associated with the mortal, material nature of human being, the most common negatively marked terms being dust, clay, and flesh, complemented by the occasional reference to corpses, worms, and maggots. This being is characterized by immorality (sin, guilt, iniquity) and by impurity (most often *niddāh*). The term *niddāh* ("menstrual impurity") is used in an extended sense already in the Bible (e.g., Ezek 36:17; Ezra 9:11) and in some places in the Hodayot (e.g., 19:14; 21:36), but in the Hodayot it often appears with other sexualized or feminized language (e.g., "fount of [menstrual] impurity" [*māqôr hannidāh*, 9:24; 20:28; cf. Lev 20:18]; "shameful nakedness" [*ʿerwat qālôn*, 5:32; 9:24; 20:28]; "one born of woman" [*yĕlûd ʾiššāh*, 5:31]), suggesting that the Hodayot associate the negativity of the human condition in its fleshly mortality with the impurity connected with the female body.[12] Finally, the human condition is associated with limited or distorted understanding (e.g., error, without understanding). These cognitive and moral defects are often expressed in terms of the "spirit" that characterizes humans. While the texts may refer to a "perverted spirit" (*rûaḥ naʿăwāh*, 5×) or an "erring spirit" (*rûaḥ hattôʿāh*, 1×), three occurrences use the term "spirit of flesh" (*rûaḥ bāśār*), suggesting that the cognitive and moral defects are also associated with the material nature of humans.[13]

Strikingly, this wretched condition does not simply characterize a wicked subset of human beings. Nor is it the result of some sort of "fall" or the consequence of some sort of angelic mischief (*pace* Hultgren).[14] Rather, this flawed being represents the fundamental human condition. The human is this way because God created it to be so.

> As for me, from dust [you] took [me, and from clay] I was [pin]ched off, to be a source of impurity and obscene shame, a heap of dust and a thing kneaded [with water, bread of magg]ots, a dwelling of darkness. And there is a return to dust for the vessel of clay at the time of [your] anger [. . .] dust returns to that from which it was taken. (20:27–30)

Though this claim may seem shocking, the wretchedness of the basic human condition serves to underscore the miraculousness of God's transformation of a select group of persons who are then suited for fellowship with the angels. Needless to say, this is a view of human nature and destiny that cannot simply be read off of the central biblical narratives and teachings about humankind. It is an extraordinarily different account. And yet, in the Qumran community such a claim could not be persuasive unless it were grounded in authoritative texts. Indeed, it acquires its own authority and persuasiveness by being shown to be the hidden meaning of the texts that outsiders have not discerned but that has been made accessible to the understanding of those transformed by God.

Even within sectarian literature from Qumran, the radical view articulated in the Hodayot is distinctive. Outside of the Hodayot from Caves 1 and 4, similar passages occur only in the Maskil's hymn in columns 10–11 of the Community Rule, a composition generally recognized as itself a hodayah-type psalm, and in one passage in the Songs of the Maskil (4Q511 28–29 4–6). Since the Songs of the Maskil appear to "sample" other sectarian texts as well, such as the Sabbath Songs and the Berakot, it is likely that it is borrowing from the Hodayot rather than being a source for it. In any event, I take the Hodayot, the Maskil psalm from 1QS, and the passage in the Songs of the Maskil as reflecting *one* anthropological conception found in a closely related group of texts, distinct from the anthropologies found in other sectarian and nonsectarian texts in the Dead Sea Scrolls. That is not to say that the Hodayot are ignorant of these other traditions. The Hodayot do, apparently, appropriate some expressions from 4QInstruction,[15] notably "spirit of flesh" (4Q416 1 10; 4Q417 1 i 17; 4Q418 81 1–2; cf. 4Q416 2 ii 2–3 and a close parallel in 8 ii 7–8; in the Hodayot 1QH^a 4:37; 5:15, 20), but the anthropology that each text develops is different. Similarly, 1QH^a 9:17–21 appears to reflect the predestinarian language and concepts of the Two Spirits Teaching but does not use its dualistic anthropology.[16]

Correlated with the distinctiveness of the nature of the anthropology in the Hodayot is the profile of the intertexts that it uses for exegesis. For example, both the Two Spirits Teaching and 4QInstruction make use of Genesis 1 for anthropological speculations, though in different ways.[17] The Hodayot contain only minor references to Genesis 1. Similarly, though the use of the phrase concerning the inclination of the thoughts of humankind in Genesis 6:5 and 8:21 can be found in numerous texts (e.g., the Plea for Deliverance, the Prayer of Levi, Barkhi Nafshi, and the Damascus Document), the Hodayot make extensive use of the term *yēṣer* but very rarely in the sense of "inclination" and never clearly in the sense of an inherent moral inclination toward evil.[18] By contrast, the Hodayot make a critical and strategic use of anthropological passages from Job, notably the negative anthropologies of Eliphaz and Bildad, but other passages as well. And yet, so far as I have been able to determine, no other text at Qumran or elsewhere draws upon Job in constructing an anthropological reflection.[19] Thus, even though authors of texts at Qumran may be aware of other compositions and even borrow certain concepts and phrases from them, each appears to develop a distinctive anthropology in part by exegetical activity based on a different configuration of texts. Even when they do use some of the same biblical texts (such as Gen 2–3), the way these are combined with other texts, what one might call the exegetical recipe, is different. Each text manifests a distinctive and disciplined exegetical practice, not a general "shopping basket" approach to conceptions and terminology.[20]

One can begin to analyze the anthropological claims in the Hodayot by noting the frequency of certain terms for human beings that occur most frequently in contexts in which humans are negatively characterized. The term "dust" (*ʿāpār*) occurs with the greatest frequency, some thirty-five times (thirty-two of which are in the Maskil hodayot).[21] Its close synonym "clay" (*ḥēmār*) occurs fourteen times (eleven in the Maskil hodayot), with "dirt" (*ʾădāmāh*) one time in an anthropological context. "Flesh" (*bāśār*), which is the animate form of this material being, appears twenty-eight times, sometimes in the more neutral sense of "human" but often with overtones of moral weakness and unreliability. Six passages employ a developed image of the human as a piece of pottery, mixed with clay or dust and water or spittle (5:32; 9:23; 11:25; 18:5–6; 20:28; 23:28; cf. 21:12). Moreover, apart from one instance in a broken context, some twenty-one or twenty-two of the thirty-two occurrences of the word *yēṣer* in the Maskil compositions have the sense of "a thing shaped," "a vessel," rather than the meaning "inclination" or "purpose," and clearly belong to the image of the human as pottery. This trope is thus at the center of the negative anthropology of the Hodayot.[22]

The image of the human as a pottery vessel naturally leads one to look at the creation story in Genesis 2–3. But do the Hodayot simply refer to a common conception? Or is there an actual intertextual allusion? It appears that there is, since clear syntactical as well as lexical relationships occur between Genesis 3:19 (*'ad šubkā 'el-hā'ădāmāh kî mimmennāh luqqāḥtā; kî-'āpār 'attāh wĕ-'el-'āpār tāšûb*) and at least ten passages in the second group of Maskil psalms (18:6, 14; 20:27, 29–30 [2x], 34; 22:8, 30; 23:24, 29). This clear allusion gives further weight to seeing other connections with Genesis 2–3 that are less explicit. The noun *yēṣer*, meaning "vessel," "thing shaped," is used only one time as a metaphor for human beings in the Hebrew Bible (Isa 29:16, "Should what is made say of the one who made it, 'He didn't make me,' or should the pot [*yēṣer*] say to its potter, 'He didn't understand'?"). Moreover, the noun does not occur with this meaning in other Qumran literature, except in the Hodayot and the related passage in the Songs of the Sage (4Q511 28–29 3).[23] In the Hodayot its use and prominence are likely derived from the presence of the verb *yāṣar* in Genesis 2:7, facilitated perhaps by comparison with Isaiah 29:16. The very prominence of the term "dust" (*'āpār*), used both absolutely and in the construct phrase "vessel of dust," points to Genesis 2–3, since *only* there and in Psalm 103:14 is the term used to refer to the material composition of humans. It is perhaps implicit in the imagery of the return to dust in Psalms 30:9; 104:29; Job 10:9; 34:15; and Qohelet 12:7. Psalm 103:14, which may itself be an allusion to Genesis 2:7, is likely another key intertext for the Hodayot. It appears to play with the vocabulary of Genesis 2:7 as it explains the basis for God's compassion toward humans: "for he knows how we are formed [*yiṣrēnû*]; he is mindful that we are dust [*'āpār*]." Even though the noun *yēṣer* there more likely refers to the process of formation than the product, the wordplay in Psalm 103:14 facilitates the development of the notion of the "vessel of dust." To an actual potter, of course, the expression "vessel of dust" would seem odd, since it is not dust/dirt per se that one uses but dirt that has particular properties; one uses clay (*ḥōmer*; in Qumran Hebrew *ḥēmer*). Thus the prophetic texts that use the general trope of the human as pottery (*ḥōmer*) and God as the potter (*yôṣēr*), such as Jeremiah 18:3 and Isaiah 45:9, are also drawn into the intertextual web. That a systematic collocation of biblical texts relevant to the conception stand behind the Hodayot's discourse is suggested by the intertextual allusion to the rather obscure passage in Job 33:6. There Elihu expresses his common status with Job by saying, "I, too, was pinched off from clay" (*mēḥōmer qōraṣtî*), a use of the *pual* or *qal* passive that occurs only in this passage. The phrase is echoed twice in the Hodayot (18:8; 20:28–29) and once in the related Maskil's psalm (1QS 11:22).

Intertextuality with known scriptural texts is not the only source for the more graphic imagery of the human as pottery vessel that one finds in the Hodayot. Other distinctive phrases may be drawn from texts no longer extant or be free elaborations on the idea of humans as pottery, constructed by the authors of the Hodayot themselves. The frequent description of the person as "a structure of dust, kneaded with water" (*mbnh ʿpr wmgbl mym*, 5:32), "a vessel of clay, kneaded with water" (*yṣr hḥmr wmgbl hmym*, 9:23; also 11:24–25; possibly 21:11–12; cf. the differently worded phrase *whwʾh mṣyrwq ḥmr qwrṣ*, 1QS 11:21), uses forms of the root *gābal* in its Mishnaic sense of "to mix" or "knead," as in making bread dough or clay for pottery. As Jonas Greenfield notes, a commonly repeated Midrash employs this trope and this term in referring to the creation of humans: "In the first hour (of 1 Tishri, which was the sixth day of creation) God thought of him (man), in the second He took counsel with the attending angels, in the third He gathered his dust, in the fourth He kneaded him, in the fifth He shaped him, in the sixth He made him a lifeless being, in the seventh He inspired into him a soul" (Lev. Rab. 21:1).[24]

The verb is used similarly in the Hodayot—with one important difference. Both the rabbinic midrash and all of the biblical passages I have cited so far that describe human creation as analogous to the making of pottery do so without any claim that human materiality is evidence of disgusting sinfulness and impurity. At most, it signifies frailty and human limitation. How, then, does the author of the Hodayot read this tradition in a way that recruits all of these neutral images into such negatively marked assertions about humans? Initially, it seemed that Psalm 103:14 might play a critical role. Was the author of the Hodayot reading Psalm 103:14 as making a connection not just with Genesis 2:7 but also with 6:5 and 8:21, with their negative use of *yēṣer* as a moral inclination judged to be radically defective? While it is certainly possible that such an intertextual play is at work in Psalm 103:14, the Hodayot make little or no use of it, even though the notion of a reified bad *yēṣer* was well known.[25]

It appears that exegetical linchpins for the transposition of the value of the biblical references are the negative anthropologies that occur in the book of Job.[26] To establish this point, one must demonstrate explicit intertextual references to Job in the Hodayot. Four terms or words meet the criteria. The most distinctive is the phrase "born of woman" (*yĕlûd ʾiššāh*), which occurs four times in 1QH[a] and once in the generically similar Psalm of the Maskil (1QS 11:21). In the Bible this phrase occurs *only* in Job 14:1, 15:14, and 25:4. Although the phrase on its own does not have a negative meaning, signifying only a mortal being, the *contexts* in Job are all negative. In Job 15:14 and 25:4 the phrase occurs at the beginning of the characterization of humans as guilty and abhorrent before God, and in 14:1 it occurs in a passage that observes that one cannot produce "a clean thing out of an unclean one," that is, out of a human being. The semantic field of uncleanness is significant, since vocabulary of ritual/moral uncleanness and of disgust (the negative counterpart to holiness and sanctity) figures prominently in the negative anthropology of the Hodayot. Indeed, one of the distinctive features of the anthropology of the Hodayot is the use of pollution terminology associated with female sexuality (see below).[27] It may well be that the occurrence in Job of the phrase "born of woman" in proximity to the semantic field of uncleanness facilitates this development.

The second distinctive phrase shared between Job and the Hodayot is "dust and ashes." This phrase occurs in Job 30:9 and 42:6, and otherwise only in Genesis 18:27 in the Hebrew Bible. It occurs in the Hodayot in 18:7 and 20:30, in contexts stressing human incapacity. Apart from these occurrences there is a likely occurrence in 4QŠir[b] (4Q511) 126 2 and in 4QD[b] (4Q267) 1 5 (= 4Q266 1a–b 22–23), though both in broken contexts. The rareness of the occurrence of both "born of woman" and "dust and ashes" in Qumran literature, and indeed, in other Second Temple literature, suggests that they were not common idioms but were invoked with a sense of intertextual allusion.

Perhaps the most unexpected but distinctive intertextual allusion to Job is the phrase "pinched off from clay" mentioned above. It occurs in 1QH[a] 18:6, 20:27, and the related 1QS 11:22. In the Bible it occurs only in Elihu's speech in Job 33:6. In that context Elihu does not intend anything negative by the phrase, using it instead simply to establish a common humanity between himself and Job. But the fact that this distinctive expression is picked up by the Hodayot suggests that the book of Job had been studied for the topic of human creation and human nature, and that its various phrases might be interpreted in light of one another, so that the negative anthropologies could be read into those phrases that were not in their own contexts negative. The picture becomes even more clear when one examines the only other occurrence of this phrase in literature from Qumran, 4QŠir[b] (4Q511) 28–29 4. There, in an extended *Niedrigkeitsdoxologie*, the speaker describes himself as "pinched off [from clay]." In the immediately preceding line the passage alludes to Eliphaz's statement from Job 4:19. Eliphaz had referred to people as "those who dwell in houses of clay, whose foundation is in the dust." In the Songs of the Maskil the speaker refers to "my foundations of dust" (*sōd ʿăpārî*). Thus the passage in 4QŠir[b] brings together Eliphaz's negative image with Elihu's neutral one and casts both as part of a description of a humanity that is guilty and disgusting in its very created nature.

In fact, it is the ability of Job to establish verbal links that makes it such an important exegetical tool. As noted above, anthropological passages in the Bible using the term "dust" occur in Genesis; those using "clay" are used in the prophets. Only in Job does poetic parallelism employ them synonymously, in 4:19, 10:9, and 30:9 (also 27:16, in a nonanthropological context). Thus through verbal association the Joban passages link the relevant Genesis passages with those in the prophets. Similarly, Job 10:9 and 34:15 use versions of the phrase "return to the dust" (*šûb* + *ʿāpār*), gesturing to Genesis 3:19.

Given the associative exegetical practice of linking verses that share common words and expressions, the anthropological passages in the book of Job appear to be a kind of exegetical key to other anthropological expressions in the Hebrew Bible. Not only do these passages from Job serve as a kind of concordance to draw together a number of passages from Genesis, the prophets, and the Psalms. They also provide the strongly negative valence that can then serve as the means of reinterpreting the other passages in a negative light.

It is significant that in Job the distinctly negative anthropology is most explicit in those passages that make a direct ontological contrast between the nature of God and the nature of humans. In all three of the key passages, Job 4:17–19, 15:14–16, and 25:4–6, Eliphaz and Bildad use a "great chain of being" trope that argues by comparison from the greater to the lesser, from God to angels/luminaries to humans. In the Hodayot of the Maskil, as in these passages from Job, the emphasis is less on the contrast between the righteous and the wicked than between God and wretched humanity. Though other biblical texts may gently allude to the gulf between God and humanity for purposes of humble expression or justification of divine compassion, only in Job is it used to qualify humans as morally loathsome and impure.

The Hodayot are distinctive even within Qumran literature in associating human creaturely existence as such with impurity and sin. Although it is difficult to pin down the precise exegetical process, it seems clear that the link is made with the notion of birth from the woman, whose body is associated with sexual impurity. As Jonathan Klawans has demonstrated, at Qumran "ritual and moral impurity were melded into a single conception of defilement."[28] The clear anchor point for the connection in the Hodayot is the phrase "born of woman," unique to Job and used three times in the Hodayot (5:31; 21:2; 23:13–14) and once in 1QS 11. Though the phrase itself simply refers to the finitude of all humanity, its occurrences in Job (14:1; 15:14; 25:4) all introduce passages in which the human is described as "unclean" (*ṭāmēʾ*), "abhorrent" (*nitʿāb*), "foul" (*neʾĕlāh*), and "guilty" (*loʾ zakkû*). Moreover, Job makes other references to birth from the female body that provide links to creation accounts. The first is in 1:21, where Job says, "Naked I came from my mother's womb; and naked I shall return there." Here, of course, the parallel between the female body and the "earth's body" is implied, and the verb "to return" establishes a potential connection with Genesis 3:19. Job 10:8–15 details the formation of the human as fetus, using the poetic pair dust and clay to describe a being who is watched and judged by God for its inevitable sinfulness. Possibly other intertexts besides Job are in play as well, such as Psalm 51:7.

The association of the female body with impurity is strongly marked in the Hodayot. The Hodayot's preferred terms for the womb are "crucible" (*kûr*) and, particularly, "source" (*māqôr*). In the three instances in which *māqôr* refers to the womb (5:32; 9:25; 20:28), it occurs in the phrase *māqôr niddāh* ("source of menstrual impurity"), and in two of these (5:32; 20:28) it is paralleled with the phrase "obscene nakedness" (*ʿerwat qālôn*), which establishes a likely connection with Leviticus 20:18, prohibiting sexual relations with a brother's wife, a transgression that is compared to or perhaps conflated with forbidden intercourse with a menstruating woman. In that text the terms *ʿerwāh* and *māqôr* occur, though *dām* rather than *niddāh* is used to refer to menstruation. The words *niddāh* and *ʿerwāh* are found together in verse 21, however. In the Hodayot it is not voluntary sexual relations with a woman that are the problem but the inescapable fact of birth itself.

By pursuing this insight it is possible to see how the image clusters of the Hodayot come together to define its distinctive anthropology. In priestly legislation the birth process renders the parturient impure. If she gives birth to a male child the period of primary and secondary impurity lasts forty days. If she gives birth to a female child, the period is eighty days (Lev 12:1–5). Although Leviticus says nothing about the transmission of impurity to the child through the birth process or contact with the impure mother, such impurity may have been assumed in some halakhic traditions.[29] In Jubilees 3:8–15, after God creates Adam and, subsequently, Eve, God waits forty days to place Adam into the holy garden of Eden, and eighty days for Eve. The same tradition is recorded in 4Q265 (4QMisc Rules) 6, 11–17. Both Jubilees and 4Q265 make these primordial events the etiological basis for the legislation concerning the parturient's impurity. But in Jubilees and 4Q265 the delay pertains to the newly created Adam and Eve themselves. Thus the implication appears to be that creation itself, analogized to birth, results in an initial period of impurity for the child/newly created humans.[30] Joseph Baumgartner, discussing these texts, refers also to an apocryphal Life of Adam, quoted by George Syncellus. "Adam was brought into Paradise on the 40th day of his creation, wherefore also they bring male children into the Temple on the 40th day according to the Law. But for a female child she is to be unclean 80 days . . . , because Eve entered into Paradise on the 80th day."[31] This tradition appears to be assumed in Luke 2:22, describing how Jesus is presented at the Temple "when the time came for their purification according to the law of Moses." Similarly, Hannah K. Harrington draws the conclusion that "a theological principle found in other Qumran texts may be surfacing here as well: humanity is born in an impure condition, coming into the world brings impurity (even for Adam and Eve)."[32]

The Hodayot certainly do seem to be drawing on this tradition, associating impurity both with the original human creation from dust and water and with all those subsequently "born of woman." But why is this problematic? Impurity associated with birth is easily dealt with in halakhic terms. The Hodayot are, of course, not legal texts and are not developing halakhic rules. Rather, they are generating conceptions of anthropology by juxtaposing fields of metaphor and imagery with all of their cognitive and affective implications. Now one can see the power of the imagery of the Hodayot and why the rather unusual image of the human as a "vessel of dust" and "vessel of clay" has been so prominent in the poetry. Unlike other items that can be purified by washing or by passing through fire, pottery contaminated with impurity cannot be purified in any manner and must be broken (Lev 11:33; 15:12). Humans—made from dust into vessels of dust and clay and born from a process that is inextricably associated with impurity—are themselves like contaminated pottery that cannot be purified but must be smashed. This is a radical and intractable impurity that makes one abhorrent before God.

Although the majority of references to human moral incapacity are associated with the materiality of human existence, the texts do not assume a simple flesh/spirit dualism. Indeed, the agential spirit associated with untransformed humans is also described negatively. Within the Maskil compositions the phrases used are "perverted spirit" (*rûaḥ naʿăwāh*, 3×, plus 2 in the Teacher psalms), "erring spirit" (*rûaḥ hattôʿāh*, 1×), and "spirit of flesh" (*rûaḥ bāśār*, 3×). It is not clear that any of these expressions are exegetically derived, and "spirit of flesh" may be appropriated from 4QInstruction, though used in the context of a different anthropology. The passage in 1QH[a] 20:27–30 (cited above), which most clearly describes God's creating of humans *to be* unclean and morally perverted creatures, makes no mention of the breath or spirit that animates humans, stressing only human materiality. The phrase "spirit of flesh," however, is a particularly apt term to refer to the kind of spirit or agency that would characterize such a creature.[33]

The entire person, body and animating spirit, must be transformed, a process that is envisioned by means of an interpretation of Ezekiel 36:25–27. In Ezekiel's model, the first action is God's purification of Israel ("I will sprinkle clean water upon you, and you will be clean," 25a). That is followed by the promise of a new heart and a new spirit (26a). The heart of stone is removed and replaced by a heart of flesh (26b). Finally God promises to "put my spirit into your body" (*wĕ-ʾet-rûḥî ʾettēn bĕqirbĕkem*, 27a), the result of which will be that "I will cause you to follow my laws and faithfully to observe my rules" (27b). In the Hodayot the clean water of Ezekiel is interpreted as God's holy spirit. Although the Hodayot prefer the unusual verb *nûp* instead of Ezekiel's more common *zāraq*, the concluding benediction in 4:38 blesses God because "you have sprinkled your holy spirit upon your servant [and you] have cleansed his heart from [. . .]" (cf. 8:30, "cleansing me by your holy spirit"). In 23:27–29 a *Niedrigkeitsdoxologie* that employs the various tropes of dust, ashes, and vessel of clay that characterize the person as originally created shifts to the theme of transformation with the claim that "over the dust you have sprinkled [your holy] spirit" (23:29). Although the following lines are broken, line 33 further claims that "your [h]oly [spirit] you have sprinkled in order to atone for guilt." The result of this transformation allows the speaker "to be united with the children of heaven" (l. 30) and to be among those "[who s]erve with your host" (l. 34). As for the other actions in Ezekiel's scenario, one hodayah does use the phrase "heart of stone" (21:12; cf. "heart of dust" in 21:10); but the negative connotations of flesh in the Hodayot make Ezekiel's image of the heart of flesh unsuitable as an image of transformation. Instead, emphasis is on God's implantation of the spirit (4:29; 5:36; 21:34), which in some cases is referred to specifically as God's holy spirit (8:20; 20:14–15). Although the "holy spirit" is not as reified as it will become in later usage, it does connote the means by which God is present.[34] Thus more is at stake here than simply the animation effected by God's breath in Genesis 2:7 or even the cognitive and moral transformation effected by God's spirit in Ezekiel 36:27. As so often, broken texts impede complete understanding, but the hodayah that concludes column 4 appears to associate the sprinkling of the holy spirit and purification with access to "all of the insight of Adam."[35] The association with Adam, made "in the image of God," may well suggest that the reception of the holy spirit effects an ontological change in the persons who receive it. Clearly, the result is that the one so transformed can now be united with the angels. Thus it may not be excessive to say that this transformation effects a kind of divinization, or, if one prefers, an angelification (e.g., 19:13–17). Nevertheless, as will become evident, the transformation is not something that is accomplished completely and at once through God's action. It is the inauguration of a process that the speaker experiences in paradoxical fashion.

Experiencing and Representing the Problem That Is Not Only "Me" but "I"

The attention given to the materiality of human existence as the key to its nature as morally abject puts the focus largely on the bodily self and its impurity. Yet as the preceding paragraph indicates, the perceiving, thinking, agential aspects of the experiencing subject are also called into question. Although the speaker has been fundamentally transformed by God, he retains continuity with his appalling material self and, indeed, with his "spirit of flesh." Although it is fairly simple to represent an objectified problematic "Me," how does one represent a destabilization of the subjective experience of the "I"? What *is* such a self? How is it experienced? How can one grasp and find verbal and aesthetic representation of such an experience? It is the extraordinary attempt to do so that gives the Hodayot such frisson. The representation of this only partially realized eschatological self focuses on two areas: epistemology and agency. The Hodayot attempt to construct a verbal experience of the self who knows divine mysteries and yet cannot possibly know such things, the self who can do acts of righteousness and yet cannot do or will anything. These are both functions of the subject or "I" quality of self-experience. The intersection of these contradictions is the experience of the self constructed in the Hodayot of the Maskil. This phenomenon is what I have elsewhere referred to as the masochistic sublime, since only through experiential immersion in the full negativity of one's abhorrent materiality is it possible to grasp the radical transformation effected by God's purification of one's self and the infusion of God's own spirit.[36]

The Hodayot, as literary compositions, have to use literary techniques to construct an analogue to the experience toward which they point. In contrast to the referential/intertextual techniques used to ground the scriptural basis for their anthropology, the experiential dimension has to be constructed in the dynamics of the flow of the speech acts. How do they do it? The primary technique is to have the speaker perform acts of speech that assert and demonstrate his knowledge of divine mysteries. Then he interrupts this outward focused speech act with a sharp turn toward himself, or perhaps one should say, to his knowledge of himself as a creature of base materiality who is by definition incapable of such knowledge. These passages are often introduced by a rhetorical question that emphasizes the impossibility of the act just performed. Although the content of the knowledge about the self implicates the "Me" of the speaker as materially base, polluted, and sinful, it also raises a question about how such "perverted spirit" can know and speak about the mysteries of God. The contradiction is resolved as the speaker turns his focus to God and specifically to God's becoming the agent of knowledge that operates through the speaker.

The hodayah that begins in 5:12 provides a good example (cf. also 9:23–33; 18:3–14; 20:14–16, 27–30; 21:2–12).[37] It opens with a Maskil heading and identifies its purpose as didactic ("to give insight to the simple," "to give insight to humankind," 5:13, 14). The introductory benediction makes reference to "a spirit of flesh," though unfortunately in a broken context. Next, the speaker refers to God's instructing him with respect to "wonderful mysteries," which he recounts in order to glorify God (5:19). The recitation of these mysteries (5:17–30) refers to God's predetermined plan for the world throughout "eternal epochs," "the ways of truth and the works of evil, wisdom and folly," and their ultimate judgment at the "everlasting visitation." Finally, the account culminates in the claim that "in the mysteries of your understanding [you] apportioned all these in order to make known your glory." As in the Two Spirits Teaching, the speaker appears to have knowledge of the very mind of God and God's intentions since before the creation of the world. To recite such things is to lose oneself in the act of adoration. Such a practice is characteristic of a variety of types of hymns of praise in the Psalms, especially those that focus on God's mighty acts in creation (e.g., Ps 104). Ben Sira, too, constructs such a form of meditative praise in Sirach 42:15–43:33. Typically, the speaker is occluded or presented as modestly acknowledging the inadequacy of praise (e.g., Ps 104:33–34; Sir 43:27–33).

The innovation in the Hodayot is to abruptly shift the focus back to the knower:

> [But how i]s a spirit of flesh to understand all these things and to discern [. . .]? What is one born of woman amid all your [gre]at fearful acts? He is a thing constructed of dust and kneaded with water. Sin[ful gui]lt is his foundation. (He is) obscene shame and a so[urce of im]purity. And a perverted spirit rules him. When he acts wickedly, he becomes [a sign for]ever and a portent for dis[ta]nt generations of flesh. (5:30–33)

This shift changes the function of the psalm so that it becomes not just an instrument for the praise of God but an instrument for highlighting the nature of the speaker's subjectivity. As an embodied person, this paradox is the speaker's reality. He is, quite literally, incapable of knowing and uttering what he has just spoken. Here the speaker of praise can no longer dissolve into the praise or be merely a modest presence beside it. His own subjectivity, his own "I," is encountered as an impossibility.

The authors of the Hodayot, of course, are not proto-existentialists attempting to explore a type of epistemological and moral nausea à la Sartre. The encounter with the abyss of one's own "spirit of flesh" is preparatory for grasping the meaning and experience of God's transformation of the speaker. At the end of the *Niedrigkeitsdoxologie,* the speaker had turned from the ontology of moral abjection to its consequences—acts of wickedness. He now begins his account of transformation with the moral dimension, "only through your goodness can a person be righteous . . ." (5:33–34), but then turns to imagery of creation that alludes to Genesis 1–2. "By your splendor you glorify him, and you give [him] dominion" (5:34). The word "dominion" points to Genesis 1:26–28, and the references to God's splendor and the glorification of the human to the claim that humanity is made in the image and likeness of God. The abundant delights (*rb ʿdnm*) are a play on the name of Eden, and the eternal peace and long life are among the eschatological gifts named in 1QS 4:7, evocative of life in the garden before the fact of death. That this is not an allusion to the original creation but to the re-creation of the elect through the new action of God is indicated by the epistemological claim in 5:35 that answers the question of how "a spirit of flesh could understand." This passage affirms that "I, your servant, know by means of the spirit that you have placed in me . . . ," alluding to the interpretation of Ezekiel 36:27 as the foundation of the Hodayot's subjectivity.

The claim that God is the source of understanding is, of course, a pietistic commonplace, as illustrated by various statements in Psalm 119: "Open my eyes, so that I may perceive the wonders of your teaching" (v. 18); "Make me understand the way of your precepts that I may meditate on your wondrous acts" (v. 19). Nehemiah, too, refers to his plans as "what my God was putting into my mind to do for Jerusalem" (*māh ʾĕlōhê nôtēn ʾel-libbî laʿăśôt lîrûšālaim*, 2:12). These are, of course, both Second Temple texts and may reflect a greater tendency to emphasize the porosity of one's thought processes to the presence of God, though the general understanding of God's ability to influence thoughts, plans, and actions is well represented in narratives that are undoubtedly older, as discussed in chapter 2. What the Hodayot do is to take that commonplace and radicalize it, examining its implications for the experience of subjectivity. They dramatize what it is like when one sharply polarizes divine and human nature and then imagines the transforming presence of God's spirit in one's body. How does an "I" represent that experience if not by cultivating the sense of acute paradox that only resolves by acknowledging the presence of God in one's own most intimate experience of selfhood, one's thoughts and perceptions. God is no longer simply encountered in the social categories of king, redeemer, protector, and so forth, but also in the *rûaḥ* of one's own being.

This altered sense of self in the Hodayot may be even more clearly represented in those passages that speak of agency. The sense of intending and willing are, like the sense of perception, aspects of the subjective "I." The self as agent is, as discussed in earlier chapters, one of the fundamental assumptions of Israelite moral discourse, even though in certain narrative texts there are explorations of the ways in which God might affect a person's agency, either through an externally envisioned charismatic *rûaḥ* or through operating in ways unperceived by the subject to "harden the heart" or otherwise direct intentions and motivations. The exploration of agency in the Hodayot, however, is largely configured by their theological commitment to God's superagency in predestining all things. How, then, does one speak of agency and, indeed, experience agency, in such a context?

Most discussions of predeterminism and moral agency at Qumran focus on concepts and their logical consistency or inconsistency rather than on the representation of experience.[38] Scholars note the presence of both deterministic claims and voluntarist claims, often within the same document and even within the same passage. One approach to such seemingly contradictory data is to assume that the sectarians were simply inconsistent or not fully systematic in their beliefs.[39] This may indeed be the case, though Jonathan Klawans argues that, properly understood, all deterministic systems are consistent with voluntarism in a rather minimal way, in that they distinguish "between intended and unintended behavior."[40] Moreover, some systems of predeterminism are more about divine foreknowledge of actions that are undertaken freely than about divine causation of actions, though that does not seem to be the perspective of Qumran texts.[41] The form of predeterminism Klawans considers most similar to that found in Qumran literature is one in which God predetermines the dispositions of persons, who then choose according to those dispositions.[42] In my opinion, Klawans is correct in identifying the predetermining of dispositions as key to understanding Qumran predestinarian beliefs, at least as these are articulated in the Hodayot. Moreover, if this is the case, then examining how moral agency is constructed and represented in the Hodayot may provide a more detailed understanding of how predeterminism functioned to provide a distinctive sense of self and agency for Qumran sectarians.

One might object, of course, that the very term "moral agency" is a voluntarist category and so incompatible with a predeterminist system of belief. I do not think that is the case, though the agency constructed within predeterminism will have different characteristics than agency within a voluntarist system of thought, as I will attempt to demonstrate.[43] One could illustrate the juxtaposition of voluntarist and predeterministic language from many texts in the Hodayot, but a particularly good example is to be found in 1QH[a] 7:23–27. The introduction to the hodayah is in lines 21–22, so this passage comes from the beginning of the composition.[44]

> (23) And I love you freely. With all (my) heart and with all (my) soul I have purified (myself) from iniquity. [And upon] my [li]fe (24) [I] have sw[orn

> no]t to turn aside from all that you have commanded. I will stand firm against the many appointed for the [day of slaughter, no]t (25) abandoning any of your statutes. *vacat* And as for me, I know, by the understanding that comes from you, that it is not through the power of flesh [that] an individual [may perfect] (26) his way, nor is a person able to direct his steps. And I know that in your hand is the inclination of every spirit [and all] its [activi]ty (27) you determined before you created it.

In the first part of the passage, the unselfconscious use of voluntarist language is evident in the adverbial phrase *bndbh* ("freely"), which claims agency with respect to the speaker's commitment to God.[45] Such language is also present in the use of *bkwl lb* and *bkwl npš*, the terms that identify the centers of will, intention, and desire, drawn from Deuteronomy 6:5 (cf. 10:12; 30:2). These efforts are directed toward the actions of moral purification and obedience. If the restoration is correct, there is also a reference to taking an oath, a strong assertion of moral agency. These self-assertions are similar to expressions that can be found elsewhere in the Hodayot (e.g., 6:28–29, 37) and in the Serek ha-Yaḥad (e.g., 1:1–18; 5:7–11). Following the *vacat,* however, the depiction of the locus of moral agency is drastically different.

The parallelism of the passage is the key to the author's thought. Although line 25 is broken and requires some restoration,[46] the basic structure of the thought of the beginning of this section is established by the repeated negative particle, verb, and infinitive that describe the activity, plus the object of that activity and a term for the human subject. Thus, human moral agency appears to be denied, at least to a significant extent. This claim is introduced with the phrase "in the power of flesh." Here "flesh" appears in its relatively neutral sense as a synonym for *'dm* and *'nwš*. The speaker appears to say that humans qua humans do not have moral agency. The next line establishes a new contrast parallel between *ky' l' byd bśr* and *ky bydk.* Here "flesh" and its incapacity are contrasted with God and God's capacity. The agency that does not belong to humans belongs to God (reinforced at the end of the statement with the repetition of the key verbal root *kwn*). The following phrase, *ky bydk yṣr kwl rwḥ*, refers to a person's moral agency, which is determined by God. The assertion is completed with a temporal reference that all of this was established "before you created it." Thus, the conceptual context is strongly predeterministic.

On the face of it there appears to be a strong contradiction between the lines before the *vacat* and those following, concerning the locus and nature of moral agency. How should one make sense of the contradiction? The issue of contradictory assertions involving self-representation has attracted the attention of anthropologists, who often encounter the phenomenon in field work. As Katharine Ewing described it,

> in all cultures people can be observed to project multiple, inconsistent self-representations that are context-dependent and may shift rapidly. At any particular moment, a person usually experiences his or her articulated self as a symbolic, timeless whole, but this self may quickly be displaced by another, quite different "self," which is based on a different definition of the situation. The person will often be unaware of these shifts and inconsistencies and may experience wholeness and continuity despite their presence. . . . [People] often keep only one frame of reference in mind at any particular moment. . . . The same individual may shift frames of reference from one context to another, even from one moment to the next, and may tolerate considerable inconsistency in his or her own beliefs and opinions, often without realizing it.[47]

These self-representations are understood by means of performance theory as "performances" of self.[48]

It is perfectly possible to explain the shifts in the Hodayot as examples of shifting frames of reference. When the speaker orients himself to the traditional voluntarist frame of reference, he speaks as a moral agent. When he orients himself to a frame of reference focused on God's sovereignty in creation, he speaks as someone whose whole activity is determined by God. The author performs one type of self, then performs another contextually appropriate type of self. Understood this way, the phenomenon would be analogous to what linguists call code-switching—the use of different dialectical forms of speech that are dependent upon the audience or social context within which one is speaking. In that case, what occurs in the hodayah would be a kind of conceptual code-switching, dependent on the cognitive framing of one's self-representation. The small *vacat* could even be a visual marker of the shift. In many respects I find this explanation appealing, because personal and cultural systems are often inconsistent, and all persons may well have a variety of inconsistent self-representations in our repertoire, even if we are not fully aware of this fact. I have used a rather similar explanation for the variety of inconsistent representations of moral agency in Qumran literature more generally, arguing that these representations shift according to the requirements of the rhetorical situation.[49] In some cases this does indeed seem to be the right explanation, especially where the inconsistent or contradictory statements are contextually separated.[50] I have reservations, however, about the adequacy of this approach for the Hodayot. I do not think that conceptual code-switching is a fully adequate explanation for what is going on here, and if one were to stop with this analysis, something vital would be missed.[51]

What the Hodayot do is to construct a model and an experience of what might be termed a dual subjectivity. The exegetically based discernment that underpins the entire rationale for the Hodayot is that the speaker is a person who, though "[pin]ched off (from clay) to be a source of impurity and obscene shame," (20:27–28), has also been elected in God's predetermined plan to be someone into whom God places God's own spirit. But what is the effect of this divine spirit that has been placed into the speaker? In Ezekiel, the transformation that is effected by the heart of flesh and the new spirit is complete moral transformation: "Thus I will cause you to follow my laws and faithfully to observe my rules" (Ezek 36:27; NJPS). Though the people will remember with loathing their previous sins (36:21–32), they will sin no more. The situation is somewhat different for the speaker of the Hodayot, however. One of the things that the gift of the spirit does is to provide knowledge: knowledge of heavenly mysteries, that is, knowledge of the plan of God. But that knowledge also includes awareness of one's own constitution as a spirit of flesh. In contrast to the situation of the re-created being in Ezekiel, where the heart of stone is removed, the spirit of flesh is not removed from the speaker of the Hodayot. He still claims the perverted spirit/spirit of flesh as his identity (4:37; 5:32; 8:18; cf. 9:23–25), and the repeated *Niedrigkeitsdoxologien* psychologically rehearse the anxiety of being created as a person without moral agency. Not only is the speaker appalled at his past sins (4:30), but he is also aware of his continuing incapacity as a mere mortal. Through God's gift of the holy spirit he has the power not to sin, but his transformation is not complete (8:29–32), and he still fears that without God's continuing action he is subject to "stumbling from the precepts of your covenant" (8:33).

The favored image of "vessel" for human beings in the Hodayot suggests that the community thought of persons metaphorically as containers. Most human beings are vessels that contain only the defective "spirit of flesh" (and the synonymous expressions that characterize it). The "I" that expresses the subjectivity of the ordinary person—the content of his consciousness—is wholly constituted by his spirit of flesh. Thus, he has no independent awareness of it. The problem of wickedness is in part, one might say, a problem of false consciousness. In Ezekiel 36, the model of subjectivity is one of replacement: the defective heart is removed and a new heart and a new divine spirit put in its place. The new subjectivity that is constituted by this transformation remains, however, simple in structure. It has the capacity to retrospectively judge the sinful actions that the person had committed and to feel self-loathing for these actions (Ezek 36:31), but it is not a divided subjectivity. Consequently, it lacks true introspection. The Hodayot, however, present a more complexly structured model. Though the transformation effected for the speaker by the gift of the divine spirit its decisive, it does not eliminate the spirit of flesh from the person. The gift of the divine spirit is what makes him aware of the spirit of flesh within him and of his desire to dissociate himself from it, though he knows this is not fully possible, at least without God's further action.

One of the implications of this model is that the speaker's subjectivity is also not fully constituted by the divine spirit, as it is in Ezekiel. Instead, the speaking subject is also aware of the divine spirit within him. The speaker does not simply say, "I know," but rather, "I know by means of the spirit that you have placed in me" (21:34; see also 4:29; 5:36; 8:20; 20:15). Even his prayer is the product of an agency that he ascribes to God's spirit within him ("I entreat you with the spirit that you have placed in me," 8:20). Indeed, all of the speaker's positive affects and actions can also be attributed to this divine source—this is what allows him to "not sin against you" (4:34, 35; 6:28; etc.).

This is not to say that the speaker experiences himself as an automaton. He has real agency—but it is a kind of co-agency in which the speaker's knowledge and will and actions are made possible through the palpable agency of God working within him:

> And as for me, dust and ashes? What can I devise unless you desire it, and what can I plan for myself without your will? How can I hold fast unless you cause me to stand firm? And how can I have insight unless you have formed it for me? (18:7–9)

> As for me, I am unable to speak. What could I say concerning this? According to my knowledge I have spoken, a thing kneaded together, a vessel of clay. What can I say unless you open my mouth? How can I understand unless you give me insight? What can I s[peak] unless you reveal it to my mind? (20:35–37)[52]

The self-conscious recognition of both the spirit of flesh and the holy spirit as constituent of the self is only part of the knowledge bestowed by the spirit that God has placed in the speaker. This spirit also gives the speaker access to an understanding of the plan of God for the world, that is, the purpose and fate of the righteous and the wicked, including God's determination of who they are "from the womb" (7:28). This knowledge is part of the speaker's agency, that is, part of his self. It allows him—quite curiously—to be virtually present at his own creation, grasping his own re-creation as part of the predetermined plan of God, who has indeed "formed every spirit" and established its "inclination" (3:26; 6:22; 7:26, 35; 9:11; 18:24). His agency is both free (he really does choose) and determined—from the womb.

To return to the question posed above about the juxtaposition of voluntarist and predeterminist language in the Hodayot, these forms of discourse are not best understood as discontinuous representations of the self and its agency accomplished through rapid conceptual code-switching. Rather, their juxtaposition is utterly essential to the representation of the distinctive form of dual agency manifested in the Hodayot. The ostensibly contradictory discourses about the nature and source of moral agency are resolved through the nature of what is predetermined. God predetermined that certain persons and not others would be given the gift of the divine spirit that then allows them to have a subjectivity that is not wholly constituted by their spirit of flesh. This new spirit, though it gives them new capacities for knowledge and moral action, does not eliminate the moral will. If one were to visualize the structure of the moral self in the Hodayot, it might be represented as a triangle. The speaking subject, the one who says "I," is aware of and observes the effects of two spirits within himself: the spirit of flesh and the holy spirit of God. Both of these are part of his complex subjectivity, though he seeks to identify with one and to reject the other. In this regard, although the Hodayot are generally not considered to be dualistic texts in the way that the Two Spirits Teaching of 1QSerek ha-Yahad is, the Hodayot also construct a subjectivity that is similarly shaped.

Since the nonbiblical writings of Qumran are not part of the canonical religious literature of either Judaism or Christianity, few scholars grant them the dignity of being taken seriously as colloquy partners in our own self-understanding. They do, however, deserve the status of classic literature and so to be admitted to the canon of texts for the wider culture that can speak across confessional lines. Indeed, though in many respects the Qumran literature may seem to operate in a theological idiom that few modern people would consider plausible and many would reject as abhorrent for its demonization of outsiders, certain perspectives to which it gives voice are uncanny in their resonance with contemporary scientific understandings of humans as sentient creatures in a vast, transcendent, yet surprisingly understandable universe. How is it that life arises out of inert matter? How is it that matter achieves consciousness? And how astonishing that not only does matter achieve consciousness but that it can grasp the very principles by which the universe is constituted, gaze into the origins of that universe, perceive its trajectory toward an end, though perhaps as only a moment in a yet stranger multiverse. Humans as a species are a mere 300,000 years old at most. And yet, we grasp so much of the rationality of the cosmos. Is it just that we are luckily clever? Or is it that the very principles that would lead to the emergence of life and sentience would, in a sense, speak through us? Martin Heidegger's essay "Language" suggests something similar about the relationship of the human being to being itself, of *logos* to *Logos*. Though the imagery he uses in the essay is marked as Christian, the basic ideas are not. In his notoriously hermetic style he says, "we enter into speaking of language in order to take up our stay with language, e.g., within *its* speaking, not within our own. Only in that way do we arrive at the region within which it may happen—or fail to happen—that language will call to us from there and grant us its nature."[53]

While one cannot equate these modern and ancient formulations of human existence, neither are they so far apart as to prevent conversation. Both posit the origin of human existence in a materiality that is as devoid of cognitive, moral, and spiritual qualities as it is possible to imagine. For both, the transformative element is associated with cognitive capacity. "Knowing" is an immediate experience of subjectivity, the very constitutive element of being an "I." And the mysteriousness of how humans can know things that transcend their own limited physical existence requires reflection. How is *logos* related to *Logos*? Although modern responses run the gamut of possibilities, Heidegger suggests that human understanding in speech is not simply a lucky shot but rather should be envisioned in the opposite direction. It is Being that speaks through beings. It is "language [that] will call to us . . . and grant us its nature." So, in the Hodayot, it is the divine spirit that is placed within the human that grants knowledge and calls forth speech. In the Hodayot, as in Heidegger, there is not simple overwriting of the human by the transcendent. Indeed, the preservation of the difference is what permits and requires the act of speech. "The intimacy of world and thing is not a fusion. Intimacy obtains only where the intimate—world and thing—divides itself cleanly and remains separated."[54] There would be no point in the Maskil's speaking if he were entirely subsumed by the divine spirit. It is only because he is aware of the spirit within him that grants him knowledge and agency, but also because he is not identical with that spirit, that he must give voice to his experience—his thanksgiving at his transformation and the knowledge it affords, as well as his abiding sense that he is and remains a mortal being.

Many Second Temple texts express the idea that God's act of creation elicits a response of astonished praise from all created beings, from angels to the lowest forms. "When all the morning stars sang together" (Job 38:7a); "When all his angels saw—for he showed them what they did not know" (4QHymn to the Creator [11QPs^{a} 26:12]); "Dew and rain, bless the Lord . . . Frost and chill, bless the Lord" (Dan 3:68–69). So, too, in the Hodayot, "You yourself created breath for the tongue. You know its words, and you determine the fruit of the lips before they exist . . . in order to make known your glory and to recount your wonders" (1QH^{a} 9:29–32). Speech from all of creation is God's own spirit, dispersed throughout creation, echoing back the joy of the act of creation itself. In its own way certain movements within Second Temple Judaism sought a "unified field theory" of reality. They articulated it through a sense of God's predestining of all things, the capacity of all reality to praise, and the special pouring out and implanting of divine spirit among Israel and the elect. Nowhere are the implications of this fundamental idea for the meaning of human subjectivity so profoundly explored as in the Hodayot.

Conclusion

Anyone who attempts to explore aspects of the cultural history of the self in antiquity has to do so with a keen sense of the limitations of the available evidence. Unlike anthropologists, we have no access to living communities where everyday speech situations can be observed and where statements about the self can be put in the context of a wider range of behaviors, interactions, and practices. The sources available come from a narrow range of literary texts, often of uncertain date and with a complex history. The frequent observation among scholars of the Dead Sea Scrolls that their task is that of putting together a jigsaw puzzle with 90 percent of the pieces missing and no picture on the cover of the box is equally applicable to many other attempts to reconstruct aspects of ancient culture. In addition, the hermeneutical task is fraught with the dangers of the unconscious tendency to assimilate ancient culture to our own assumptions, but equally to the dangers of an overcorrection that leads to exoticizing ancient culture and ancient selves. Despite the limitations and the risks, there is much that can be discovered.

Throughout this inquiry I have attempted to avoid reifying culture, but rather to see it as a series of improvisational responses to changing contextual circumstances. One of the questions that has been present in all of my inquiries, sometimes explicitly and sometimes implicitly, is the relationship between a fundamental neurophysiology of self functions that is common to all humanity as members of the same species and the diverse and changing cultural forms that representation of the self takes. This is not to say that I think we are all "the same" and that culture is simply a superficial overlay. Not at all. The very thoughts we think and the ways in which we think them—especially if they are part of cultural practices that are frequently repeated and imbued with emotional significance—can affect the synaptic patterns of the brain. Culture and neurophysiology are complexly related. This is one reason why cultural histories of the self are important. The neurophysiology of the self includes a number of phenomena that are essential to successfully negotiating the world, including ways of self-monitoring, managing conflicting impulses, and speculating on the dispositions and intentions of socially important others. Particular cultures may or may not focus their attention on these phenomena and make use of them. If and when they do, however, then those who practice such attention experience themselves differently. By cultivating these self functions and embedding them in larger symbolic structures of meaning, intimate experiences of the self become ways of participating in transcendent realities. Clifford Geertz oversimplified when he assumed that symbolic forms and self-experience are transparent to one another. They are not. But they are closely related. Symbolic forms are tools for shaping experience. The member of the Qumran community trained by the Maskil who used the Two Spirits Teaching and the Hodayot to instruct initiates had a far different set of tools to use for grasping and shaping his self-experiences than did the pupil of the sage who used the instructions and sayings of Proverbs. Indeed, the member of the Qumran community may have been equipped with both of these, as well as many others. Since we have no access to the actual persons of antiquity, we cannot judge how they used their cultural tools. We can, however, study the tools themselves.

In the first three chapters of this work I have attempted to look at some of the symbolic forms relating to self and agency that form a cultural baseline and aid in recognizing where change and variation occur. As biblical scholars have recognized for generations, the body is key to the vocabulary of the self in ancient Israel. As interesting as what one finds in the texts is what one does not find or finds only occasionally. Using William James's heuristic distinction between the self as subject ("I") and the self as object ("Me"), one can see that most ancient Israelite texts were not much interested in exploring and exploiting the "I-Me" relationship, even though it is one of the basic and essential features of the neurophysiological self. That relationship remained largely culturally opaque. Even in those contexts, such as wisdom instructions in Proverbs, where one of the primary concerns is the development of self-regulation, one finds only a modest development of the potentialities of body language in representing

"I-Me" relationships. Consequently, where such symbolizations of the body do begin to appear and develop, one is able to raise questions about what changed historical and cultural conditions may have made this a tool worth developing, and to what perhaps unanticipated additional uses it might be turned in later contexts.

Since agency is such a fundamental aspect of the self, I was surprised to discover how little research has been done on the representation of agency in general in ancient Israel. Yet this is a highly useful category within which to bring together various lines of scholarly inquiry that have perhaps not always been in conversation. Not surprisingly, the biblical texts appear to be particularly interested in the ways in which divine and human agency interact. Some of the assumptions about divine-human interaction are clearly self-conscious and are referred to explicitly in the texts. Other assumptions, however, appear to have been tacit, and it is not even certain that if we could have interviewed ancient Israelites, they would even have been aware of their assumptions. "Unknown knowledge," however, can be some of the most significant. The clearly divergent patterns of prepositions and verbs used for different forms of interactions with divine spirit, and the similarly divergent patterns of imagery in speaking of *nepeš* or *rûaḥ* in the context of death, are markers at the level of syntax and discourse of shared but seldom articulated understandings of how the individual self and divine spirit are related. How much more might one discover by further searching for such tacit knowledge in the literary remains?

One of the useful aspects of thinking of cultural models and symbolic forms as tools rather than simply as beliefs is that it becomes possible to see how particular rhetorical tasks call for different assemblages of tools. Even if an analysis of the narrative literature demonstrates how easily ancient Israelites could conceive of the human mind and agency as being permeable to divine mind and agency, a context like that of the covenant relationship as it is presented in Deuteronomy requires a strongly autonomous model of human agency. Other ways of thinking about the nature of agency are not discarded; they are just not relevant. The plural nature of self models becomes increasingly evident in texts from the Second Temple period, when a larger variety of models for understanding self and agency were developed. In many cases speakers may simply have moved between one and another model in a likely unconscious process of cultural code-switching. In some cases, however, the juxtaposition of different self models may have provided the impetus for sophisticated hybrid models for experiencing the self and its agency, as I argue is the case in the Hodayot of the Maskil.

When I began this project, it was with the hypothesis that the destruction of the kingdom of Judah was the central event responsible for what appeared to be a significant shift in models of self and agency in the Second Temple period. The reality, of course, turns out to be much more complicated. But the impact of 586 BCE cannot be underestimated. Especially given the immense investment of ancient Israelite culture in a model of the divine-human relationship that stressed the autonomous moral agency of the human covenant partners, the devastating losses could only have been read as evidence of catastrophic moral failure. A number of texts whose composition bridged the events of 586 BCE and their aftermath show the impact of this terrible experience and the early attempts to envision rhetorical and symbolic ways in which it might be absorbed and accommodated. The late additions to Deuteronomy, Jeremiah, and Ezekiel all attempted to grapple with the massive failure of human moral agency on the part of Judah and yet recognized that it was impossible to envision a future as a people without the capacity for robust agency. Each finds a way to displace the source of agency onto God, who gifts it securely back to the people. Whereas the earlier models for strengthening moral agency, such as one finds in Proverbs and Deuteronomy, relied on personal discipline grounded in strong social bonds, the post-586 BCE models are all grounded in tropes of radical transformation. To varying degrees moral abjection is the necessary starting point for the restoration of agency. Of the various models Ezekiel's is the most extreme. His exceptional rhetoric is grounded not only in the particular circumstances of his role as prophet among the first group exiled from Judah to Babylonia, but above all in the resources of his priestly imagination. In contrast to the strongly social models of divine-human relationship in Deuteronomy and Jeremiah, Ezekiel's priestly imagination works through the logic of holiness and what is, essentially, an exploration of the ontological gulf between the divine and the human. It is this, as much as his particular imagery of the heart and spirit, that has profound consequences for the ways in which Second Temple Judaism began to envision the moral self in relation to God.

The Second Temple–era texts examined in chapter 4 stand at the heart of my project. In many respects the texts are quite heterogenous. Although their provenance is often uncertain, they exhibit different systems of imagery, patterns of intertextual engagement, and rhetorical stances. Most, but not all, are first-person-singular prayers. What they all have in common, however, is an interest in representing the "I-Me" relationship as an experience of fundamental importance, and, indeed, a troubled and troubling experience. By locating the focus of distress as an aspect of the self in the context of first-person-singular prayer, an act of introspection is naturally created. The very fact that these texts do not all represent the relationship of the I and its Me by means of the same imagery is significant. When one finds the same or an analogous gesture repeated in different symbolic forms, then one has evidence of a culturally dispersed interest in a particular experience. I have termed this experience "self-alienation," since in almost all of the texts the "I-Me" relationship is constituted as one of distress at a sinful condition that one is powerless to affect. As with Deuteronomy, Jeremiah, and Ezekiel's attempts to envision a solution to failed moral agency, the resolution involves transformation of the self by God. But whereas those texts were concerned with the problem of the nation, the texts examined in chapter 4 are mostly framed in relation to the individual's experience. It is quite possible that the spread of sin and guilt language into the domain of personal prayer, where it had previously been largely absent, was an unconscious attempt to relocate the dynamic of sin, reconciliation, and restoration from the national level, where the process seemed incomplete, to the realm of personal religion, where it could be a present experience. Whatever the forces that initially led to the introduction of tropes of self-alienation into the language of prayer and the development of the spaces of introspection, the dynamics came to be used in the creation of novel forms of spiritual experience focused on intimacy with the divine.

One of the odd problems in working on this project was where to locate a discussion of the text of Genesis 2–3, and, indeed, what to make of it. While the significance of the text is clear if one is engaged in a history of the self in early Christianity, it is an enigma when viewed from the perspective of Second Temple Judaism. It is largely ignored, and when it is engaged from about the second century BCE onward, it is engaged in a manner that seems to ignore or dismiss its narrative force. Yet through a variety of "strong misreadings" it becomes a fruitful source for tropes and images that are incorporated into novel understandings of self and agency, both strongly positive and shockingly negative. Combined in innovative exegetical ways with the passage about the creation of humankind "in the image and likeness of God" from Genesis 1:26–27, it can be used to generate a view of human purpose and destiny that is exalted. But combined with the growing attention to the ontological abyss between the divine and the human, it figures human physicality itself as an index of moral abjection. Even this, however, becomes a powerful tool for the experience of sublime transformation.

It should come as no surprise that the "heroes" of my narrative are the two great texts from Qumran—the Two Spirits Teaching, as it is incorporated into the Community Rule, and the Hodayot, especially those of the Maskil. The distinctive needs of a sectarian community that developed during the middle Second Temple period created the perfect environment for the cultivation of a focus on the self and its experience, as the Yahad attempted to form persons for perfect obedience to torah. In addition to the social story of the origins of the community as it is narrated in columns 1–4 of the Damascus Document, the Two Spirits Teaching, as it is incorporated into the Community Rule, provides the metaphysical story of the origins and destiny of the members of the community told as a story of the self and its agency. The Hodayot of the Maskil take up the tradition of first-person-singular prayer that develops the "I-Me" relation as a mode of spiritual experience. But they do so in a way that dissolves not only the unselfconscious unity of I and Me in traditional psalmody but even the self-consistent I of Second Temple prayer. Through a remarkable reinterpretation of Genesis 2–3 and Ezekiel 36, these compositions construct a subjectivity that is simultaneously aware of its ontological sinfulness and its radical transformation by the very spirit of God. As I intuited but did not fully understand in my earlier work on these texts, the self at Qumran is truly symbolic space.

The scope and focus of this project have remained within the confines of texts from ancient Israel and the Hebrew and Aramaic literature of Second Temple Judaism. No attempt has been made to set these developing models of the self in relation to those of Jewish literature composed in Greek or to other cultures of the Hellenistic world. At the same time, it would be myopic to imagine that the discourse about the self in Second Temple Judaism developed in isolation from wider currents. The analyses I have presented in these chapters are merely the first steps in understanding the significance of the texts in their larger cultural context. The Qumran texts, in particular, with their subtle and sophisticated accounts of the nature of human selfhood in its relation to cosmological realities and ethical imperatives, need to be seen and analyzed as part of a wider Hellenistic cultural interest in these matters. Even where one might not speak of direct connections, the issues and ideas concerning the self in these texts can be put in fruitful conversation with contemporary and later works that make the self central to the exploration of religious and philosophical ideas and experiences. Some of these connections have been noted in the past, but I hope that my efforts to uncover more of the discourses about the self in the Hebrew literature will encourage a new consideration of these comparisons.

Closest to hand, of course, would be a comparison of the moral psychology of the Second Temple writings with that of the Testaments of the Twelve Patriarchs, a text that has a complex development within both Hebrew- and Greek-speaking Jewish cultures, as well as early Christian communities. This text is a particularly valuable example of how different folk theories concerning agency and character could converge and meld in Hellenistic culture. The role of demonic spirits that one finds in the Testaments is derived from aspects of the Semitic trajectory of moral agency I discuss in chapter 4. But the psychological mechanisms by which these spirits work appear to blend such notions with those derived from earlier Greek models of the mind and emotions.[1]

A different sort of comparison is invited by the Hodayot and the Odes of Solomon, a Jewish-Christian text probably composed no later than the early second century CE. Earlier work tended to focus somewhat narrowly on questions of influence and even authorship.[2] While those are intriguing questions and some sort of relationship is assumed even by cautious critics, it might be more productive to prescind from worries about identifying specific relationships and to ask rather how the Odes and the Hodayot model similar but distinctive ways of constructing a self who is transformed through intimate infusion of God's divine spirit, how knowledge is constitutive of subjectivity in each tradition, and how cosmology and the self are related. What is equally worthy of closer investigation is the use of confessional first-person-singular poetry as a means for cultivating the religious experience of salvation, enlightenment, and transformation. Certain notable differences between the Odes and the Hodayot in the way in which they depict the self and its relation to God may well correlate with different strands of Hellenistic philosophy that formed part of the intellectual atmosphere of eastern Mediterranean religious cultures.

Although comparisons between Pauline anthropology and that of the Dead Sea Scrolls have a long history, recent scholarship has reinvigorated this discussion and emphasized the significance of these texts for Pauline understanding of the human condition, especially in relation to Pauline anthropology and the problem of moral agency.[3] This conversation, however, has tended not to intersect with the parallel interest in the ways in which Pauline anthropology can be fruitfully related to similar concerns in Hellenistic moral philosophy, in particular late Stoic philosophy.[4] I would like to suggest, however, that an important next step is to bring these two conversations together. The Qumran texts are especially important because they share with Paul significant elements of a Jewish sapiential/apocalyptic worldview, even as they share important perspectives and concerns with Stoicism, some of which are quite different from what one finds in Paul.

Although it is not common to discuss Qumran literature in the context of Hellenistic philosophy, certain of its conceptual categories invite such comparison, especially in the areas of cosmology and anthropology. Rüdiger Bartelmus has suggested that some of the innovative expressions involving the verb *hāyāh* ("to be"), such as *tʿwdt hwwh* ("the testimony of what exists"), which is "what shall be, without end" (*why'h thyh w'yn 'ps*, 1QH 20:12–13), are comparable to the Hellenistic philosophical concept of *to ōn* ("that which exists," "Being"). The distinctive Qumran conception of God that focuses on "knowledge" (*'l dʿwt*, 1QS 3:15) and the fundamental structures of creation by which God predetermines all things, both in cosmology and in history (e.g., *mḥšbt*, *dbwdw*, *swd*, *'mt*, *rz*, *nhyh*), arguably have more in common with the Zeus of Stoic thought than with the God of Deuteronomy, though, to be sure, Qumran literature merges the two streams of reflection on the divine. With respect to the person, the fundamental emphasis on knowledge as constitutive of selfhood in the Two Spirits Teaching and in the Hodayot provides an intriguing analogy to the role of rationality that is constitutive of mature humanity in Stoicism. This is all the more the case in that both traditions emphasize the essential divinity of that rationality,[5] though the way they conceptualize the relationship is different. Certainly, the assumptions about agency are quite different, and have different implications for the nature of the "technologies of the self" that were developed in each tradition. Yet even here common concerns can be recognized. For the late Stoics the task was to give "assent" to those things in accord with rationality. At Qumran, the use of "truth" (*'mt*) as a virtue term and its frequent pairing with "righteousness" (*ṣdq*) also suggest that bringing affects and actions into accord with divine order is the understanding of the ethical task. In the predestinarian contexts of Qumran, the gift of divine spirit becomes the mechanism for instilling a functioning human agency in the elect, and so one finds repeated reference to the task of choosing what God loves and rejecting what God hates (e.g., 1QH[a] 6:21–22; 1QS 1:4; 4:24–25; CD 2:15). Although there is no parallel in Stoic thought to the strong anthropological binarism and dualism characteristic of Qumran literature that play such an important role in generating a self-reflexive subjectivity, scholars often note that Stoicism's strong psychological monism is qualified in middle and late Stoicism, facilitating a turn toward self-examination as part of self-discipline, a practice of "I-Me" self-awareness.[6] To be sure, practices such as Seneca's were more private and individualistic than those at Qumran, which were embedded in a context of communal examination and evaluation. But the development of first-person prayer practices in the Hodayot that modeled the self's confrontation with its sinful nature marks the importance of the speaking voice also at Qumran.

This very brief sketch of common elements between Qumran and Stoic concerns for the self is not meant to suggest a model of "influence," as was often the case in earlier studies of Greek philosophy and Second Temple wisdom. In vibrant multicultural societies, such as the Hellenistic-Roman eastern Mediterranean, traditional and newly encountered intellectual concerns, concepts, and models frequently hybridized and were creatively combined in ways that render simple notions of influence utterly inadequate. For the historical scholar with an interest in moral hermeneutics, what may be most profitable is to construct the kind of dialogue that Mikhail Bakhtin saw in Dostoevsky's work. Dostoevsky, he says, "brought together ideas and worldviews, which in real life were absolutely estranged and deaf to one another, and forced them to quarrel."[7] So, too, it is possible to see that it might be productive not simply to bring together Paul and the Stoics but to include the Qumran Maskilim in the gathering.

These suggestions for future work are only some of the many ways in which issues of self and agency in Second Temple Judaism might be explored. As I indicated at the end of chapter 1, the interest in other minds in narrative, the aesthetic challenge of representing complex mental states in dramatic poetry, and the development of sophisticated spiritual practices of retrospective introspection are other directions yet to be explored in detail. Moreover, what is one to make of the widespread use of forms of first-person-singular testimony that one finds in such divergent genres as apocalyptic accounts of heavenly journeys, deathbed moral testaments, autobiographical reports, pietistic psalms, and wisdom instructions? But why, for all the attention given to new forms of representing the self, is so little attention given to the construction of individualized personae, as one finds in contemporary Greco-Roman culture? Much remains to be explored. This study can be only one modest contribution to the efforts of many to reinvigorate the study of the self in ancient Israel and early Judaism. But to put together a few more pieces of the jigsaw puzzle is not without its own satisfaction.

Abbreviations

AARSR	American Academy of Religion Studies in Religion Series
AB	Anchor Bible
ABS	Archaeology and Biblical Studies
AESP	*Advances in Experimental Social Psychology*
AJEC	Ancient Judaism and Early Christianity
ANEM	Ancient Near East Monographs/Monografías sobre el Antiguo Cercano Oriente
AP	*American Psychologist*
ARA	*Annual Review of Anthropology*
ARP	*Annual Review of Psychology*
AT	*Anthropological Theory*
AYBRL	Anchor Yale Bible Reference Library
BA	*Biblical Archaeologist*
BAAAS	*Bulletin of the American Academy of Arts and Sciences*
BASOR	*Bulletin of the American Schools of Oriental Research*
BETL	Bibliotheca Ephemeridum Theologicarum Lovaniensium
BibInt	Biblical Interpretation Series
BJS	Brown Judaic Studies
BN	*Biblische Notizen*
BTS	Biblical Tools and Studies
BWANT	Beiträge zur Wissenschaft vom Alten und Neuen Testament
BZAW	Beihefte zur Zeitschrift für die alttestamentliche Wissenschaft

BZNW	Beihefte zur Zeitschrift für die neutestamentliche Wissenschaft
CBET	Contributions to Biblical Exegesis and Theology
CBQ	*Catholic Biblical Quarterly*
CBQMS	Catholic Biblical Quarterly Monograph Series
CC	Continental Commentary
CDPS	*Current Directions in Psychological Science*
COS 2	Hallo, William W., ed. *Monumental Inscriptions from the Biblical World*. Vol. II of *The Context of Scripture*. Leiden: Brill, 2000.
CQS	Companion to the Qumran Scrolls
CRPGRW	Culture, Religion, and Politics in the Greco-Roman World
DSD	*Dead Sea Discoveries*
DSSE	Dead Sea Scrolls Editions
DSSR	*The Dead Sea Scrolls Reader*. Edited by Donald W. Parry and Emanuel Tov. 6 vols. Leiden: Brill, 2004–2005.
EJL	Early Judaism and Its Literature
ExAud	*Ex Auditu*
FAT	Forschungen zum Alten Testament
FAT 2	Forschungen zum Alten Testament 2. Reihe
FP	*Frontiers in Psychology*
FRLANT	Forschungen zur Religion und Literatur des Alten und Neuen Testaments
HALOT	*The Hebrew and Aramaic Lexicon of the Old Testament*. Ludwig Koehler, Walter Baumgartner, and Johann J. Stamm. Translated and edited under the supervision of Mervyn E. J. Richardson. 4 vols. Leiden: Brill, 1994–1999.
HBS	Herders biblische Studien
HeBAI	*Hebrew Bible and Ancient Israel*
HeyJ	*Heythrop Journal*
HSM	Harvard Semitic Monographs
IEJ	*Israel Exploration Journal*
JAJ	*Journal of Ancient Judaism*

JAJSup	Journal of Ancient Judaism Supplements
JAOS	*Journal of the American Oriental Society*
JAR	*Journal of Anthropological Research*
JBL	*Journal of Biblical Literature*
JCH	*Journal of Cognitive Historiography*
JJS	*Journal of Jewish Studies*
JNES	*Journal of Near Eastern Studies*
JQR	*Jewish Quarterly Review*
JSJSup	Supplements to Journal for the Study of Judaism
JSOTSup	Journal for the Study of the Old Testament Supplement Series
JSPSup	Journal for the Study of the Pseudepigrapha Supplement Series
JTS	*Journal of Theological Studies*
LHBOTS	The Library of Hebrew Bible/Old Testament Studies
LNTS	The Library of New Testament Studies
MSDSS	*Meghillot: Studies in the Dead Sea Scrolls*
NEBTh	Neue Echter Bibel: Themen
OBO	Orbis Biblicus et Orientalis
ORA	Orientalische Religionen in der Antike
OTL	Old Testament Library
PPS	*Perspectives on Psychological Science*
PR	*Psychological Review*
PT	*Poetics Today*
QD	Quaestiones Disputatae
QRB	*Quarterly Review of Biology*
RB	*Revue biblique*
RC	*Religion Compass*
RevQ	*Revue de Qumran*
SNT	Studien zum Neuen Testament
SSA	Schriften der Sektion für Altertumswissenschaft
STDJ	Studies on the Texts of the Desert of Judah
SUNT	Studien zur Umwelt des Neuen Testaments

TBN	Themes in Biblical Narrative
TCS	*Trends in Cognitive Science*
TDOT	*Theological Dictionary of the Old Testament*. Edited by Johannes G. Botterweck, Helmer Ringgren, Heinz-Josef Fabry, and Holger Gzella. Translated by John T. Willis, David E. Green, and Douglas W. Stott. 16 vols. Grand Rapids, MI: Eerdmans, 1974–2018.
TEG	Traditio Exegetica Graeca
THAT	*Theologisches Handwörterbuch zum Alten Testament*. Edited by Ernst Jenni, with assistance from Claus Westermann. 2 vols. Munich: Chr. Kaiser Verlag; Zürich: Theologischer Verlag, 1971–1976.
ThWQ	Fabry, Heinz-Josef, and Ulrich Dahmen, eds. *Theologisches Wörterbuch zu den Qumrantexten*. 3 vols. Stuttgart: Kohlhammer, 2011–2016.
TSAJ	Texte und Studien zum antiken Judentum
VT	*Vetus Testamentum*
VTSup	Supplements to Vetus Testamentum
VWGT	Veröffentlichungen der Wissenschaftlichen Gesellschaft für Theologie
WLAW	Wisdom Literature from the Ancient World
WMANT	Wissenschaftliche Monographien zum Alten und Neuen Testament
WUNT	Wissenschaftliche Untersuchungen zum Neuen Testament
ZAH	*Zeitschrift für Althebräistik*
ZABR	*Zeitschrift für Altorientalische und Biblische Rechtsgeschichte*
ZAW	*Zeitschrift für die alttestamentliche Wissenschaft*

Discoveries in the Judaean Desert Volumes

DJD 7	Baillet, Maurice. *Qumrân Grotte 4.III (4Q482–4Q520)*. DJD 7. Oxford: Clarendon, 1982.
DJD 29	Chazon, Esther G., et al. *Qumran Cave 4.XX: Poetical and Liturgical Texts, Part 2*. DJD 29. Oxford: Clarendon, 1999.

DJD 40 Stegemann, Hartmut, with Eileen Schuller. *1QHodayot[a] with Incorporation of 1QHodayot[b] and 4QHodayot[a–f]: Qumran Cave 1, III.* With translation of texts by Carol Newsom. DJD 40. Oxford: Clarendon, 2009.

Notes

Chapter 1. The Self in Israelite Culture

1. Antonio Damasio, *Self Comes to Mind: Constructing the Conscious Brain* (New York: Vintage, 2010) is an excellent guide to understanding the neurophysiology of the origins and operations of subjectivity, consciousness, and selfhood. Damasio considers the "simple self" or "core self" to be a property of many animals. It is in many respects the sense of "*me*," which includes: "(1) the *perspective* in which the objects [of consciousness] are being mapped (the fact that my mind has a standpoint of viewing, touching, hearing, and so on, and that the standpoint is my body); (2) the feeling that the objects are being represented in a mind belonging to me and to no one else (*ownership*); (3) the feeling that I have *agency* relative to the objects and that the actions being carried out by my body are commanded by my mind; and (4) *primordial feelings*, which signify the existence of my living body independently of how objects engage it or not" (196–97, italics in original). Humans, and in all likelihood some birds and social mammals, also have an autobiographical self that is built up of layers of memory and the reworking of memory as biographical objects (27, 223, 226). With humans, the symbolic capacities of the mind, especially but not exclusively language, create an exceptionally developed autobiographical self.
2. The subfield of cultural neuroscience attempts to investigate these phenomena. For an overview see Lynda C. Lin and Eva H. Telzer, "An Introduction to Cultural Neuroscience," in *The Handbook of Culture and Biology*, ed. José M. Causadias, Eva H. Telzer, and Nancy A. Gonzales (New York: John Wiley & Sons Inc., 2018), 399–420. For the interaction of culture and the brain see Shihui Han and Yina Ma, "A Culture–Behavior–Brain Loop Model of Human Development," *TCS* 19 (2015): 666–76.
3. This concern has been at the heart of the work of David Lambert. See, in particular, *How Repentance Became Biblical: Judaism, Christianity, and the Interpretation of Scripture* (New York: Oxford University Press, 2016).

4. In addition to Damasio's work, cited above, I draw on the perceptive analysis of Christian Frevel, "Person–Identität–Selbst: Eine Problemanzeige aus alttestamentlicher Perspektive," in *Anthropologie(n) des Alten Testaments*, ed. Jürgen van Oorschot and Andreas Wagner (Leipzig: Evangelische Verlagsansalt, 2015), 65–89.
5. For attempts to uncover traces of the personality of individuals in such self-presentations from ancient Israel, see Saul Olyan, "The Search for the Elusive Self in Texts of the Hebrew Bible," in *Religion and the Self in Antiquity*, ed. David Brakke, Michael L. Satlow, and Steve Weitzman (Bloomington, IN: Indiana University Press, 2003), 40–50; Susan Niditch, *The Responsive Self: Personal Religion in Biblical Literature of the Neo-Babylonian and Persian Periods*, AYBRL (New Haven: Yale University Press, 2015), 53–71. A pioneering study in identifying traces of the distinctive individual self in conventionalized self-accounts is Janet Gyatso, *Apparitions of the Self: The Secret Autobiographies of a Tibetan Visionary* (Princeton, NJ: Princeton University Press, 1998).
6. Clifford Geertz, *Local Knowledge: Further Essays in Interpretive Anthropology* (New York: Basic Books, 1983), 58.
7. Unni Wikan, *Managing Turbulent Hearts: A Balinese Formula for Living* (Chicago: University of Chicago Press, 1990).
8. Melford E. Spiro, "Is the Western Conception of the Self 'Peculiar' within the Context of World Cultures?" *Ethos* (1993): 107–53, similarly discovered that despite the normative views of Theravada Buddhism, the Buddhist Burmese villagers that he studied were quite dismissive of the normative view. "I discovered that the Burmese villagers with whom I lived and worked do not internalize the doctrine of *Anatta*. Instead, they strongly believe in the very ego or soul that this doctrine denies. They do so on two accounts, experiential and pragmatic. . . . Having learned the hard way that one cannot validly infer actors' conception of the self, let alone their mental representations of their own self, from the normative cultural conception, it is not surprising that I was rather skeptical of Geertz's claim" (119, 120).
9. Wikan, *Managing Turbulent Hearts*, 80–93.
10. Carol A. Newsom, *The Self as Symbolic Space: Constructing Identity and Community at Qumran*, STDJ 52 (Leiden: Brill, 2004). There, for example, I make the argument that the dualistic structure of the self in the Two Spirits Teaching from the Serek ha-Yahad is a reflex, likely unconscious, of the political dualism that had been developing in early Jewish thought since the time of Second Isaiah. "Concern about political domination can be displaced onto anthropology, reshaping the structure of the human self according to the dynamics of the repressed struggle. . . . This displacement accounts for the energy that can be invested specifically in knowledge of the nature of the self. On that level the contradiction [in history] can be grasped and overcome not only through symbolic speech but even in the practices of everyday life" (89).

11. The most comprehensive anthropology of ancient Israel, including the anthropology of the self, is the magisterial work by Bernd Janowski, *Anthropologie des Alten Testaments: Grundfragen, Kontexts, Themenfelder* (Tübingen: Mohr Siebeck, 2019). In general, German scholarship has led the renewed interest in ancient Israelite anthropology, as the following essay collections attest: Bernd Janowski and Kathrin Liess, eds., *Der Mensch im Alten Israel: Neue Forschungen zur alttestamentlichen Anthropologie*, HBS 59 (Freiburg im Breisgau: Herder, 2009); Andreas Wagner, ed., *Anthropologische Aufbrüche: Alttestamentliche und interdisziplinäre Zugänge zur historischen Anthropologie*, FRLANT 232 (Göttingen: Vandenhoeck & Ruprecht, 2009); Christian Frevel, ed., *Biblische Anthropologie: Neue Einsichten aus dem Alten Testament*, QD 237 (Freiburg im Breisgau: Herder, 2010); Jürgen von Oorschot and Andreas Wagner, eds., *Anthropologie(n) des Alten Testaments* (Leipzig: Evangelische Verlagsanstalt, 2015); Andreas Wagner and Jürgen van Oorschot, eds., *Individualität und Selbstreflexion in den Literaturen des Alten Testaments*, VWGT 48 (Berlin: Evangelische Verlagsanstalt, 2017).
12. Johannes Pedersen, *Israel: Its Life and Culture*, 2 vols., trans. A. Møller and A. I. Fausbell (London: Oxford University Press, 1926–49), 99–181; Georges Pidoux, *L'homme dans l'Ancien Testament* (Neuchâtel: Delachaux & Niestlé, 1953); Ludwig Köhler, *Hebrew Man: Lectures Delivered at the Invitation of the University of Tübingen, December 1–16, 1952. With an Appendix on Justice in the Gate*, trans. Peter R. Ackroyd (London: SCM, 1956).
13. Hans Walter Wolff, *Anthropologie des Alten Testaments* (München: C. Kaiser, 1973); published in English as *Anthropology of the Old Testament*, trans. Margaret Kohl (Philadelphia: Fortress, 1974). Analysis of the body was only the first part of Wolff's anthropology. The second part considered concepts of time, which he treated under the heading of "biographical anthropology," and the third part examined social relations and categories under the heading of "sociological anthropology."
14. Wolff, *Anthropology*, 7. As Katrin Müller observes, claims that such a somatic anthropology was somehow distinctive of Hebrew or Semitic thought are inaccurate (Katrin Müller, "Die synthetische Körperauffassung—keine Besonderheit des Hebräischen Denkens" in *Individualität und Selbstreflexion*, 67–77). As cognitive linguistics has shown, thinking by means of the body is fundamental to human cognition per se, though the patterns and usage of the body in cognition differ in each culture. Homeric era Greek thought was also deeply somatic, and the analysis of the use of the body in Homeric literature provides an informative parallel for the study of ancient Israelite usage. The influential work of Bruno Snell, *The Discovery of the Mind: The Greek Origins of European Thought*, trans. T. G. Rosenmeyer (Oxford: Blackwell, 1953), unfortunately drew some inappropriate conclusions, suggesting that, because there was no single term for "body," the Homeric Greeks lacked the conception of the body as a unity.

That view was robustly dismantled by Bernard Williams in *Ethics and the Limits of Philosophy* (Cambridge, MA: Harvard University Press, 1985). The most methodologically sophisticated analysis of the body and its role in Homeric anthropology of the self and cognition is Michael J. Clarke, *Flesh and Spirit in the Songs of Homer: A Study of Words and Myths* (Oxford: Clarendon, 1999).

15. Wolff, *Anthropology*, 7.
16. Wolff, *Anthropology*, 17.
17. Bernd Janowski, in Hans Walter Wolff, *Anthropologie des Alten Testaments; Mit zwei Anhängen neu herausgegeben von Bernd Janowski* (Gütersloh: Gütersloher Verlagshaus, 2010), 386.
18. Andreas Wagner, "Wider die Reduktion des Lebendigen: Über das Verhältnis der sog. anthropologischen Grundbegriffe und die Unmöglichkeit, mit ihnen die alttestamentliche Menschenvorstellung zu erfassen," in Wagner, ed., *Anthropologische Ausbrüche*, 183–99.
19. Though it can be argued that the ancient Israelites, like the Homeric Greeks, lacked a specialized term for the body as a whole, it is certainly not because they lacked the notion of the body as an entity. When they needed such a term, they used the term *gĕwiyyah* (specifically, "trunk") to refer either to living (Gen 47:18; Neh 9:37) or dead (1 Sam 31:10–12; Ps 110:6) bodies. Similarly, various terms might be used for the more abstract concept of "person." The terms *pānîm* and *nepeš*, in particular, are attested with this significance.
20. See Janowski, *Anthropologie*, 138–59, for a systematic overview of the organs of the body and their significance in Israelite thought. One can get a good sense of both the richness and the differentiation in the use of the parts of the body to represent the human experience in the popular and somewhat idiosyncratic book by Thomas Staubli and Sylvia Schroer, *Body Symbolism in the Bible*, trans. Linda M. Maloney (Collegeville, MN: Liturgical, 2001; originally published as *Die Körpersymbolik der Bibel* [Darmstadt: Wissenschaftliche Buchgesellschaft, 1998]). Particularly instructive are the rich iconographic representations of the body, both as disarticulated and stylized symbols and as parts of more realistically depicted scenes. For the significance of *nepeš* see Katrin Müller, "*Lobe den Herrn, meine 'Seele'": Eine kognitiv-linguistische Studie zur næfæš des Menschen im Alten Testament*, BWANT 215 (Stuttgart: Kohlhammer, 2018). I discuss aspects of *nepeš* and *rûaḥ* in the following chapter.
21. Bernd Janowski, "Das Herz—ein Beziehungsorgan: Zum Personverständnis des Alten Testaments," in *Das hörende Herz* (Göttingen: Vandenhoeck & Ruprecht, 2018), 31–75.
22. Thomas Krüger, "Das 'Herz' in der alttestamentlichen Anthropologie," in Andreas Wagner, ed., *Anthropologische Aufbrüche*, 106. Krüger positions his arguments specifically in relation to the claims of Christian Frevel and Oda Wischmeyer, *Menschsein*, NEBTh 11 (Würzburg: Echter, 2003), 33, 37; and Silvia Schroer and Thomas Staubli, *Die Körpersymbolik*, 58.

23. William James, *The Principles of Psychology* (New York: H. Holt, 1890); *Psychology* (New York: H. Holt, 1892).
24. James, *Psychology*, 175, italics in original.
25. The clearest account of the use of the "I-Me" distinction in contemporary cognitive studies is the essay by Mateusz Woźniak, "'I' and 'Me': The Self in the Context of Consciousness, *FP* 9 (2018): 1–14.
26. Woźniak ("'I' and 'Me,'" 5) argues that the "I" is, properly speaking, a metaphysical construct and that what is typically called the "I" might better be referred to as the "higher-level phenomenal Me" and the "Me" as the "lower-level phenomenal me."
27. Mark Johnson and George Lakoff, *Philosophy in the Flesh: The Embodied Mind and Its Challenge to Western Thought* (New York: Basic Books, 1999). See especially chapter 13, "The Self" (267–89). Johnson and Lakoff leave open the question "how universal are experiences of inner life and the metaphors used to reason about them," noting that little research has been conducted concerning the inner life of other cultures (284). Their hypothesis is that they are common, if not universal.
28. Janowski ("Die hörende Herz," 67–70) specifically contests Krüger's analysis of Prov 15:28, 16:23, and 17:22. Although Krüger discusses a broader variety of texts, many would be subject to the same objections that Janowski brings against these three examples. I am focusing in this discussion on the aspect of Krüger's analysis concerning the distinction between "center and periphery" in the self. Other aspects of his argument, including the heart's role in defining "inner" experience and the problematic issues arising from the corruption of the heart, are quite compelling.
29. The works of E. B. Tylor, James Frazer, Andrew Lang, and Lucien Lévy-Bruhl in various ways asserted the existence of a primitive mentality that contrasted with modern cognition.
30. H. Wheeler Robinson, *Corporate Personality in Ancient Israel* (Philadelphia: Fortress, 1964).
31. John W. Rogerson, "The Hebrew Conception of Corporate Personality: A Re-Examination," *JTS* 21 (1970): 1–16.
32. Frevel, "Person–Identität–Selbst," 75–78. Jan Dietrich, *Kollektive Schuld und Haftung*, ORA 4 (Tübingen: Mohr Siebeck, 2010), 21–29, provides a brief history of the discussion of collective and individual identity in biblical studies.
33. See, for example, Franz Boas, *The Mind of Primitive Man* (New York: Macmillan, 1911).
34. Important studies from the 1980s include Richard A. Shweder and Edmund J. Bourne, "Does the Concept of the Person Vary Cross-Culturally?" in *Culture Theory*, ed. Richard A. Shweder and Robert A. LeVine (Cambridge: Cambridge University Press, 1984), 158–99; Louis Dumont, "A Modified View of Our Origins: The Christian Beginnings of Modern Individualism," in *The*

Category of the Person, ed. Michael Carrithers, Steven Collins, and Steven Lukes (Cambridge: Cambridge University Press, 1985), 93–122; John Kirkpatrick and Geoffrey M. White, "Exploring Ethnopsychologies," in *Person, Self, and Experience: Exploring Pacific Ethnopsychologies* (Berkeley: University of California Press, 1985), 3–32; Edward E. Samson, "The Debate on Individualism: Indigenous Psychologies of the Self and Their Role in Personal and Societal Functioning," *AP* 43 (1988): 15–22.

35. Clifford Geertz, "From the Native's Point of View," *BAAAS* 28 (1974): 31.
36. Geertz, "From the Native's Point of View," 35.
37. Hazel Rose Markus and Shinobu Kitayama, "Culture and the Self: Implications for Cognition, Emotion, and Motivation," *PR* 98 (1991): 225.
38. Markus and Kitayama, "Culture and the Self," 224.
39. Robert A. Di Vito, "Old Testament Anthropology and the Construction of Personal Identity," *CBQ* 61 (1999): 217–38.
40. Charles Taylor, *Sources of the Self* (Cambridge, MA: Harvard University Press, 1989).
41. Di Vito, "Old Testament Anthropology," 221.
42. The most thorough critique is that by Melford E. Spiro, "The Western Conception of the Self," but Charles Lindholm, "Does the Sociocentric Self Exist? Reflections on Markus and Kitayama's 'Culture and the Self'," *JAR* 53 (1997): 405–22, is particularly incisive in pointing out logical and methodological problems with the Markus and Kitayama study. In addition, he presents evidence from medieval Japan that demonstrates how inadequate the label "interdependent" is for a description of the Japanese experience of the self.
43. Lindholm, "Does the Sociocentric Self Exist?" 405.
44. Dorothy Holland, William Lachicotte, Jr., Debra Skinner, and Carole Cain, *Identity and Agency in Cultural Worlds* (Cambridge, MA: Harvard University Press, 1998), 28.
45. Frevel, "Person–Identität–Selbst," 78.
46. Di Vito, "Old Testament Anthropology," 232.
47. Frevel, "Person–Identität–Selbst," 80–81. A similar point is made in Holland, et al., *Identity and Agency*, 33.
48. See Sean Burt, *The Courtier and the Governor: Transformations of Genre in the Nehemiah Memoir*, JAJSup 17 (Göttingen: Vandenhoeck & Ruprecht, 2014).
49. Niditch, *The Responsive Self*, 53–71.
50. Di Vito, "Old Testament Anthropology," 225.
51. Di Vito, "Old Testament Anthropology," 225.
52. To be sure, ancient Israelite texts do not exhibit the range of explicit practices for the cultivation of the inner self that one finds in some other cultures, both from antiquity and from subsequent periods.
53. See, for example, the analysis of agency in laments in Amy C. Cottrill, *Language, Power, and Identity in the Lament Psalms of the Individual*, LHBOTS 493 (New York: T&T Clark, 2008).

54. See the essays collected in Joëlle Proust and Martin Fortier, eds., *Metacognitive Diversity: An Interdisciplinary Approach* (New York: Oxford University Press, 2018). The essays by Rolf Reber and Ara Norenzayan, "Shared Fluency Theory of Social Cohesiveness: How the Metacognitive Feeling of Processing Fluency Contributes to Group Processes," 47–67, and Tanya M. Luhrmann, "Prayer as Metacognitive Activity," 297–318, are particularly relevant to the role of metacognition in religious dimensions of culture.
55. The following paragraphs are a summary of a longer and more technical discussion of the psalm in Carol A. Newsom, "'If I had said. . . .' (Ps 73:15): Retrospective Introspection in Didactic Psalmody of the Second Temple Period," in *Petitioners, Penitents, and Poets: On Prayer and Praying in Second Temple Judaism*, ed. Timothy J. Sandoval and Ariel Feldman, BZAW 524 (Berlin: De Gruyter, 2020), 69–82.
56. Self-talk is one of the important forms of cognitive control of emotions. See K. O. Ochsner and J. J. Gross, "Cognitive Emotion Regulation," *CDPS* 17 (2008): 153–58; T. F. Heatherton, "Neuroscience of Self and Self-Regulation," *ARP* 62 (2011): 363–90. Little if any research appears to have been done on cross-cultural differences in practices of self-talk, however.
57. Clinton McCann, "Psalm 73: An Interpretation Emphasizing Rhetorical and Canonical Criticism" (PhD diss., Duke University, 1985), 212, notes that numerous scholars have attempted to explain what happens with suggestions that "range from the possible to the ridiculous."
58. Divine agency in the mind of individuals in narrative is examined in chap. 2.
59. As Reber and Norenzayan, "Shared Fluency Theory," 48–49, describe it, "shared exposure promotes shared beliefs; shared beliefs increase interpersonal fluency; behavioral coordination independently increases interpersonal fluency; interpersonal fluency in turn increases mutual liking; mutual liking feeds back to behavioral coordination; shared exposure increases shared object fluency; shared object fluency, in turn, increases liking of the objects that interacting individuals or members of a group are exposed to; mutual liking and shared liking (together constituting social cohesiveness) increase the likelihood that interacting individuals or group members will expose themselves again to the same object."
60. See, for example, the analyses of Lam 3:18–21 and Job 16:13 in Christian Frevel, "'Quellen des Selbst'? Charles Taylor's Einfluss auf die alttestamentliche Anthropologie," in *Im Dienste der Gerechigkeit und Einheit: Festschrift für Heinrich J. F. Reinhardt zur Vollendung seines 75. Lebensjahres*, ed. Rüdiger Althaus, Judith Hahn, and Matthias Pulte (Essen: Ludgerus Verlag, 2017), 447–63. See also Bernd Janowski, "Das erschöpfte Selbst: Zu Semantik der Depression in den Psalmen und in Ijobbuch," in *Das hörende Herz*, 77–123. More generally, Janowski, *Anthropologie des Alten Testaments*, 168–77.
61. Martin Buber, *The Prophetic Faith*, trans. Carlyle Witton-Davies (New York: Macmillan, 1949), 192.

62. I have developed these points more fully elsewhere. See esp. Carol A. Newsom, *The Book of Job: A Contest of Moral Imaginations* (Oxford: Oxford University Press, 2003), 164–68.
63. In literary criticism this phenomenon is often referred to as "theory of mind" or "mindreading." Although theory of mind has a more technical meaning in psychology, in literature it is used more broadly to describe the imaginative construction of the states of mind of others, including feelings, thoughts, and intentions. For a good introduction see Paula Leverage, Howard Mancing, Richard Schweickert, and Jennifer Marston William, eds., *Theory of Mind and Literature* (Purdue, IN: Purdue University Press, 2011). Narrative representation of such mental states remains limited, at least in western literature, until the rise of the novel. It reaches its peak in modernist novels such as those by Henry James and Virginia Wolff. James's ability to represent mental processes is so highly regarded that it is sometimes held up as a model in neuroscientific literature. See, for example, Merlin Donald, *A Mind So Rare: The Evolution of Human Consciousness* (New York: W. W. Norton & Co., 2001), 78–83. Some experimental studies even attempt to show how literary fiction enhances readers' skills in practical mindreading (David Comer Kidd and Emanuele Castano, "Reading Literary Fiction Improves Theory of Mind," *Science* 342 [2013]: 377–80). Although the narrative literature of Second Temple Judaism does not reach the psychological sophistication of the modern novel, the centrality of theory of mind to the narrative construction of many of the stories suggests a distinct change in cultural attention.
64. I will examine the case of Abimelech of Gerar in Genesis 20 in the following chapter.

Chapter 2. Agency in Biblical Narrative

1. Damasio, *Self Comes to Mind*, 197, 217.
2. Alfred Bandura, "Toward a Psychology of Human Agency," *PPS* 1 (2006): 164.
3. The classic study is Lee Ross and Richard E. Nisbett, *The Person and the Situation: Perspectives of Social Psychology* (New York: McGraw-Hill, 1991). They demonstrate persuasively the extent to which both cognitive and moral decisions are influenced by situational factors, and especially the influence of the opinions of the reference group.
4. Andrew Lock, "Universals in Human Conception," and Paul Heelas, "The Model Applied: Anthropology and Indigenous Psychologies," in *Indigenous Psychologies: The Anthropology of the Self*, ed. Paul Heelas and Andrew Lock (London: Academic, 1981), 19–36, 38–63.
5. See R. G. Lienhardt, *Divinity and Experience: The Religion of the Dinka* (New York: Oxford University Press, 1961), 149.
6. Paul Heelas, "The Model Applied," 46–47.

7. William S. Sax, "Agency," in *Theorizing Rituals*, vol. 1: *Issues, Topics, Approaches, Concepts*, ed. Jens Kreinath, Jan A. M. Snoek, and Michael Stausberg (Leiden: Brill, 2006), 477–79.
8. Laura M. Ahearn, "Language and Agency," *ARA* 30 (2001): 112.
9. David Haig, "Intrapersonal Conflict," in *Conflict*, ed. Martin Jones and A. C. Fabian (Cambridge: Cambridge University Press, 2006), 12–16.
10. By that term I mean what passes for "common sense" among average, secular, modern persons.
11. The experience alluded to in Genesis has, perhaps, a modern analogy in the American evangelicals studied by T. R. Luhrmann in *When God Talks Back: Understanding the American Evangelical Relationship with God* (New York: Random House, 2012). These modern subjects for the most part grew up with a psychology in which hearing the voice of God was not a simple or intuitive concept. They had to learn to discern the voice of God, "God's interjected thoughts," as one informant puts it, amid the stream of their own thoughts (46). As they became proficient in this form of attention, however, they did attribute certain perceptions and decisions as emanating from a source beyond themselves. Thus I would argue that the representation of agency in the fashion that one finds in Gen 31:1–3 points to a construction of the self in which certain aspects or functions of the self are experienced as externalized.
12. Josh 11:20 uses the same trope in a situation of collective agency by the cities of Canaan.
13. See "The Power of the Situation," chap. 2 in Ross and Nisbett, *The Person and the Situation*.
14. Heidi M. Ravven, *The Self Beyond Itself: An Alternative History of Ethics, the New Brain Sciences, and the Myth of Free Will* (New York: New Press, 2013), 244–45, 272. Claims that persons do not have free will at all, however, tend to be provocative overstatements and conflate various levels of decisionmaking, conscious and unconscious. For a balanced discussion see the work of Eddy Nahmias, "Your Brain as the Source of Free Will Worth Wanting: Understanding Free Will in the Age of Neuroscience," in *Neuroexistentialism: Meaning, Morals, and Purpose in the Age of Neuroscience*, ed. Gregg D. Caruso and Owen J. Flanagan (New York: Oxford University Press, 2018), 251–68. Nahmias humorously calls the radical deniers of free will "willusionists."
15. See, e.g., Dirk Geeraerts, "Deliteralization and the Birth of 'Emotion,'" in *Approaches to Language, Culture, and Cognition*, 50–67, and Benjamin Blount, "Situating Cultural Models in History and Cognition," same, 271–98.
16. Blount, "Situating Cultural Models," 274. For an overview see David B. Kronenfeld et al., eds., *A Companion to Cognitive Anthropology* (Chichester: Blackwell, 2011).
17. Dorothy Holland and Naomi Quinn, "Culture and Cognition," in *Cultural Models in Language and Thought*, ed. Dorothy Holland and Naomi Quinn (Cambridge: Cambridge University Press, 1987), 4.

18. Naomi Quinn, "How to Reconstruct Schemas People Share, from What They Say," in *Finding Culture in Talk: A Collection of Methods*, ed. Naomi Quinn (New York: Palgrave Macmillan, 2005), 45.
19. Claudia Strauss, "Analyzing Discourse for Cultural Complexity," in *Finding Culture in Talk*, 35–82.
20. The literature on *rûaḥ* in biblical studies is vast. For a critical overview see Rainer Albertz and Claus Westermann, "*rûaḥ*," *THAT* 2: 726–53; Sven Tengström and Heinz-Josef Fabry, "*rûaḥ*," *TDOT* 13: 365–402; John R. Levison, *Filled with the Spirit* (Grand Rapids, MI: Eerdmans, 2009); Eibert J. C. Tigchelaar, "Historical Origins of the Early Christian Concept of the Holy Spirit: Perspectives from the Dead Sea Scrolls," in *The Holy Spirit, Inspiration, and the Cultures of Antiquity*, ed. Jörg Frey, John R. Levison, and Andrew Bowden, Ecstasis 5 (Berlin: de Gruyter, 2014), 167–240.
21. John Levison, *Filled with the Spirit*, 12.
22. Geeraerts, "Deliteralization," 64–66.
23. See Ingrid E. Lilly, "*Rûaḥ* Embodied: Job's Internal Disease from the Perspective of Mesopotamian Medicine," in *Borders: Terminologies, Ideologies, and Performances*, ed. Annette Weissenrieder, WUNT 366 (Tübingen: Mohr Siebeck, 2016), 323–36.
24. Tengström, "*rûaḥ*," 377; Ed Noort, "Taken from the Soil, Gifted with the Breath of Life: The Anthropology of Genesis 2:7 in Context," in *Dust of the Ground and Breath of Life (Gen 2:7): The Problem of a Dualistic Anthropology in Early Judaism and Christianity*, ed. Jacques T.A.G.M. van Ruiten and George H. van Kooten, TBN 20 (Leiden: Brill, 2016), 3–4. Elihu, who seems to allude to Gen 2–3, uses *rûaḥ* and *nĕšāmāh* in parallel lines in Job 32:8, 33:4, and 34:14–15.
25. Choon Leong Seow, *Ecclesiastes: A New Translation and Commentary*, AB 18C (New York: Doubleday, 1997), 337, notes that "bones" is used in the sense of "body" of the fetus.
26. Similarly, Walther Eichrodt, *Ezekiel: A Commentary*, OTL (Philadelphia: Westminster, 1970), 61.
27. So Klaus Koch, "Der Güter Gefährlichstes, die Sprache, dem Menschen gegeben . . . ; Überlegungen zu Gen 2, 7," *BN* 48 (1988): 50–60; Andreas Schuele, "The Notion of Life: *npš* and *rwḥ* in the Anthropological Discourse of the Primeval History," *HeBAI* 1 (2012): 484.
28. Noort, "Taken from the Soil," 8–9, comes to similar conclusions, following a slightly different line of reasoning.
29. The compound expression in Gen 7:22 (*nišmat-rûaḥ ḥayyim*) is usually attributed to a redactor.
30. The English word "animal" captures this sense as well, since it derives from the Latin *animalis*, "having breath."
31. Ezek 36:26–27 does associate the implantation of God's *rûaḥ* into the house of Israel with the capacity for obedience to divine commandments, which it

previously lacked. Ezekiel's claim marks an innovation in thinking about the relationship between God's *rûaḥ* and human existence that has profound implications for Second Temple religious thought, as I explore in the following chapter.

32. Tengström, "*rûaḥ*," 375.
33. Staubli and Schroer, *Body Symbolism*, 58.
34. See the recent study by Katrin Müller, *Lobe den Herrn, meine "Seele."* In her careful study she demonstrates how many of the meanings of the word *nepeš* are developed through the cognitive-metonymic relationships of body part for function and body part for person.
35. Aubrey Johnson, *The Vitality of the Individual in the Thought of Ancient Israel* (Cardiff: University of Wales Press, 1949), 5–26; Christian Frevel ("Struggling with the Vitality of Corpses: Understanding the Rationale of the Ritual in Numbers 19," in *Les vivants et leurs morts*, ed. Jean-Marie Durand, Thomas Römer, and Jürg Hutzli, OBO 257 [Fribourg: Academic Press, 2012], 225) glosses *nepeš* as "vitality, presence, personality."
36. Seth L. Sanders, "The Appetites of the Dead: West Semitic Linguistic and Ritual Aspects of the Katumuwa Stele," *BASOR* 369 (2013): 44.
37. Joachim Schaper, "Elements of a History of the Soul in North-West Semitic Texts: *npš/nbš* in the Hebrew Bible and the Katumuwa Inscription," *VT* 70 (2020): 165–68.
38. Frevel, "Vitality of Corpses," 224, argues that after death, "the *nepeš* of the deceased then abides in the netherworld (*šĕʾôl*) during the process of decomposition (Pss 16, 10; 30, 4; 49, 26, etc.) but is, at the same time, not completely absent from the world of the living because of the anamnetic remembrance of his former social environment." David Schloen and Amir S. Fink ("New Excavations at Zincirli Höyük in Turkey [Ancient *Samʾal*] and the Discovery of an Inscribed Mortuary Stele," *BASOR* 365 [2009]: 11) refer to "the traditional West Semitic conception that one's soul resides in one's bones after death." At least one psalm, however, appears to resist the notion of the *nepeš*'s residence in Sheol (Ps 16:10–11) and suggests an alternative fate for the pious in the presence of God. See Schaper, "History of the Soul," 169–70. Much about that psalm is contested, however, including its date.
39. Richard C. Steiner, *Disembodied Souls: The Nefesh in Israel and Kindred Spirits in the Ancient Near East, with an Appendix on the Katumuwa Inscription*, ANEM 11 (Atlanta: SBL, 2015), 11. Schaper, "History of the Soul," 160–65.
40. Frevel, "Vitality of Corpses," 225.
41. Yitzhaq Feder, "Contagion and Cognition: Bodily Experience and the Conceptualization of Pollution," *JNES* 72 (2013): 161. In a subsequent essay Feder undertakes a broader analysis of the issues of corpse pollution, "Death, Afterlife and Corpse Pollution: The Meaning of the Expression *ṭameʾ la-nepeš*," *VT* 69 (2019): 408–34.

42. E.g., Horst Seebass, "*nepeš*," TDOT, 511–12, "a person does not *have* a vital self but *is* a vital self."
43. James Barr, *The Garden of Eden and the Hope of Immortality* (Minneapolis: Fortress, 1993), 36–41. Richard Steiner, *Disembodied Souls*, 125–26, attempts to construct a logically consistent synthesized model. The notion of divine spirit as essential in constituting human life but not ordinarily experienced as an alien presence has an intriguing parallel in recent scientific recognition of the vast biome that lives upon and within humans and indeed is necessary to constitute a person as a functioning entity. Though the divine spirit is hardly the same as gut bacteria, both are models of nonautonomous modes of human being in which the presence of the "other" is ordinarily not experienced as an alien presence but simply as an essential part of what it means to be human. But there are conditions in which this other can make its presence felt.
44. Strauss, "Analyzing Discourse," 223.
45. The syntax may mark the evil spirit as instrumental and not some aspect of Yhwh himself (but see 19:9, *rûaḥ yhwh rāʿāh*).
46. Notably, all of these texts refer to the effect of divine spirit on individual persons. Beginning in the exilic or early postexilic period, however, the transformation of the entire people of Israel by divine spirit is also figured in ways that use a model of external contact. But in these instances the divine spirit is metaphorically represented as a liquid that is poured out, either like rain (see Isa 32:15; 44:3–4) or splashed out, as one pours water from a container onto some object (see Ezek 39:29; Joel 3:1, 2; Zech 10:12). In only one late instance is the image used to refer to the spiritual transformation of the individual prophetic seer (1 En 91:1). I discuss this metaphor for spirit more fully in "In Search of Cultural Models for Divine Spirit and Human Bodies," *VT* 70 (2020): 118–22.
47. Unfortunately, there is no indication of how the spirit enters the body of a human. It may be assumed to enter via the breath. Or perhaps the ancient Israelites simply did not theorize how this entry takes place.
48. For the semantics of *pittāh* (pi.) see D.J.A. Clines and D. M. Gunn, "'You Tried to Persuade Me' and 'Violence! Outrage!' in Jeremiah XX 7–8," *VT* 23 (1978): 23.
49. James C. VanderKam, *Jubilees: A Commentary in Two Volumes*, Hermeneia (Minneapolis: Fortress, 2018), 1: 441.
50. Tengström, "*rûaḥ*," 377.
51. Levison, *Filled with the Spirit*, 11–12, argues strongly that they are one and the same, but he makes an essentialist argument. The syntactical evidence, discussed above, suggests that ancient Israelites did tend to differentiate, though not without some sense of how the phenomena overlap.
52. It is also possible that the use of *ʿal* is chosen to associate the expected king with the charismata of David (1 Sam 16:13). The qualities named, however, are distinctly sapiential. For *gĕbûrāh* as "acuity" see the analysis of P. Wernberg-

Moller, *The Manual of Discipline*, STDJ 1 (Leiden: Brill, 1957), 74, who cites Job 12:13 and Prov 8:14 as contexts in which *gěbûrāh* has connotations of wisdom.

53. This passage, with its possible reference to music (*zěmirôt*, v. 1), may be the basis for "David's Compositions" in 11QPs[a] XXVII, which says that "Yhwh gave him a brilliant and discerning spirit, so that he wrote [enumeration of compositions]. All these he composed through prophecy given him by the Most High" (ll. 2, 11).

Chapter 3. Moral Agency in Israelite Perspective

1. Genesis 2–3 is the text that most explicitly reflects on the origins and limits of agency, including moral agency. That text will be considered in the following chapter.
2. Michael V. Fox, "Words for Folly," *ZAH* 10 (1977): 4–17; *Proverbs 1–9*, AB 18A (New York: Doubleday, 2000), 38–43.
3. David Lambert, "'Desire' Enacted in the Wilderness: Problems in the History of the Self and Bible Translation," in *Self, Self-Fashioning, and Individuality in Late Antiquity: New Perspectives*, ed. Maren R. Niehoff and Joshua Levinson, CRPGRW 4 (Tübingen: Mohr Siebeck, 2019), 25–49. Lambert focuses on the semantics of the verbal root *'wh* and the noun *ta'awāh*, though his findings are broadly informative.
4. One rare exception, discussed above, is Job 31:1.
5. Lambert, "'Desire' Enacted," 37–38.
6. Michael V. Fox, "The Pedagogy of Proverbs 2," *JBL* 113 (1994): 241.
7. The implicit model of the moral self as having cognitive, affective, and volitional dimensions suggests a certain resemblance to the Platonic tripartite soul with its rational (*logistikon*), appetitive (*thumodes*), and spirited (*epithumetikon*) elements. But the differences are far more significant than the similarities. The three categories apply to somewhat different things. Plato's appetitive element is focused more narrowly on the body's demands for pleasure, whereas the area of desire in the Israelite moral self is much broader in scope. What concerns Israelite thought about volition is specifically how it relates to the regulation of legitimate external authority, which is not the issue that concerns Plato.
8. See most recently the discussion by Bernd U. Schipper, "'Teach Them Diligently to Your Son!': The Book of Proverbs and Deuteronomy," in *Reading Proverbs Intertextually*, ed. Katharine Dell and Will Kynes, LHBOTS 629 (London: T&T Clark, 2019), 21–34.
9. As summarized in Michael Fox, "Who Can Learn? A Dispute in Ancient Pedagogy," in *Wisdom, You Are My Sister: Studies in Honor of Roland E. Murphy, O. Carm.*, ed. M. L. Barre, CBQMS 29 (Washington, DC: Catholic Biblical Association, 1997), 62–77. Fox notes H. Brunner, *Altägyptische Erziehung* (Wiesbaden: Harrassowitz, 1957), 112–16, as "the standard study of the issues."

10. Cited by Fox, "Who Can Learn?" 70. The positive counterpart is articulated in Papyrus Insinger 9.19: "It is the god who gives the heart, gives the son, and gives the good character" (trans. Lichtheim; cited by Fox, "Who Can Learn?" 71).
11. See, e.g., James L. Crenshaw, *Old Testament Wisdom: An Introduction*, rev. and enl. ed. (Louisville: Westminster John Knox, 1998), 67; and John Barton, *Understanding Old Testament Ethics: Approaches and Explanations* (Louisville: Westminster John Knox, 2003), 67. These views are discussed and refuted by Anne W. Stewart (*Poetic Ethics in Proverbs: Wisdom Literature and the Shaping of the Moral Self* [Cambridge: Cambridge University Press, 2016], 80–101), who argues that the culture of rebuke in Proverbs points to a model of "educated moral selfhood" in which a person's "moral equipment is innate, but exists in potential only" and requires discipline in order to mature (98).
12. Fox, "Who Can Learn?" 70, 71.
13. Stewart, *Poetic Ethics in Proverbs*, 98–99.
14. The only saying that might entertain such a notion is Prov 25:26, "A muddy spring, a ruined well, such is a righteous person who totters before a wicked one" (*maʿyān nirpāś ûmāqôr mošḥāt / ṣaddîq māṭ lipnê-rāšāʿ*). Even there, however, the "tottering" may refer to being overcome rather than giving way morally, though the imagery of a muddied spring could point to being morally dirtied. However one construes the saying, the topic is virtually ignored as a matter of concern in Proverbs.
15. Sun Myung Lyu, *Righteousness in the Book of Proverbs*, FAT 2/55 (Tübingen: Mohr Siebeck, 2012), 60.
16. Michael V. Fox, "The Epistemology of the Book of Proverbs," *JBL* 126 (2007): 675–84. Fox draws on "coherence theory."
17. Timothy J. Sandoval, *The Discourse of Wealth and Poverty in the Book of Proverbs*, BibInt 77 (Leiden: Brill, 2006); Christine Roy Yoder, "The Shaping of Erotic Desire in Proverbs 1–9," in *Saving Desire: The Seduction of Christian Theology*, ed. F. LeRon Shults and Jan-Olav Henriksen (Grand Rapids, MI: Eerdmans, 2011), 148–63; Anne Stewart, "The Model of Desire," in *Poetic Ethics in Proverbs*, 130–69.
18. New technologies of surveillance now threaten to alter this cultural pattern profoundly.
19. Carol A. Newsom, "Woman and the Discourse of Patriarchal Wisdom: A Study of Proverbs 1–9," in *Rhetoric and Hermeneutics: Approaches to Text, Tradition and Social Construction in Biblical and Second Temple Literature*, FAT 130 (Tübingen: Mohr Siebeck, 2019), 39.
20. R. D. Branson and G. J. Botterweck, "*yāsar, mûsār*," *TDOT* 6: 131.
21. As noted above, Proverbs schools the desires by associating and redirecting "natural" desires for wealth, food, sex, and other basic elements to wisdom itself. Similarly, the act-consequence relationship is engrained not, as Stewart points

out, through "a set of rigid moral axioms" but instead by presenting "a host of scenarios" (*Poetic Ethics in Proverbs*, 14). The student thus learns through repeated and varied examples how to recognize relationships and connections between phenomena and to evaluate outcomes.

22. Bernd U. Schipper, *Proverbs 1–15*, trans. Stephen Germany, Hermeneia (Minneapolis: Fortress, 2019), 128–29.
23. It is possible that this image, too, alludes to an inscribed amulet. See Schipper, *Proverbs 1–15*, 129.
24. David Carr, *Writing on the Tablet of the Heart: Origins of Scripture and Literature* (New York: Oxford University Press, 2005), 127–29, discusses the idiom in relation to memorization of written texts as part of the education-enculturation process. He notes that the image is also attested in Egyptian and Greek sources.
25. Although Proverbs represents this as agential activity on the part of the student, the book of Jeremiah recasts this image to suggest the failure of teaching and a radical remedy (31:33; cf. 17:1 for internalized guilt).
26. Fox, *Proverbs 10–31*, 678–79, following Arnold B. Ehrlich (*Randglossen zur hebräischen Bibel*, vol. 6 [Hildesheim: Georg Olms, 1913]), repoints *bĕrāʿ* as *bĕrēaʿ* in the first stich and renders: "Severe bruises scour the mind, and they smite the chambers of the belly."
27. Fox, *Proverbs 10–31*, 677.
28. Richard Clifford, *Proverbs: A Commentary*, OTL (Louisville: Westminster John Knox, 1999), 186; Fox, *Proverbs 10–31*, 677.
29. Tyler Duckworth, "Cultivating *Rûaḥ* in the Ethos of Proverbs," 1 (paper presented at the Society of Biblical Literature International Meeting, Helsinki, Finland, August 2, 2018). I wish to thank Mr. Duckworth for giving me permission to cite his unpublished work.
30. Duckworth, "Cultivating *Rûaḥ*," 3.
31. Clarke, *Flesh and Spirit in the Songs of Homer*, 73–89.
32. As Fox (*Proverbs 10–31*, 637) observes, the variant of the saying in 14:29 refers to patience (*ʾerek ʾappayim*), favoring the *ketib* (*qar rûaḥ*, "cool of spirit") rather than the *qere* (*yĕqar rûaḥ*, "precious of spirit"). He also notes the similar contrast in Egyptian wisdom between the "cool" and the "hot" person.
33. Students of cognitive metaphor have studied cross-cultural metaphors for anger extensively. Anger as hot liquid in a container is a widely attested cognitive metaphor. Its resemblance to the hot breath model in Israelite literature suggests that the Israelite model was analogous. See, in general, Zoltán Kövecses, *Metaphor and Emotion: Language, Culture, and Body in Human Feeling* (Cambridge: Cambridge University Press, 2000), especially chap. 8 ("Universality in the Conceptualization of Emotions," 139–63) and chap. 9 ("Cultural Variation in the Conceptualization of Emotions," 164–81).
34. Duckworth, "Cultivating *Rûaḥ*," 4.

35. Duckworth, "Cultivating *Rûaḥ*," 9.
36. Juha Pakkala, "The Influence of Treaties on Deuteronomy, Exclusive Monolatry, and Covenant Theology," *HeBAI* 8 (2019): 182.
37. For a translation of de Wette's dissertation see Paul B. Harvey, Jr., and Baruch Halpern, "W.M.L. de Wette's 'Dissertatio Critica . . .': Context and Translation," *ZAR* 14 (2008): 47–85.
38. A helpful review of the course of the scholarly debate can be found in the introductory essay by Cynthia Edenburg and Reinhard Müller, "Editorial Introduction: Perspectives on the Treaty Framework of Deuteronomy," *HeBAI* 8 (2019): 73–86. Also useful is the thoughtful survey of critical issues in John Collins, *The Invention of Judaism: Torah and Jewish Identity from Deuteronomy to Paul* (Berkeley: University of California Press, 2017), 21–43, 195–207.
39. The post-586 BCE perspective is most clear in Deut 4:25–31 and 28:69–30:20.
40. George E. Mendenhall, "Covenant Forms in Israelite Tradition," *BA* 17 (1954): 50–76. Mendenhall's focus of comparison was with the Hittite Treaties. Given the chronological difficulties in establishing a connection between the Hittite treaty tradition and Israelite scribes, most scholars focus instead on the Neo-Assyrian treaties, especially the Vassal Treaties of Esarhaddon. It is possible, however, that a West-Asian Aramaic treaty tradition preserved aspects of the Hittite model and transmitted knowledge of those forms to Israelite scribes. See Billie Jean Collins, *The Hittites and Their World*, ABS 7 (Atlanta: SBL, 2007), 222. Although some scholars—including Lothar Perlitt, *Bundestheologie im Alten Testament*, WMANT 36 (Neukirchen-Vluyn: Neukirchener Verlag, 1969), Ernest W. Nicholson, *God and His People: Covenant and Theology in the Old Testament* (Oxford: Clarendon, 1986), and Christoph Levin, *Die Verheissung des neuen Bundes: In ihrem theologiegeschichtlichen Zusammenhand ausgelegt* (FRLANT 137; Göttingen: Vandenhoeck & Ruprecht, 1985)—reject the impact of the treaty tradition upon covenant traditions, those views are a distinct minority.
41. Collins, *The Invention of Judaism*, 34.
42. Avishai Margalit, *On Betrayal* (Cambridge, MA: Harvard University Press, 2017), 52–55.
43. Margalit, *On Betrayal*, 149–50.
44. I draw on and adapt the categories developed by Moral Foundations Theory for the cross-cultural study of moral systems. The most accessible presentation of this theory is Jonathan Haidt, *The Righteous Mind: Why Good People Are Divided by Politics and Religion* (New York: Pantheon Books, 2012). For a more technical discussion see Jesse Graham et al., "Moral Foundations Theory: The Pragmatic Validity of Moral Pluralism," *Advances in Experimental Social Psychology* 47 (2013): 55–130. The basic moral foundations that this theory argues are common to all cultures (though they may be formulated in differing ways) are care/harm, fairness/cheating (sometimes referred to as reciprocity), loyalty/

betrayal, authority/subversion, and sanctity/degradation, though the researchers acknowledge that there are likely others. I have discussed the possibilities and limitations of Moral Foundations Theory for analyzing moral systems in ancient Israel in "'The Righteous Mind' and Judean Moral Culture: A Conversation between Biblical Studies and Moral Psychology," in *Worship, Women, and War: Essays in Honor of Susan Niditch*, ed. John J. Collins, Tracy M. Lemos, and Saul M. Olyan, BJS 357 (Providence: Brown University, 2015), 117–34; and "Moral 'Recipes' in Deuteronomy and Ezekiel: Divine Authority and Human Agency," *HeBAI* 4 (2017): 488–509.

45. C. Boehm, *Hierarchy in the Forest: The Evolution of Egalitarian Behavior* (Cambridge, MA: Harvard University Press, 1999), 64–89.
46. Franz de Waal, *Peacemaking among Primates* (Cambridge, MA: Harvard University Press, 1990), 245–47. Hierarchies have a variety of functions among different species and human groups, though social harmony is a widely attested effect.
47. For translation and critical notes, see "The Kulamuwa Inscription," trans. K. Lawson Younger, Jr., *COS* 2.30: 147–48.
48. Moshe Weinfeld, "The Covenant of Grant in the Old Testament and in the Ancient Near East," *JAOS* 90 (1970): 194; Moshe Weinfeld, *Social Justice in Ancient Israel and in the Ancient Near East* (Jerusalem: Magness, 1995), 45–56; Frank M. Cross, "Kinship and Covenant in Ancient Israel," in *From Epic to Canon: History and Literature in Ancient Israel* (Baltimore: Johns Hopkins University Press, 1998), 3–21.
49. The emotion of disgust invoked in the rhetoric against other gods (e.g., Deut 7:26) does draw on the concern for purity and so can be related to the sanctity foundation. See Thomas Staubli, "Disgusting Deeds and Disgusting Gods: Ethnic and Ethical Constructions of Disgust in the Hebrew Bible," *HeBAI* 6 (2017): 471–74. In Deuteronomy, however, this motive is incorporated within the overarching political rhetoric.
50. The care/harm moral foundation is not prominent in the hortatory portions of the book, though it finds some expression in the legal material. Although the hortatory material does emphasize the protection and benefits given to the people by Yhwh, the framing of the material indicates that it functions more in terms of the reciprocity foundation. If the benefits were cast in terms of care/harm, then the recipients would be more strongly characterized in terms of their vulnerability and neediness, as they occasionally are (e.g., Deut 10:18). More often, however, the issues are framed in terms of the gratitude or ingratitude of the recipients. See also the discussion by Thomas Kazen, "Emotional Ethics in Biblical Texts: Cultural Construction and Biological Bases of Morality," *HeBAI* 6 (2017): 441–42, who contrasts the strongly empathetic language of the Covenant Code with the "drier" formulations in Deuteronomy 10:17–19 and 24:10–22.
51. Haidt, *The Righteous Mind*, 125.

52. The foundational study is that of R. L. Trivers, "The Evolution of Reciprocal Altruism," *QRB* 46 (1971): 35–57. For further discussion of the roles of biology and culture in shaping altruistic behavior and its relevance for biblical texts, see Kazan, "Emotional Ethics."
53. M. E. McCullough, M. B. Kimeldorf, and A. D. Cohen, "An Adaptation for Altruism? The Social Causes, Social Effects, and Social Evolution of Gratitude," *CDPS* 17 (2008): 281–85.
54. McCullough, Kimeldorf, and Cohen, "Adaptation for Altruism?" 282–83.
55. In Moral Foundations Theory, the foundation of loyalty is largely discussed in terms of human groupishness, which involves dedication to one's family, tribe, or nation, often paired with hostility toward outsiders. Here, I think, Moral Foundation Theory's analysis is limited by its dependence on data drawn largely from modernized societies. While there is a certain degree of ethnic construction in Deuteronomy, loyalty *to* the ethnic group is not a strong motivating feature in Deuteronomy. Its imagination is strongly vertical, not horizontal. Loyalty is directed toward the person of Yhwh (e.g., 12:29–31, 18:9–14).
56. Margalit, *On Betrayal*, 149.
57. The classic study is that of William L. Moran, "The Ancient Near Eastern Background of the Love of God in Deuteronomy," *CBQ* 25 (1963): 77–87.
58. Jacqueline E. Lapsley, "Feeling Our Way: Love for God in Deuteronomy," *CBQ* 65 (2003): 350–69.
59. It also appears likely that portions of Prov 1–9 are aware of and trope on portions of Deuteronomy. So Schipper, "'Teach Them Diligently to Your Son!'"
60. Occasional elements in Proverbs present a contrary position, especially the words of Agur in Prov 30:1–14. See the discussion by Bernd U. Schipper, "'Teach Them Diligently to Your Son!'" 29–31.
61. Although "fear of Yhwh" is a central motif in the framing of Proverbs (1:7; 9:10) and has emotive significance, it is never grounded in the kind of dramatic punishment imagery that Deuteronomy employs.
62. Most recently, see Barat Ellman, *Memory and Covenant: The Role of Israel's and God's Memory in Sustaining the Deuteronomic and Priestly Covenants*, Emerging Scholars (Minneapolis: Fortress, 2013).
63. Werner E. Lemke, "Circumcision of the Heart," in *A God So Near: Essays on Old Testament Theology in Honor of Patrick D. Miller*, ed. Brent A. Strawn and Nancy R. Bowen (Winona Lake, IN: Eisenbrauns, 2003), 306–7.
64. In a passage similar to Deut 4:29–31, the tradents of Jeremiah envision the people in exile "calling" upon God, "praying," "searching," and "seeking," eliciting a positive response from Yhwh (Jer 29:12–14).
65. The Deuteronomistic History resolved the problem by "back-dating" the critical moral failure to Manasseh (2 Kgs 21:11–15). The Deuteronomistic History, however, makes the agency of the kings more significant than the distributed agency of the whole people. Chronicles, by contrast, includes the moral failures

of the people as well as the kings and does not employ the notion of intergenerational moral guilt.

66. Marc Zvi Brettler, "Predestination in Deuteronomy 30:1–10," in *Those Elusive Deuteronomists: The Phenomenon of Pan-Deuteronomism*, ed. Linda S. Schearing and Steven L. McKenzie, JSOTSup 268 (Sheffield: Sheffield Academic, 1999), 174–78.
67. Brettler, "Predestination in Deuteronomy," 177.
68. Brettler, "Predestination in Deuteronomy," 181.
69. Brettler also notes that 4QMMT alludes to this passage with the assumption that it refers to the events of the eschatological age ("And we are aware that the range of blessings and curses that are written in the Book of Moses have transpired, and this is the end of days when those of Israel will return forever" [4Q398 11–13, 3–5; trans. Brettler]). Thus a divinely determined eschatological timetable rather than human agency is responsible for the return of Israel.
70. The most extensive recent study is Michael Lyons, *From Law to Prophecy: Ezekiel's Use of the Holiness Code*, LHBOTS 507 (New York: T&T Clark, 2009). Although Lyons makes a strong case that Ezekiel draws explicitly on formulations from the Holiness Code, some scholars assess the chronological relationships differently, seeing Ezekiel as earlier or the two corpora overlapping chronologically in their development. For an updated discussion and a plea for a more nuanced model of relationships, see Christophe L. Nihan, "Ezekiel and the Holiness Legislation: A Plea for Nonlinear Models," in *The Formation of the Pentateuch: Bridging the Academic Cultures of Europe, Israel, and North America*, ed. Jan Christian Gertz, Bernard M. Levinson, Dalit Rom-Shiloni, and Konrad Schmid, FAT 111 (Tübingen: Mohr Siebeck, 2016), 1015–39.
71. Haidt, *The Righteous Mind*, 146–53.
72. C. Nemeroff and P. Rozin, "The Contagion Concept in Adult Thinking in the United States: Transmission of Germs and Interpersonal Influence," *Ethos* 22 (1994): 158–86.
73. Yitzhaq Feder, "Contagion and Cognition," 165. In "Defilement and Moral Discourse in the Hebrew Bible: An Evolutionary Framework," *JCH* 3 (2016): 157–89, Feder demonstrates how pollution terminology was extended to bring a variety of norm violations within the orbit of the sanctity foundation, including bloodshed, adultery, promiscuity, illicit sexual behavior, idolatry, and intermarriage.
74. Contrast, for example, the explicit material advantages of loyalty to Yhwh that form such a frequent theme in Deuteronomic motivational rhetoric (e.g., Deut 6:3, 10–11; 7:13–15; 8:1–6).
75. Jay Sklar, "Sin and Impurity: Atoned or Purified? Yes!" in *Perspectives on Purity and Purification in the Bible*, ed. Baruch Schwartz et al., LHBOTS 474 (New York: T&T Clark, 2008), 24. See also Jonathan Klawans, *Impurity and Sin in Ancient Judaism* (New York: Oxford University Press, 2000), 26–31.

76. Tikva Frymer-Kensky, "Pollution, Purification, and Purgation in Biblical Israel," in *The Word of the Lord Shall Go Forth*, ed. C. L. Meyers and M. O'Connor (Winona Lake, IN: Eisenbrauns, 1983), 405.
77. Baruch J. Schwartz, "The Ultimate Aim of Israel's Restoration in Ezekiel," in *Birkat Shalom: Studies in the Bible, Ancient Near Eastern Literature, and Post-biblical Judaism Presented to Shalom M. Paul on the Occasion of His Seventieth Birthday*, vol. 1, ed. C. Cohen and S. M. Paul (Winona Lake, IN: Eisenbrauns, 2008), 305.
78. Schwartz, "Israel's Restoration in Ezekiel," 306.
79. E. Royzman et al., "'CAD or MAD?' Anger (Not Disgust) as the Predominant Response to Pathogen-Free Violations of the Divinity Code," *Emotion* (2014): 904.
80. See R. Müller, "A Prophetic View of the Exile in the Holiness Code: Literary Growth and Tradition History in Leviticus 26," in *The Concept of Exile in Ancient Israel and Its Historical Contexts*, ed. Ehud Ben Zvi and Christophe Levin (Berlin: De Gruyter, 2010), 208 n. 6, for a review of various scholarly views. My interest is not in the chapter's chronological relationship to Ezekiel but in its conceptual relationship to the common issue of how restoration is to be envisioned.
81. Jacob Milgrom, *Leviticus 17–22*, AB 3A (New York: Doubleday, 2000), 1404.
82. Frymer-Kensky, "Pollution," 411–12, suggests that the exile functions similarly to the set periods of time after which a person becomes pure without further purification rituals, though there is no indication that such a provision was envisioned before the exile itself happened. It appears to be a creative ex post facto extension of purity logic.
83. Jacqueline E. Lapsley, *Can These Bones Live? The Problem of the Moral Self in the Book of Ezekiel*, BZAW 301 (Berlin: De Gruyter, 2000), 78–103. Casey A. Strine ("The Role of Repentance in the Book of Ezekiel: A Second Chance for the Second Generation," *JTS* 63 [2012]: 467–91) argues that the people's repentance is an essential act of agency that is necessary to the accomplishment of Yhwh's restoration of the people to the land, even if this restoration occurs solely as an act of divine choice. To be sure, not even Ezekiel could eliminate all traces of moral agency from his theocentric account of the people's condition and future. It may be the case that oracles had different rhetorical or redactional contexts, so that foregrounding the role of human agency was strategic in some cases, whereas agency was denied in others. There is evidence also for redactional reworking that shifts agency from humans to God, as in the relationship between Ezek 11:16–21 and 36:23c–32. There is no doubt, however, that Ezekiel radically departs from the traditions of moral agency that were common in monarchical Judah.
84. Klawans, *Impurity and Sin*, 30–31. As Anja Klein notes ("From the 'Right Spirit' to the 'Spirit of Truth,'" in *Dynamics of Language and Exegesis at Qumran*,

ed. Devorah Dimant and Reinhard Kratz, FAT 2/35 [Tübingen: Mohr Siebeck, 2009], 174), the passage in Ezek 36:23c–32 does not occur in the Greek Pap. 967 and so represents a redactional addition after the text tradition from which P. 967 derives split from what became the MT. See Johan Lust, "Ezekiel 36–40 in the Oldest Greek Manuscript," *CBQ* 43 (1981): 522–25; and the thorough discussion by Ingrid E. Lilly, *Two Books of Ezekiel: Papyrus 967 and the Masoretic Text as Variant Literary Editions*, VTSup 150 (Leiden: Brill, 2012), 194–213. Lust provides evidence that the scribe who reworked Ezek 11:16–21 in 36:23c–32 was also influenced by Deuteronomic phraseology from the book of Jeremiah. Thus the development of this passage is to be dated to the Persian period.

85. In the similar passage in Ezek 11:17–21, as in Deut 30:1–10, it is possible to read the text as implying some limited moral agency on the part of the people that is enhanced by the gift of "a heart of flesh" and "a new spirit." The redactional reworking of Ezek 11:17–21 in 36:23c–32 shifts the source of agency wholly to God (see Lilly, *Two Books of Ezekiel*, 204–5). The overall orientation of Ezekiel's view of the future is one in which a morally abject and incapacitated people is re-created and given agency through God's agency and by means of God's own spirit, a perspective that was enhanced in the redactional activity of the tradents responsible for Ezek 36:23c–32.

Chapter 4. Sin-Consciousness, Self-Alienation, and the Construction of Interiority

1. Werner E. Lemke, "Circumcision of the Heart," 306–7. Anja Klein, *Schriftauslegung im Ezekielbuch: Redactionsgeschichtliche Untersuchungen zu Ez 34–39*, BZAW 391 (Berlin: De Gruyter, 2008), 99–106, argues for the influence of Jeremiah's language about the heart in Jer 24:6–7a; 31:31–34; and 32:37–41 on the formulations in Deuteronomy and Ezekiel.
2. Jeremiah's image is a reversal of his earlier trope for intractable sin: "The sin of Judah is inscribed with an iron stylus, engraved with a diamond point on the tablet of their heart" (17:1).
3. In fact, some non-Israelite peoples also practiced circumcision. For Jeremiah, however, even circumcision of the penis counts for nothing if there is no circumcision of the heart (Jer 9:24–25).
4. Klein, *Schriftauslegung im Ezekielbuch*, 94, plausibly suggests that the image itself is an elaboration on the motifs of the "stubborn heart" (*ḥizqê-lēb*) in 2:4 and the "hard heart" (*qĕšê-lēb*) in 3:7.
5. Lambert, *How Repentance Became Biblical*, 160–71. Although Christian Frevel does not directly engage Lambert's work, he makes a vigorous case for significantly more psychological interiority and reflexivity in biblical texts than Lambert allows for ("Von der Selbstbeobachtung zu inneren Tiefen," 13–43).

6. Lambert, *How Repentance Became Biblical*, 154, contrasts "repentance" with "cessation of sin" according to eight features. Repentance is (1) an "act, a discrete event," (2) a "mental act," (3) "retrospective," (4) utilizing an "emotion of sorrow," (5) implying an "agent" who has "autonomy," (6) focused on "a specific sin or series of sins," (7) performable by the "righteous" as well as sinners, and (8) "an efficacious act."
7. Earlier in 6:9 and 20:43 Ezekiel also uses the motif of self-loathing (*qwṭ*) in connection with the people's recognition that "I am Yhwh," though in these cases no mention is made of the transformation of the people by God.
8. For a discussion of the shame terminology in Ezekiel and its significance, see Lapsley, *Can These Bones Live?*, 129–42. Lapsley considers the construction of shame in Ezekiel to have psychological as well as social aspects.
9. Erich Zenger (Erich Zenger and Frank-Lothar Hossfeld, *Psalms 2: A Commentary on Psalms 51–100*, trans. Linda Maloney, Hermeneia [Minneapolis: Fortress, 2005], 21) notes not only the influence of Ezek 36 but also echoes of Jeremiah and Second Isaiah in the psalm. As Werner Lemke ("Circumcision of the Heart," 315) observes, "the conjoining of 'spirit' and 'heart' is unique to Ezekiel and not found in either Deuteronomy or Jeremiah." Thus the prominent use of the pair here in Ps 51 is a strong indication that Ezekiel is the primary intertext. For a more recent analysis see Anja Klein, *Schriftauslegung im Ezekielbuch*, 106–10. Her arguments are also summarized in "From the 'Right Spirit' to the 'Spirit of Truth,'" 175–76.
10. Lesley R. DiFransico, *Washing Away Sin: An Analysis of the Metaphor in the Hebrew Bible and Its Influence*, BTS 23 (Leuven: Peeters, 2016), 80–118, 130–42, discusses the imagery in Ps 51 and Ezek 36, and their interrelationships and possible allusions to other prophetic texts.
11. See the insightful and humorous account by Mark Turner and Gilles Fauconnier, "A Mechanism of Creativity," *PT* 20 (1999): 397–418.
12. Contra Miriam Brand, *Evil Within and Without: The Source of Sin and Its Nature as Portrayed in Second Temple Literature*, JAJSup 9 (Göttingen: Vandenhoeck & Ruprecht, 2013), 62, n. 12, who argues that the problem in Ps 51 is specific sins. Since there never was a time when the speaker was not enmeshed in sin, it does not seem that the specific sins can be separated from the sinful condition that has characterized the speaker since conception.
13. DiFransico, *Washing Away Sin*, 104–7.
14. DiFransico, *Washing Away Sin*, 97–98.
15. Klein, "From the 'Right Spirit' to the 'Spirit of Truth,'" 173.
16. Nathan D. MacDonald, "The Spirit of Yahweh: An Overlooked Conceptualization of Divine Presence in the Persian Period," in *Divine Presence and Absence in Exilic and Post-Exilic Judaism*, ed. Nathan MacDonald and Izaak J. de Hulster, FAT 2/61 (Tübingen: Mohr Siebeck, 2013), 95–120.

17. The work called Barkhi Nafshi is a collection of perhaps ten poetic compositions preserved in five badly damaged manuscripts (4Q434–438) that were either composed by the Qumran community or at least were influential there. Some of the compositions describe God's providential care for a beleaguered community. Others focus on the speaker as a leader of a community and bear some resemblance to the collection of Teacher psalms in the Hodayot (1QH[a] 10–17). Two compositions are described by Daniel Falk as having "highly personal diction, in which the speaker praises God directly for help toward himself" ("Barkhi Nafshi," *T&T Clark Companion to the Dead Sea Scrolls*, ed. George J. Brooke and Charlotte Hempel [London: T&T Clark, 2019], 286). In one, the aid is deliverance from enemies. In the passage considered here God is thanked for "spiritual assistance." For the critical text see Moshe Weinfeld and David Seely, "Barkhi Nafshi," in *Qumran Cave 4. XX: Poetical and Liturgical Texts, Part 2*, ed. Esther G. Chazon et al., DJD 29 (Oxford: Clarendon, 1999), 255–334. Possible contexts for the collection are discussed by Mika S. Pajunen, *The Land to the Elect and Justice for All: Reading Psalms in the Dead Sea Scrolls in Light of 4Q381*, JASJ 14 (Göttingen: Vandenhoeck & Ruprecht, 2013), 66–70; and George J. Brooke, "Body Parts in *Barkhi Nafshi* and the Qualifications for Membership of the Worshipping Community," in *Sapiential, Liturgical & Poetical Texts from Qumran: Proceedings of the Third Meeting of the International Organization for Qumran Studies, Published in Memory of Maurice Baillet*, STDJ 34, ed. Daniel K. Falk, F. García Martínez, and Eileen M. Schuller (Leiden: Brill, 2000), 79–94. The fundamental study of the body language is that of David R. Seely, "Implanting Pious Qualities as a Theme in the *Barki Nafshi* Hymns," in *The Dead Sea Scrolls—Fifty Years after Their Discovery: Proceedings of the Jerusalem Congress, July 20–25, 1997*, ed. Lawrence H. Schiffman et al. (Jerusalem: Israel Exploration Society, 2000), 322–31.
18. Weinfeld and Seely, DJD 29, 301.
19. Menachem Kister ("'Inclination of the Heart of Man,' the Body and Purification from Evil," in *MSDSS* 8, ed. Moshe Bar-Asher and Devorah Dimant [Jerusalem: Bialik Institute and Haifa University, 2010], 243–84 [Heb]) associates the passage with other "purification prayers for the organs" in early Judaism (270). Similarly, Brand, *Evil Within and Without*, 45, emphasizes that the problem in this section of the composition is not specific sins but a sinful condition over which the speaker has no control.
20. The translation follows Brand's adaptation of the DJD translation, emphasizing the physical identity of the organs (Brand, *Evil Within and Without*, 43–44).
21. Cf. also the reference to the "broken heart" (*lb* [*nd*]*kh*) in 1. ii 4, an allusion to Ps 51:19.
22. Eibert Tigchelaar, "The Evil Inclination in the Dead Sea Scrolls, with a Re-Edition of 4Q468i (4QSectarian Text?)," in *Empsychoi Logoi: Religious Innova-*

tions in Antiquity: Studies in Honour of Pieter Willem van der Horst, ed. Alberdina Houtman et al., AJEC 73 (Leiden: Brill, 2008), 351.

23. Brand, *Evil Within and Without*, 40.
24. Brand thinks it is an internal disposition (*Evil Within and Without*, 209). David Flusser ("Qumran and Jewish 'Apotropaic' Prayers," *IEJ* 16 [1966]: 205) and Armin Lange ("Considerations Concerning the 'Spirit of Impurity' in Zech 13:2," in *Die Dämonen: Die Dämonologie der israelitisch-jüdischen und frühchristlichen Literatur im Kontext ihrer Umwelt*, ed. Armin Lange, Hermann Lichtenberger, and K. F. Diethard Römheld [Tübingen: Mohr Siebeck, 2003], 260–61) take it as a demonic spirit.
25. Menachem Kister, "Demons, Theology and Abraham's Covenant," in *The Dead Sea Scrolls at Fifty: Proceedings of the 1997 Society of Biblical Literature Qumran Section Meetings*, ed. Robert A. Kugler and Eileen M. Schuller, EJL 15 (Atlanta: Scholars, 1999), 170.
26. Ishay Rosen-Zvi argues that one line of development in early Rabbinic thought treats the *yēṣer* as a kind of internalized demonic force (Ishay Rosen-Zvi, *Demonic Desires:* Yetzer Hara *and the Problem of Evil in Late Antiquity* [Philadelphia: University of Pennsylvania Press, 2011], 127.
27. The most thorough recent study of the development of the *yēṣer* in Second Temple and Rabbinic literature is Rosen-Zvi, *Demonic Desires*. Earlier studies—such as Geert H. Cohen Stuart, *The Struggle in Man between Good and Evil: An Inquiry into the Origin of the Rabbinic Concept of Yeser Hara* (Kampen: Kok, 1984), and Frank C. Porter, "The Yeçer Hara: A study in the Jewish Doctrine of Sin," in *Biblical and Semitic Studies: Critical and Historical Essays by the Members of the Semitic and Biblical Faculty of Yale University* (New York: Scribner's, 1901), 93–156—are still valuable but must be used with caution. More helpful is Roland E. Murphy, "*Yēṣer* in the Qumran Literature," *Biblica* 39 (1958): 334–43.
28. The word *rāṣôn* might be translated as either "desire" or "will," both terms that have collected a lot of theological baggage in Christian thought. In this context the term seems to indicate the person's impulse to do what he or she wishes to do, even though God opposes it. Thus it is not surprising that it is used in conjunction with both "lustful eyes" and "stubbornness of heart."
29. "[Practicing self-regulation] requires the executive aspects of the self (the 'I' as knower) that allow people to change according to social context, including altering their thoughts, actions, and emotions. Thus people need to inhibit their impulses, stifle their desires, resist temptations, undertake difficult or unpleasant activities, banish unwanted and intrusive thoughts, and control their emotional displays, all of which are difficult to do but are necessary for staying in the good graces of others" (Heatherton, "Neuroscience of Self and Self-Regulation," 366).
30. See the discussion in Yoder, "The Shaping of Erotic Desire in Proverbs 1–9."

31. There is general agreement that 4 Ezra was composed sometime after 70 CE, perhaps around 100 CE. For a discussion of the issues see Michael E. Stone, *Fourth Ezra*, Hermeneia (Minneapolis: Augsburg Fortress, 1990), 9–10.
32. Stone, *Fourth Ezra*, 63 n. 18; Karina Martin Hogan, *Theologies in Conflict in 4 Ezra: Wisdom Debate and Apocalyptic Solution*, JSJSup 130 (Leiden: Brill, 2008), 114.
33. See the nuanced discussion in Hindy Najman, *Losing the Temple and Recovering the Future: An Analysis of 4 Ezra* (Cambridge: Cambridge University Press, 2014), 79–83, who makes a strong case that one should not expect to find a clearly defined theory about the origin of sin in 4 Ezra. One can, however, see how certain anxieties about sin repeatedly resurface. Though Hogan (*Theologies in Conflict*, 112–20) notes the inconsistent imagery in Ezra's own formulations, she sees a discernible difference in the positions articulated by Ezra and Uriel.
34. Najman, *Losing the Temple*, 82, prefers to translate "clothed himself with," which would suggest "not so much an internal tempter as an external and inauthentic guise, perhaps freely adopted but hard to shed."
35. Stone, *Fourth Ezra*, 224.
36. This is Stone's preferred translation for Latin *sensus*, which probably reflects Greek *nous* and Hebrew *lēb*.
37. Stone, *Fourth Ezra*, 225–26.
38. Dualism is a term that is used in many different ways. I use the term to designate what can perhaps be called "mirror-image" dualism, that is, two phenomena that are similar in structure but opposite in valance. In addition, the phenomena relate to one another in a pattern of hostility. Zoroastrian dualism and the dualism in the Two Spirits Teaching are clear examples. In other cases the mirroring may be somewhat less exact but is still identifiable. The trope of "battle" or "war" often serves to identify a dualistic relationship, since opposing fighters or armies are a form of mirror-image opposition. I differentiate this dualism from other types of binary relationships that may involve opposition but in which the entities are not at the same time similar to one another. Thus a human being and its objectified evil inclination may be in a relationship of struggle but they are not mirror-image opposites of each other. Binary opposition and dualistic opposition bear some family resemblance to each other, of course, but it is important to attend to how they differ. Other ways of defining dualism and binarism are certainly legitimate and may be used for a variety of conceptual purposes. It is simply important to clarify how one uses the terms. For another approach to the issues see Jörg Frey, "Different Patterns of Dualistic Thought in the Qumran Library: Reflections on Their Background and History," in *Legal Texts and Legal Issues: Proceedings of the Second Meeting of the International Organization for Qumran Studies, Cambridge, 1995: Published in Honour of Joseph M. Baumgarten*, ed. Moshe Bernstein, Florentino García Martínez, and John Kampen, STDJ 23 (Leiden: Brill, 1997), 275–309.

39. I examine this aspect of dualistic models of selfhood in *The Self as Symbolic Space*, 77–90.
40. Esther Eshel, "Apotropaic Prayers in the Second Temple Period," in *Liturgical Perspectives: Prayer and Poetry in Light of the Dead Sea Scrolls: Proceedings of the Fifth International Symposium of the Orion Center for the Study of the Dead Sea Scrolls and Associated Literature, 19–23 January, 2000*, ed. Esther G. Chazon, Ruth Clements, and Avital Pinnick, STDJ 48 (Leiden: Brill, 2003), 81.
41. Brand, *Evil Within and Without*, 205 n. 35. She persuasively argues why Qimron's suggested translation, "arteries," is unlikely. See Elisha Qimron, "Notes on the 4Q Zadokite Fragment on Skin Disease," *JJS* 42 (1991): 256–59.
42. Kenneth Burke, *A Grammar of Motives* (Berkeley: University of California Press, 1969), xv–xxiii.
43. Brand, *Evil Within and Without*, 201.
44. Jubilees 10:1–3 understands the spirits of the dead giants to be demonic spirits that attack and lead astray the children of Noah.
45. Although it is possible that the Two Spirits Teaching may be a pre-Yahad composition secondarily incorporated into 1QS, as Armin Lange and others have suggested (*Weisheit und Prädestination: Weisheitliche Urordnung und Prädestination in den Texfunden von Qumran*, STDJ 18 [Leiden: Brill, 1995], 127–28), recent scholarship makes a strong case for seeing it as a sectarian composition. See Peter Porzig, "The Place of the 'Treatise of the Two Spirits' (1QS 3:13–4:26) within the Literary Development of the Community Rule," and Mieke Christian, "The Literary Development of the 'Treatise of the Two Spirits' as Dependent on Instruction and the Hodayot," in *Law, Literature, and Society in Legal Texts from Qumran: Papers from the Ninth Meeting of the International Organization for Qumran Studies, Leuven 2016*, ed. Jutta Jokiranta and Molly Zahn, STDJ 128 (Leiden: Brill, 2019), 127–52, 153–84. Also, the dissertation of Arjen Bakker, "The Figure of the Sage in Musar le-Mevin and Serek ha-Yahad" (PhD diss., Katholieke Universiteit Leuven, 2015), examines the patterns of relationship between 4QInstruction and the Two Spirits Teaching and the implications for the provenance of both. Even if the Two Spirits Teaching should be an earlier and pre- or non-Yahad composition, the fact that it was given a *lmśkyl* heading and incorporated into at least one version of the Community Rule is ample evidence that it not only could be but was read as a "sectarian" document. Since my interests are in the significance for the text in its relation to the formation of self and agency, I am particularly concerned with its role in the sectarian context.
46. Although many scholars translate the term *twldwt* as "history," in recognition of the temporal scope outlined in the heading, that translation misses the etymological relationship of the term to "birth," a nuance that is present in the account's concern with origins as much as with eschatological destinies. Thus I prefer the term "genealogy," which gestures toward origin, generational con-

tinuity, and inheritance, all of which are central concerns of the discourse. The term may in fact be an allusion to Gen 5:1, the genealogy of Adam. See further below.

47. Hermann Lichtenberger, *Studien zum Menschenbild in Texten der Qumrangemeinde*, SUNT 15 (Göttingen: Vandenhoeck & Ruprecht, 1980), 129, 136–41.

48. Peter von der Osten-Saken, *Gott und Belial: Traditionsgeschichtliche Untersuchungen zum Dualism in den Texten aus Qumran*, SUNT 6 (Göttingen: Vandenhoeck & Ruprecht, 1969), 22–23.

49. Newsom, *The Self as Symbolic Space*, 127–34.

50. Wernberg-Møller, *The Manual of Discipline*, 67, notes several of the intertextual echoes and observes that "the whole of the essay is based on Gen. i ff." Cf. also Michael A. Knibb, *The Qumran Community* (Cambridge: Cambridge University Press, 1987), 96–97.

51. After I submitted this manuscript to Yale University Press, I discovered the recently published essay by Ethan Schwartz, "The Exegetical Character of 1QS 3:13–4:26," *DSD* 27 (2020): 31–65. Although we note many of the same points of connection between the two texts, the nature and direction of our analyses are quite different.

52. Baillet, DJD 7: 163.

53. Although Gen 2–3 became an influential text in the middle Second Temple period, its view that God prohibited access to the knowledge of good and evil was contested in a number of interpretive compositions, as I will discuss more fully in the following chapter.

54. 4QVisions of Amram prefers the language of "righteousness" and "wickedness" rather than "truth" and "perversity." The proximate text that the Two Spirits Teaching engages may not be Amram itself but some other tradition that is perhaps closer to a Zoroastrian articulation of the dualistic opposition. Although the monotheistic assumption of Judaism is incompatible with Zoroastrian dualism, a narrower focus on the relation of "truth" and "perversity" in the Two Spirits Teaching yields the conclusion that "the system of 1QS is almost wholly parallel to the Iranian one," in the judgment of Albert de Jong, "Iranian Connections in the Dead Sea Scrolls," in *The Oxford Handbook of the Dead Sea Scrolls*, ed. Timothy H. Lim and John J. Collins (New York: Oxford University Press, 2010), 493. See also Carol A. Newsom, *ʿāwel*, *ThWQ* III, 47–54. The most thorough reexamination of *ʾĕmet* is Eibert Tigchelaar, "Changing Truths: *ʾĕmet* and *qōšeṭ* as Core Concepts in the Second Temple Period," in *Congress Volume Stellenbosch 2016*, ed. Louis C. Jonker, Gideon R. Kotzé, and Christl M. Maier, VTSup 177 (Leiden: Brill, 2017), 395–415.

55. As Bakker ("The Figure of the Sage," 199) observes, the phrase "great or little" is an allusion to Num 26:56, which refers to "the inheritance of the promised land and its division among the Israelites." Here, however, the inheritance is not in land but in proportions of the two spirits.

56. Sarianna Metso with Michael Knibb, *The Community Rule: A Critical Edition with Translation*, EJL 51 (Atlanta: SBL, 2019).
57. Siegfried Wibbing, *Die Tugend- und Lasterkataloge im Neuen Testament und ihre Traditionsgeschichte unter besonderer Berücksichtigung der Qumrantexte*, BZNW 25 (Berlin: Töpelmann, 1959), 44; H. Lichtenberger, *Studien zu Menschenbild*, 134. Given that the second part of the section is introduced by the phrase "to the spirit of perversity (belong) . . ." (4:9), it is possible that a similar heading has been lost from 4:2, though there is no textual evidence to that effect. See Wernberg-Møller, *The Manual of Discipline*, 73; Knibb, *The Qumran Community*, 99.
58. See, e.g., 4QInstruction[c] (4Q417 1 i 17–18), in which the "fleshly spirit" has no access to meditation (*hgwy*) "because it did not know (how to distinguish) between [goo]d and evil."
59. For a discussion of the specific qualities in the lists and the extent to which the lists have been shaped for a sectarian context, see Newsom, *Self as Symbolic Space*, 128–32.
60. George Brooke, "Body Parts in *Barkhi Nafshi*," 88, suggests that the signs "are best understood as physical features which reflect a person's spiritual status." Though an intriguing idea in light of the physiognomy texts such as 4QZodiacal Physiognomy (4Q186) and 4QPhysiognomy (4Q561), the context seems to point more in the direction of deeds and dispositions rather than physical appearance. On the physiognomy texts see Mladen Popović, *Reading the Human Body: Physiognomics and Astrology in the Dead Sea Scrolls and Hellenistic-Early Roman Period Judaism*, STDJ 67 (Leiden: Brill, 2007).
61. Lichtenberger, *Studien zum Menschenbild*, 139.
62. Bakker (*The Figure of the Sage*, 195–209) has proposed a striking interpretation of 4QInstruction[c] (4Q417) 1 i 13–18 that would articulate a view of creation and human destiny in that text similar to the one I am suggesting for the Two Spirits Teaching. Bakker suggests that the "vision of contemplation," a form of heavenly knowledge, was assigned both to angels and to humans ("And he has assigned it to mankind as a portion together with a nation of spirit," trans. Bakker). The reason humans are granted access to such knowledge is because God "fashioned him according to the structure of the holy ones." But humans did not immediately receive access to such knowledge ("But he had not yet given contemplation to the fleshly spirit"). The reason that access to heavenly knowledge was postponed was because "he [humankind] did not know how to distinguish between good and evil according to the judgment of his spirit." According to the Two Spirits Teaching the eschatological purification of the elect has as its purpose "so that the upright may have understanding in the knowledge of the Most High, and the perfect of way insight into the wisdom of the sons of heaven" (trans. Knibb). If Bakker's rendering is correct—and the text in question is difficult and subject to several divergent interpretations—

then both 4QInstruction and the Two Spirits Teaching understand that God's original intention in creating humankind was to endow people with access to heavenly knowledge similar to that of the angels. But such knowledge could only be granted once humans had become like God and angels in "knowing good and evil," which, as the Two Spirits Teaching suggests, involves walking in the ways of both spirits and gaining understanding of them.

63. Jonathan Klawans, "Josephus on Fate, Free Will, and Ancient Jewish Types of Compatibilism," *Numen* 56 (2009): 44–90. This study is incorporated into his book *Josephus and the Theologies of Ancient Judaism* (New York: Oxford University Press, 2012), 44–91.
64. Ted Chiang, "Story of Your Life," in *Stories of Your Life and Others* (New York: Vintage Books, 2016), 91–145. The story was made into the feature film "Arrival," though unfortunately that film does not do justice to the philosophical dimensions of the story.
65. Chiang, *Stories of Your Life*, 114.
66. Chiang, *Stories of Your Life*, 116.
67. Chiang, *Stories of Your Life*, 124.
68. Chiang, *Stories of Your Life*, 119.
69. Chiang, *Stories of Your Life*, 134.
70. Chiang, *Stories of Your Life*, 132
71. Chiang, *Stories of Your Life*, 137.

Chapter 5. Rational Agency and the Birth of the Human

1. David M. Carr, *The Formation of the Hebrew Bible: A New Reconstruction* (New York: Oxford University Press, 2011), 456–69, has again taken up the case that the non-P primeval history might be an early monarchic text. See also Walter Bührer, "The Relative Dating of the Eden Narrative Gen *2–3," *VT* 65 (2015): 369–72. The prevailing scholarly consensus, however, remains in favor of an early Second Temple date. See, among others, Eckhart Otto, "Die Paradieserzählung Genesis 2–3: Eine nachprieserschriftliche Lehrerzählung in ihrem religionshistorischen Kontext," in *"Jedes Ding hat seine Zeit": Studien zu israelitischen und altorientalischen Weisheit (FS D. Michel)*, ed. Anja A. Diese et al., BZAW 241 (Berlin: De Gruyter, 1996), 173–89; Jean Louis Ska, "Genesis 2–3: Some Fundamental Questions," in *Beyond Eden: The Biblical Story of Paradise (Genesis 2–3) and Its Reception History*, ed. Konrad Schmid and Christoph Riedweg, FAT 2/34 (Tübingen: Mohr Siebeck, 2008), 16–20; Mark S. Smith, *The Genesis of Good and Evil: The Fall(out) and Original Sin in the Bible* (Louisville: Westminster John Knox, 2019), 45–48.
2. See Luis Alonso Schökel, "Sapiential and Covenant Themes in Genesis 2–3," in *Studies in Ancient Israelite Wisdom*, ed. James L. Crenshaw (New York: Ktav, 1976), 468–80; Joseph Blenkinsopp, *The Pentateuch: An Introduction to the First*

Five Books of the Bible (New York: Doubleday, 1992), 65–57; Markus Witte, *Die biblische Urgeschichte: Redaktions- und theologiegeschichtliche Beobachtungen zu Genesis 1,1–11,26*, BZAW 265 (Berlin: De Gruyter, 1998), 200–205; Konrad Schmid, "Die Unteilbarkeit der Weisheit: Überlegungen zur sogenannten Paradieserzählung Gen 2f. und ihrer theologischen Tendenz," *ZAW* 114 (2002): 21–39; Michaela Bauks, "Erkenntnis und Leben in Gen 2–3: Zum Wandel eines ursprünglich weisheitlich geprägten Lebensbegriffs," *ZAW* 127 (2015): 20–42.

3. See Carol A. Newsom, ed., *Seeking Knowledge: The Intellectual Project of Apocalypticism in Cultural Context, HeBAI* 5 (2016); Seth L. Sanders, *From Adapa to Enoch: Scribal Culture and Religious Vision in Judea and Babylon*, TSAJ 167 (Tübingen: Mohr Siebeck, 2017), 129–52; Annette Yoshiko Reed, *Demons, Angels, and Writing in Ancient Judaism* (Cambridge: Cambridge University Press, 2020).
4. My reading of Gen 2–3 is congenial to, though somewhat different from, that of Konrad Schmid, "Die Unteilbarkeit der Weisheit." He captures the wry realism of the narrative well.
5. "The breath of life then means simply being alive, and the breathing in of this breath, the giving of life to humans, nothing more (cf. Ps 104:28f.; Gen 7:22)," Claus Westermann, *Genesis 1–11: A Commentary*, trans. John J. Scullion, S.J., CC (Minneapolis: Augsburg, 1984), 207; Noort, "Taken from the Soil," 5–9; Smith, *The Genesis of Good and Evil*, 52. To be sure, the breath from God is interpreted in more transformative ways in several Second Temple texts, as will be discussed below. See T. Storalden, *Echoes of Eden: Genesis 2–3 and Symbolism of the Eden Garden in Biblical Hebrew Literature*, CBET 25 (Leuven: Peeters, 2000), 235–37. But it is important not to retroject these interpretations into the text itself.
6. See the rich collection of essays in Douglas Estes, ed., *The Tree of Life*, TBN 27 (Leiden: Brill, 2020); also Michaela Bauks, "Sacred Trees in the Garden of Eden and Their Ancient Near Eastern Precursors," *JAJ* 3 (2012): 267–301, and "Erkenntnis und Leben in Gen 2–3: Zum Wandel eines ursprünglich weisheitlich geprägten Lebensbegriffs," *ZAW* 127 (2015): 27–34.
7. Even the claim in Prov 13:12 that "a desire realized is a tree of life" occurs in a larger context that makes it clear that this is not simply an observation about hedonistic psychology but rather the desire that is formed in the wise. See vv. 13–14, 19. Bauks, "Erkenntnis und Leben," 24–27, notes the significant number of semantic overlaps between this passage and Gen 2–3.
8. Bauks, "Erkenntnis und Leben," 26.
9. Howard N. Wallace, *The Eden Narrative*, HSM 32 (Atlanta: Scholars, 1985), 121–30, reviews the proponents of this view and gives a nuanced but generally positive assessment of the interpretation. As Smith (*The Genesis of Good and Evil*, 122 n. 52) notes, however, some of the examples Wallace relies upon have a slightly different syntax.

10. Susan Niditch, "Genesis," in *Women's Bible Commentary*, 3rd ed., ed. Carol A. Newsom, Sharon H. Ringe, and Jacqueline E. Lapsley (Louisville: Westminster John Knox, 2012), 31.
11. Erhard S. Gerstenberger, "'... (He/They) Shall Be Put to Death': Life-Preserving Divine Threats in Old Testament Law," *ExAud* 11 (1995): 47.
12. David J. A. Clines, "The Tree of Knowledge and the Law of Yahweh (Psalm XIX)," *VT* 24 (1974): 9.
13. Westermann, *Genesis*, 228.
14. Qoh 3:19–21, after asserting that both humans and animals have "the same lifebreath" (*rûaḥ 'eḥād lakkōl*), gives a shrugging "who knows?" as he considers whether the breath of a human might go upward and an animal's go downward at death. He is not drawing a significant distinction between the two forms of existence, however, since his thesis is that "the fate of the human and the fate of the animal is the same fate"—both die.
15. This is, in fact, how Jubilees understands the episode. Drawing on the language of Gen 1, Jub 3:3 assumes that God has created the animals not only in different species but in sexual pairs. "Adam was looking at all of these—male and female among every kind that was on the earth. But he himself was alone; there was no one whom he found for himself who would be for him a helper who was like him" (trans. VanderKam). Thus Jubilees understands Gen 2:18–24 as explaining the mechanism by which God created the human as "male and female" (Gen 1:27).
16. Niditch, "Genesis," 31.
17. Anne Carson, *Eros the Bittersweet* (Princeton, NJ: Princeton University Press, 1986), 30.
18. Carson, *Eros the Bittersweet*, 33.
19. As various biblical scholars have noted, the transformation of Enkidu, the wild man who consorts with animals, into a companion fit for Gilgamesh involves, among other things, that he is clothed. Robert A. Oden, Jr. (*The Bible without Theology: The Theological Tradition and Alternatives to It* [Urbana and Chicago: University of Illinois Press, 2000], 104), also argues on the basis of the role of Anu's giving Adapa clothing in the Adapa myth that clothing also indicates the differentiation of the human from the divine. His larger argument is that clothing is closely associated with status and changes in status. That seems to fit the narrative of Gen 2–3 quite well. First the humans make clothes for themselves. Subsequently, God recognizes their different status and makes clothes (from animal skins!) for them.
20. Baird Callicott, "Genesis and John Muir," in *Beyond the Land Ethic: More Essays in Environmental Philosophy* (Albany: SUNY Press, 1999), 208.
21. Many scientists have documented animal cognition. Frans de Waal is perhaps the best-known popularizer of the recent research. See, in particular, *Are We Smart Enough to Know How Smart Animals Are?* (New York: W. W. Norton & Co., 2017).

22. Since male "rule" is articulated specifically in relation to female desire, I take the phrase to refer to the male role in sexual intercourse. Even if a woman desires sexual intercourse, she cannot force a male to become physically ready. He and his body "rule" in such decisions. Women are, therefore, depicted as persuaders and seductresses when they desire sexual intercourse. Men are simply said to "go in."
23. Death, however, does not appear to be one of the consequences or punishments of the action. The reference to the man's "return to the ground" (3:19) only serves to indicate the lifelong duration of his toil. Moreover, the "return to the ground" is related to the materials of the body ("for from it you were taken; for dust you are, and to dust you shall return"), not to any action that the man committed.
24. Scholars have often noted the tension between this view of the place of humans in the world and that of Gen 1, in which the elevated status of humans as made "in the image and likeness" of divine beings is itself part of the natural order of things. It is possible that the tension created by the juxtaposition of the two accounts is an intentional engagement constructed in the redaction of Gen 1–11, though I think it unlikely that Gen 2–3 was composed specifically *as* a response to Gen 1. Jan Christian Gertz ("The Formation of the Primeval History," in *The Book of Genesis: Composition, Reception, and Interpretation*, ed. Craig A. Evans et al., VTSup 152 [Leiden: Brill, 2012], 115–18) discusses the scholars who "argue that the Eden narrative itself should be seen as Midrash-like exegesis of, or correction to, Gen 1." His own view, with which I agree, is that "Gen 2:4b–3:24* was not written as a supplement to the priestly creation account and was probably also unaware of it" (118). Nevertheless, the juxtaposition invited reading the narratives in relation to one another, an opportunity richly exploited in Second Temple interpretations.
25. Henrike Frey-Anthes, *Unheilsmächte und Schutzgenien, Antiwesen und Grenzgänger: Vorstellung von "Dämonien" in alten Israel*, OBO 227 (Fribourg: Academic Press; Göttingen: Vandenhoeck & Ruprecht, 2007).
26. The association of moral freedom with the creation story is attested in Second Temple and early Christian interpretation, though more frequently as an assumption that moral freedom is a given from creation itself, much as one finds in 2 Baruch's claim that "each of us has become his own Adam" (54:19). See Benjamin Wold, "Genesis 2–3 in Early Christian Tradition and 4QInstruction," *DSD* 23 (2016): 329–46; Elaine Pagels, *Adam, Eve and the Serpent* (New York: Vintage Books, 1989), 73–74. I am more interested in the interpretation that it is through the act of eating from the tree that the capacity for moral agency is achieved. Thomas Krüger associates it with the Enlightenment figures of Kant and Schiller ("Sündenfall? Überlegungen zur theologischen Bedeutung der Paradiesgeschichte," in *Beyond Eden*, ed. Konrad Schmid and Christoph Riedweg, FAT 2/34 [Tübingen: Mohr Siebeck, 2008], 102). Smith (*The Genesis of Good and Evil*, 38) notes that such an interpretation "can be found in the

1526 *Christian Catechism* of the Anabaptist Balthasar Hubmaier." He also lists numerous biblical scholars from Gunkel onwards who have embraced a similar interpretation.

27. The article by Carly L. Crouch, "*ḥṭ't* as Interpolative Gloss: A Solution to Gen 4,7," *ZAW* 123 (2011): 250–58, and the response by Matthew Richard Schlimm, "At Sin's Entryway (Gen 4,7)," *ZAW* 124 (2012): 409–15, discuss the difficulties and some of the various solutions proposed.
28. Gen 5:28–29 is generally taken to be non-P. See Gertz, "The Formation of the Primeval History," 123; and Robin B. ten Hoopen, "Genesis 5 and the Formation of the Primeval History: A Redaction Historical Case Study," *ZAW* 129 (2017): 180.
29. The position taken by the non-P narrative bears some resemblance to that later found in 4 Ezra. Although 4 Ezra argues that humanity is burdened by an "evil heart" from creation, the angel insists that a few manage to be righteous (7:45–60).
30. Schmid ("Die Unteilbarkeit der Weisheit," 37) notes the anti-eschatological stance of Gen 2–3, though he characterizes it as not fatalistic but rather realistic.
31. See, for example, Michael E. Stone, "Adam and Enoch and the State of the World," in *Ancient Judaism: New Visions and Views* (Grand Rapids, MI: Eerdmans, 2011), 31–58.
32. M. D. Johnson, "Life of Adam and Eve," in *The Old Testament Pseudepigrapha*, vol. 2, ed. James H. Charlesworth (Garden City, NY: Doubleday, 1985), 279.
33. Ariel Feldman, "4Q422 (Paraphrase of Genesis and Exodus)," in Ariel Feldman and Liora Goldman, *Scripture and Interpretation: Qumran Texts That Rework the Bible*, ed. Devorah Dimant, BZAW 449 (Berlin: De Gruyter, 2014), 88. In translating Second Temple texts I generally render *ṭôb wāra'* as "good and evil" rather than as "good and bad," since there seems to be a moralizing drift in the understanding of the phrase.
34. Feldman, "4Q222 (Paraphrase of Genesis and Exodus)," 90.
35. Shane Berg, "Ben Sira, the Genesis Creation Accounts, and the Knowledge of God's Will," *JBL* 132 (2013): 143. As Berg notes, Sir 16:24–17:14 focuses on knowledge of the law. A second passage, 15:11–20, deals with the capacity for obeying the law (145).
36. Sir 17:5 is a gloss added in the Greek tradition and so is omitted in many translations.
37. Patrick W. Skehan and Alexander A. Di Lella, *The Wisdom of Ben Sira*, AB 39 (New York: Doubleday, 1987), 282.
38. The term used for "discernment" (*diaboulion*) is the one also used to translate Hebrew *yēṣer* in 15:14b, where it has the meaning of "natural disposition" or "temperament" (so Samuel L. Adams, *Wisdom in Transition: Act and Consequence in Second Temple Instructions*, JSJSup 125 [Boston: Brill, 2008], 185).
39. Adams, *Wisdom in Transition*, 186.

40. It is possible that Sir 25:24 ("For from a woman sin had its beginning, and because of her we all die," NRSV) refers to Gen 3:1–6, though some have argued that the context points to Ben Sira's view of women in general, not to the mythic Eve. So John R. Levison, "Is Eve to Blame? A Contextual Analysis of Sir. 25.24," *CBQ* 47 (1985): 617–23. If it is a reference to Eve, the verse may be a later insertion, as it is inconsistent with 17:7 and Ben Sira's carefully developed views there (Samuel L. Adams, private communication). To be sure, such interpretations of the dire consequences of the first disobedience did develop, though it is difficult to find in Second Temple sources a formulation as pointed as Paul's in Rom 5:12 ("Therefore, just as sin came into the world through one man, and death came through sin . . ."). I, however, am interested in tracing out a different trajectory of interpretation.
41. *episkeptetai*, perhaps translating Hebrew *pāqad*.
42. "corrupt, adj." OED Online, March 2020, Oxford University Press, https://www-oed-com.proxy.library.emory.edu/view/Entry/42034?rskey=NaGAQJ&result=1 (accessed May 14, 2020).
43. See the analysis of Wold, "Genesis 2–3 in Early Christian Tradition," 329–46.
44. Wold, "Genesis 2–3," 332.
45. Wold, "Genesis 2–3," 333 n. 12.
46. Matthew J. Goff, *4QInstruction*, WLAW 2 (Atlanta: SBL, 2013), 15.
47. See Tigchelaar, "Changing Truths."
48. See Eibert Tigchelaar, "'Spiritual People,' 'Fleshly Spirit,' and 'Vision of Meditation': Reflections on *4QInstruction* and 1 Corinthians," in *Echoes from the Caves: Qumran and the New Testament*, ed. Florentino García Martínez (Leiden: Brill, 2009), 111 n. 34, for a careful discussion of the reading.
49. Tigchelaar, "'Spiritual People,'" 113–14, argues that the phrase "vision of meditation" explicates the meaning of "book of remembrance" and refers to "the predestined plan of history itself."
50. Cana Werman, "What Is the *Book of Hagu*?" in *Sapiential Perspectives: Wisdom Literature in Light of the Dead Sea Scrolls: Proceedings of the Sixth International Symposium of the Orion Center for the Study of the Dead Sea Scrolls and Associated Literature, 20–22 May, 2001*, ed. John G. Collins, Gregory E. Sterling, and Ruth A. Clements, STDJ 51 (Leiden: Brill, 2004), 137–38.
51. John J. Collins, "In the Likeness of the Holy Ones: The Creation of Humankind in a Wisdom Text from Qumran," in *The Provo International Conference on the Dead Sea Scrolls: Technological Innovations, New Texts, and Reformulated Issues*, ed. Donald W. Parry and Eugene Ulrich, STDJ 30 (Leiden: Brill, 1998), 612, 615.
52. The second occurrence of *'m* is written interlinearly.
53. Cana Werman, "What Is the Book of Hagu?" 137. See also Wold, *4QInstruction: Divisions and Hierarchies*, STDJ 123 (Leiden: Brill, 2018), 106.
54. Collins, "In the Likeness of the Holy Ones," 615–18.

55. Wold (*4QInstruction,* 106) observes that "the emphasis is on humanity possessing a spirit, and a segment of humanity (i.e., *rwḥ bśr*) is wayward and dispossessed of revealed wisdom."
56. Lange, *Weisheit und Prädestination*, 88–89.
57. Bakker, "The Figure of the Sage," 204.
58. Bakker, "The Figure of the Sage," 197. One might compare the enigmatic passage in 1 En 32:3-6, where Enoch sees the "paradise of righteousness," including the "tree of wisdom, whose fruit the holy ones eat and learn great wisdom" (trans. Nickelsburg). This is the tree from which the first humans "ate and learned wisdom." Thus Adam and Eve did acquire access to heavenly wisdom. But in contrast to Bakker's interpretation of 4QInstruction, in Enoch the heavenly wisdom was forbidden to Adam and Eve and resulted in their expulsion from paradise. Such wisdom is, however, provided to Enoch through his instruction by the holy ones.
59. Jean-Sébastian Rey, *4QInstruction: Sagesse et eschatologie*, STDJ 81 (Leiden: Brill, 2009), 304.
60. Bakker, "The Figure of the Sage," 230–36, has a somewhat different interpretation. He also takes "spirit of flesh" as a description of human creation as dust/flesh imbued with spirit. But he argues that *ʿwd* should be rendered as "still" or "not yet" (cf. 2 Chr 20:33), translating: "But He had not yet given contemplation to the fleshly spirit, because he did not know how to distinguish between good and evil according to the judgment of his spirit." Thus *hāgû* is not something taken away but something not immediately given. As Bakker explains, "God apportions heavenly knowledge to mankind, but He had not yet given it at the moment of creation." Nevertheless, 4Q417 1 i 6–8 seems to assume that the *mēbîn* has the present capacity to meditate on the mystery of existence and that this is what results in understanding good and evil. Bakker's reading would seem to imply that one would have to achieve such knowledge before being granted access to meditation or contemplation.
61. Judith H. Newman, "Words of the Luminaries," in *T&T Clark Companion to the Dead Sea Scrolls*, ed. George J. Brooke and Charlotte Hempel (London: T&T Clark, 2019), 365–66. Although first published by Maurice Baillet in DJD 7: 237–75, the reconstruction of the text in the edition of the *DSSR* follows the reconstruction by Esther Chazon, *The Words of the Luminaries: Critical Edition, Commentary, and Socio-Historical Implications*, DSSE (Leiden: Brill, forthcoming).
62. Michael A. Knibb, "The Exile in the Literature of the Intertestamental Period," *Heythrop Journal* 17 (1976): 253–72.
63. Maurice Baillet, DJD 7: 163. Since references to the glory of Adam occur in several Second Temple texts, it is unlikely that the author of 4QDibHam is innovating here, rather than appropriating an established interpretation.
64. Though šmr does occur in l. 8.

65. Baillet (DJD 7: 163) indicates that the reading of *samekh* in *s*[*wr*] is certain.
66. Tantalizingly, although there are no clear allusions to Ezek 28, the presentation of Adam in 4QDibHam is strongly evocative of that text, especially Ezek 28:12b–16. The similarities include a glorious human who is endowed with wisdom, placed in Eden, given royal responsibilities, but nevertheless becomes "filled with lawlessness" (Ezek 28:16).
67. Esther Chazon ("The Creation and Fall of Adam in the Dead Sea Scrolls," in *The Book of Genesis in Jewish and Oriental Christian Interpretation: A Collection of Essays*, ed. Judith Frishman and Lucas van Rompay, TEG 5 [Leuven: Peeters, 1997], 15) suggests it may be an allusion to Gen 6:3, thus "foreshadowing the *antediluvian* sin and its punishment" (italics in original).
68. Jörg Frey ("Flesh and Spirit in the Palestinian Jewish Sapiential Tradition and in the Qumran Texts: An Inquiry into the Background of Pauline Usage," in *The Wisdom Texts from Qumran and the Development of Sapiential Thought*, ed. Charlotte Hempel, Armin Lange, and Hermann Lichtenberger, BETL 159 [Leuven: Peeters, 2002], 397–400) analyzes the emergence of "flesh" as a category for moral weakness, though he does not discuss this passage.
69. Baillet, DJD 7: 163. Chazon, "Creation and Fall," 15.
70. As Baillet (DJD 7: 162) and Chazon ("Creation and Fall," 15) suggest, the wording "[filling the]earth with [vi]olence and sheddi[ng blood]" is similar to 1 En 9:3.
71. See the discussion above concerning the ambiguity of the syntax in Deut 30:1–2. Most interpreters take those verses as referring to human agency in returning to God, who then circumcises the heart to prevent future failure. As Marc Zvi Brettler ("Predestination," 175–79) notes, it is possible to read Deut 30:1–2 as referring to preparatory divine action.
72. Harold Bloom, *Agon: Towards a Theory of Revisionism* (New York: Oxford University Press, 1982), 285.

Chapter 6. The Hodayot of the Maskil and the Subjectivity of the Masochistic Sublime

1. The distinction between Teacher and Community hodayot has recently been questioned on various grounds by Angela Kim Harkins, *Reading with an "I" to the Heavens: Looking at the Qumran Hodayot through the Lens of Visionary Traditions*, Ekstasis 3 (Berlin: De Gruyter, 2012); and Michael Johnson, "Reassessing the Genres of the Hodayot: Thanksgiving Psalms from Qumran" (PhD diss., McMaster University, 2019).
2. Cols. 1–3 are almost wholly missing, and it is possible that col. 18 serves as a conclusion to the Teacher collection.
3. See Carol A. Newsom, "A Farewell to the Hodyaot of the Community," *DSD* 28 (2021): 1–19.

4. Newsom, *The Self as Symbolic Space*, 165–74, 277–84.
5. This differentiation is most apparent in the recension of the Self-Glorification Hymn that is incorporated into the Hodayot in cols. 25–27.
6. The reasons for distinguishing the formulas that introduce the beginnings of compositions from those that introduce subsections are given by Hartmut Stegemann, "The Number of Psalms in *1QHodayot*[a] and Some of Their Sections," in *Liturgical Perspectives: Prayer and Poetry in Light of the Dead Sea Scrolls: Proceedings of the Fifth International Symposium of the Orion Center for the Study of the Dead Sea Scrolls and Associated Literature, 19–23 January, 2000*, ed. Esther G. Chazon, with Ruth Clements and Avital Pinnick, STDJ 48 (Leiden: Brill, 2003), 191–234.
7. The opening benediction is restored in these cases based on the practice of scribe A of leaving a vacat at the end of the section. Thus the vacats visible in 4:20, 28, and 37 are indications of a new psalm or subsection beginning in the following line.
8. The most extensive study of the epistemic formulae ("I know") and its relationship to the emplacement of spirits within the speaker is that of Rony Kozman, "Ezekiel's Promised Spirit as *adam*'s Revelatory Spirit in the Hodayot," *DSD* 26 (2019): 30–60.
9. Cf. also similar expressions in Ezek 11:19 and 37:6, 14.
10. This term was coined by Heinz-Wolfgang Kuhn, *Enderwartung und gegenwärtiges Heil*, SUNT 3 (Göttingen: Vandenhoeck & Ruprecht, 1966), 26–29.
11. Small and occasional passages reflecting this negative anthropology also occur in the Teacher Hodayot but do not seem to be a standard element of them.
12. Lichtenberger, *Studien zum Menschenbild*, 84–85; Nicholas A. Meyer, *Adam's Dust and Adam's Glory in the Hodayot and the Letters of Paul: Rethinking Anthropology and Theology*, SNT 168 (Leiden: Brill, 2016), 33–34. Meyer's forthcoming study "Born of Woman, Fashioned from Clay: Tracking the Homology of Earth and Womb from the Hebrew Bible to the Psalms of Thanksgiving," *DSD* 28 (2021), is the most thorough investigation of this motif.
13. The new study by John Francis Elwolde ("The Human Spirit and the Holy Spirit in the Qumran Hodayot," in *Sacred Texts and Disparate Interpretations: Qumran Manuscripts Seventy Years Later: Proceedings of the International Conference Held at the John Paul II Catholic University of Lublin, 24–26 October, 2017*, ed. Henryk Drawnel, STDJ 133 [Leiden: Brill, 2020], 281–315) appeared too late for me to engage.
14. Stephen J. Hultgren, *From the Damascus Covenant to the Covenant of the Community: Literary, Historical and Theological Studies in the Dead Sea Scrolls*, STDJ 66 (Leiden: Brill, 2007), 436–37. See the effective refutation by Meyer, *Adam's Dust*, 38.
15. Matthew Goff, "Reading Wisdom at Qumran: 4QInstruction and the Hodayot," *DSD* 11 (2004): 263–88; Eibert Tigchelaar, *To Increase Learning for the*

Understanding Ones: Reading and Reconstructing the Fragmentary Early Jewish Sapiential Text 4QInstruction, STDJ 44 (Leiden: Brill, 2001), 203–7.

16. Armin Lange, *Weisheit und Prädestination*, 220–22.
17. See the previous chapter for a discussion of Gen 1 and the Two Spirits Teaching. Although the anthropology of 1Q/4QInstruction remains debated, 4Q417 1 I 16–18 clearly constructs its anthropological speculation on the basis of a combination of Gen 1 and 2–3. See Matthew J. Goff, *4QInstruction*, 162–68.
18. Of the forty-two occurrences of the noun in the Hodayot, only two might possibly refer to a fixed evil disposition in humans (13:8 and 19:23), and these are equally subject to different interpretations. See further discussion below.
19. 4Q267 (4QD[b]) 1 5 uses the phrase "dust and ashes," though in a broken context. 4Q301 (4QMyst[c]?) 4 3 preserves the words "what is ash[. . . ," though it is not clear that this is an allusion to Job. See also Sir 17:32, 19:9, and 40:3, which use the phrase for human weakness. Only in 17:32 is there a possible allusion to moral weakness. See the discussion of Sir 17:20–32 in chap. 5 above.
20. I discuss the methodology for discerning implicit exegesis and intertextuality more fully in "Deriving Negative Anthropology through Exegetical Activity: The Hodayot as Case Study," in *Is There a Text in This Cave? Studies in the Textuality of the Dead Sea Scrolls in Honour of George J. Brooke*, ed. Ariel Feldman, Maria Cioată, and Charlotte Hempel, STDJ 119 (Leiden: Brill, 2017), 262–64.
21. Statistics are based on the word list in Eileen M. Schuller and Carol A. Newsom, *The Hodayot (Thanksgiving Psalms): A Study Edition of 1QH[a]*, EJL 36 (Atlanta: SBL, 2012).
22. The term "spirit" (*rûaḥ*) also figures prominently as an anthropological term in the Hodayot, most often in a neutral sense, referring to the human self and its various dispositions. But it also occurs in expressions of negative anthropology, and in statements referring to the positive transformation of the speaker through God's action. This topic will be taken up below.
23. The term in 4Q299 appears to be a verb, not a noun, contra the Qumran Concordance. Martin G. Abegg, Jr., with James E. Bowley and Edward M. Cook, *The Dead Sea Scrolls Concordance,* vol. 1: *The Non-Biblical Texts from Qumran* (Leiden: Brill, 2003), 319.
24. Jonas C. Greenfield, "The Root 'GBL' in Mishnaic Hebrew and in the Hymnic Literature from Qumran," *RevQ* 2(1960): 157–58.
25. The Hodayot of the Maskil do use the term to refer to "the *yēṣer* of every spirit" (7:26), a possibly predeterministic usage, implying some good and some bad spirits. Similarly, they refer to the bad *yēṣer* of the wicked (21:29, 30). In one case in 19:23 ("and trouble was not hidden from my eyes when I knew the *yiṣrê* of humans") the term might possibly refer to the notion of general human tendencies toward evil, but the following phrase suggests it may instead simply refer to mortality ("and I un[derstood] to what mortals return"). In the Teacher

Hodayot it can refer to an individual's bad impulses (13:8), especially that of the wicked (15:6), and to general intentions, whether good or bad (15:16, 19). Possibly the phrase "vessel/inclination of flesh" (*yēṣer bāśār*) in 24:6 is analogous to the phrase "spirit of flesh," though the context is broken. Had the authors of the Hodayot wished to exploit Gen 6:5 and 8:21, one would expect clearer intertextual allusions.

26. Frey, "Flesh and Spirit," 398, notes but does not elaborate on the role of Job 4: 17–21, 14:1–4, and 15:14–16 in the anthropology of the Hodayot.
27. Lichtenberger, *Studien zum Menschenbild*, 84–85; Meyer, *Adam's Dust*, 33–34, 47–53.
28. Jonathan Klawans, *Impurity and Sin*, 90.
29. 4Q266 [4QD[a]] 6 ii 11 seems to suggest that the child is born pure but can become unclean if it nurses from its unclean mother. Thus it is to be supplied with a wet nurse.
30. James VanderKam, *Jubilees*, 1:214, notes that Jubilees itself says nothing about the purity or impurity of the first couple but discusses only the time periods associated with each. Baumgarten and Harrington, cited below, do assume that a connection with impurity is implied.
31. Joseph M. Baumgarten, "Purification after Childbirth and the Sacred Garden in 4Q265 and Jubilees," in *New Qumran Texts and Studies: Proceedings of the First Meeting of the International Organization for Qumran Studies, Paris 1992*, ed. George Brooke and Florentino García Martínez, STDJ 15 (Leiden: Brill, 1994), 6 n. 5.
32. Hannah K. Harrington, *The Purity Texts* (London: T&T Clark, 2004), 62, 100. Harrington refers to 1QS 9:9–10, an apparent error for 1QS 11:9–10 and 1QH[a] 9:22 (now renumbered as 9:24), that is to say, the *Niedrigkeitsdoxologien*.
33. In certain predestinarian passages in the Hodayot another kind of reference to spirit occurs. The speaker says of God, "You created every spirit" (using the verb *yṣr*, 7:26, 35; 9:11, 17; 18:24), sometimes with further references to the fate of the righteous and the wicked. Other passages claim that God casts the lot for persons "according to their spirit" (6:22; cf. 3:26; 8:28). These passages may represent the traces of an alternative understanding of creation that is more dualistic. Perhaps it is the case that, as in the book of Job, different assumptions about anthropology and moral agency come into play depending on whether the speaker is thinking "horizontally" in terms of the righteous and the wicked and their fates, or thinking "vertically" in terms of all humans vis-à-vis God. It is not impossible, of course, to coordinate both ways of speaking, since God has apparently predetermined which humans are to be transformed. But neither is it necessary to make a fully self-consistent discourse out of the Hodayot. The tension between a sharp divide between the righteous and the wicked and the need to posit moral struggles within the sectarian self is analogous to that

which appears in the Two Spirits Teaching. Thus it is not improbable that different formulations could make their appearance according to the context of speech.

34. Nathan MacDonald, "The Spirit of God," 95–120.
35. In the final subsection of that composition in 4:38–41 God is blessed for having sprinkled God's holy spirit upon the speaker and purified him. Then in l. 39 a reference is made either to "the whole covenant of Adam" (*kwl bryt 'dm*) or to "all the insight of Adam" (*kwl bnyt 'dm*). The reading is difficult, but I think that, contextually, the phrase is more likely to be "all the insight of Adam."
36. Newsom, *Self as Symbolic Space*, 220.
37. Newsom, *Self as Symbolic Space*, 209–29.
38. As in Armin Lange's important monograph, *Weisheit und Prädestination*, which focuses on the content of the ideas and their derivation.
39. So E. H. Merrill, *Qumran and Predestination: A Theological Study of the Thanksgiving Hymns*, STDJ 8 (Leiden: Brill, 1975), 58; Eileen M. Schuller, "Petitionary Prayer and the Religion of Qumran," in *Religion in the Dead Sea Scrolls*, ed. J. J. Collins and R. A. Kugler (Grand Rapids, MI: Eerdmans, 2000), 45; Alex Jassen, "Religion in the Dead Sea Scrolls," *RC* 1 (2007): 11.
40. Klawans, "Compatibilism," 63.
41. Klawans, "Compatibilism," 63.
42. Klawans, "Compatibilism," 64, citing Schuller, "Petitionary Prayer," 40–41.
43. Since "moral agency" could be subject to somewhat different definitions, it is important to specify how I use the term here. When I speak of a moral agent, I mean a self who has (1) personal awareness and knowledge, coupled with (2) emotional investment (desire/aversion), which can be directed toward (3) intentional, purposeful action. Agency is "moral" in that the person is held accountable for his or her understanding, affect, and action.
44. This assessment of the beginning of the psalm assumes Stegemann's reconstruction of the scroll and the placement of frg. 10 in col. 7:11–21, which is debated. If frg. 10 is incorrectly placed, then it is likely that the psalm began at or near the top of col. 7.
45. This is the way the noun *ndbh* is normally understood (*HALOT* 2:672, "free motivation"; *TDOT* 9:226, "free decision," "free motivation"). Recently, Menachem Kister has argued that the nuance of *ndbh* is more properly "zealousness." See "The Root NDB in the Scrolls and the Growth of Qumran Texts: Lexicography and Theology," in *Meghillot: Studies in the Dead Sea Scrolls*, 11–12, ed. J. Ben-Dov and M. Kister (Haifa: Haifa University; Jerusalem: Bialik Institute and The Hebrew University Magness, 2015), 111–30 (Heb). However one resolves the semantics of that noun, the context of lines 23–25 is clearly voluntarist.
46. See Stegemann and Schuller, DJD 40:103, for discussion of the basis for the restoration. Qimron's restoration differs (*ky' l' byd bśr* [*rwḥw wl' l*]*'dm drkw*), but it

expresses a comparable sentiment. See Elisha Qimron, *The Dead Sea Scrolls: The Hebrew Writings*, 3 vols. (Jerusalem: Yad Izhak Ben-Zvi, 2020), 1: 66.

47. Katherine Ewing, "The Illusion of Wholeness: Culture, Self, and the Experience of Inconsistency," *Ethos* 18 (1990): 251, 258.
48. Naomi Quinn, "The Self," *AT* 6 (2006): 365.
49. Carol Newsom, "Models of Moral Agency: Hebrew Bible and Second Temple Judaism," *JBL* 131 (2012): 15.
50. Claudia Strauss ("Research on Cultural Discontinuities," in *A Cognitive Theory of Cultural Meaning*, ed. Claudia Strauss and Naomi Quinn [Cambridge: Cambridge University Press, 1997], 210–51) has investigated the phenomenon of "discrepant ideas" in the discourse of individuals in an attempt to discover how these discrepancies are internalized by persons. Where contradictory or discrepant discourses are reported in separate conversations, it appears that individuals are compartmentalizing their beliefs without examining them in relation to one another. Where such discourses are closely juxtaposed, informants tend to partly integrate one discourse with another, more dominant one in a way that reduces discordant implications (215). Analogously, it seems more likely that discrepant conceptual frameworks in Qumran texts that appear at some distance from one another may reflect compartmentalization, whereas one should investigate the possibility of complex integration when such discrepancies are more closely juxtaposed. This is the approach that I take here.
51. Also, the model of the self as nothing more than a sequence of contextual performances is increasingly being challenged within anthropological theory as inadequate and requires reconsideration in itself. See Quinn, "The Self," 362–84.
52. Although one could see this account as a theorizing of the narrative depictions of dual agency discussed in chap. 2, it does not appear that the Hodayot draw on these models self-consciously.
53. Martin Heidegger, "Language," in *Hermeneutical Inquiry*, vol. 1: *The Interpretation of Texts*, ed. David E. Klemm, AARSR 43 (Atlanta: Scholars, 1986), 142.
54. Heidegger, "Language," 149–50.

Conclusion

1. I address the relationship of these traditions briefly in "Toward a Genealogy of the Introspective Self in Second Temple Judaism," in *Functions of Psalms and Prayers in the Late Second Temple Period*, ed. Mika Pajunen and Jeremy Penner, BZAW 486 (Berlin: De Gruyter, 2017), 73–76. David Lambert (*How Repentance Became Biblical*, 151–71) notes the close relationship between the development of a discourse of repentance and assumptions about interiority and subjectivity. He discusses what appears to be a Jewish adaptation of notions of subjectivity that were earlier developed in Greek culture in a number of late Second

Temple texts, including the Testaments of the Twelve Patriarchs. See also Ishay Rosen-Zvi, "Bilhah the Temptress: The Testament of Reuben and 'The Birth of Sexuality,'" *JQR* 96 (2006): 65–94, who discusses the shift from a focus on the morality of action to the morality of desire in this text. More generally, see Tom de Bruin, *The Great Controversy: The Individual's Struggle between Good and Evil in the Testaments of the Twelve Patriarchs and in Their Jewish and Christian Contexts* (Göttingen: Vandenhoeck & Ruprecht, 2013).

2. Jean Carmignac, "Les affinités qumrâniennes de la onzième Ode de Salomon," *RevQ* 3 (1961): 71–102; "Un Qumrânien converti au Christianisme: L'auteur des Odes de Salomon," in *Qumran-Probleme: Vorträge des Leipziger Symposions* über *Qumran-Probleme vom 9. bis 14. Oktober 1961*, ed. Hans Bardtke, SSA 42 (Berlin: Akademie-Verlag, 1963), 75–108. James H. Charlesworth, "Les Odes de Salomon et les manuscrits de la mer Morte," *RB* 77 (1970): 522–49; "The *Odes of Solomon* and the Jewish Wisdom Texts," in *The Wisdom Texts from Qumran and the Development of Sapiential Thought*, ed. Charlotte Hempel, Armin Lange, and Hermann Lichtenberger, BETL 159 (Leuven: Peeters, 2001), 323–49. See also Charlesworth's valuable annotated bibliography in *Critical Reflections on the Odes of Solomon*, vol. 1: *Literary Setting, Textual Studies, Gnosticism, the Dead Sea Scrolls and the Gospel of John*, JSPSup 22 (Sheffield: Sheffield Academic, 1998), 261–85.

3. See, e.g., Meyer, *Adam's Dust and Adam's Glory*; John M. G. Barclay, *Paul and the Gift* (Grand Rapids, MI: Eerdmans, 2015), 239–65; Jason Maston, *Divine and Human Agency in Second Temple Judaism: A Comparative Study*, WUNT 297 (Tübingen: Mohr Siebeck, 2010); John M. G. Barclay and Simon J. Gathercole, eds., *Divine and Human Agency in Paul and His Cultural Environment*, LNTS 335 (London: T&T Clark, 2006); Jörg Frey, "Flesh and Spirit" and "The Notion of 'Flesh' in 4QInstruction and the Background of Pauline Usage," in *Sapiential, Liturgical and Poetical Texts from Qumran*, ed. F. García Martínez, STDJ 35 (Leiden: Brill, 2000), 197–226.

4. The most programmatic analyses are those of Troels Engberg-Pedersen, *Cosmology and Self in the Apostle Paul: The Material Spirit* (Oxford: Oxford University Press, 2010); and *Paul and the Stoics* (Louisville: Westminster John Knox, 2000). His approach has been criticized for sidelining Paul's indebtedness to a Jewish theological and specifically apocalyptic worldview. See the extended review essay by J. Louis Martyn, "De-apocalypticizing Paul: An Essay Focused on *Paul and the Stoics* by Troels Engberg-Pedersen," *JSNT* 24 (2002): 61–102. The most subtle and insightful recent study of Paul's similarities to and differences from late Stoic views on personhood is that of Susan Grove Eastman, *Paul and the Person: Reframing Paul's Anthropology* (Grand Rapids, MI: Eerdmans, 2017). Her study is analogous to my own inquiries in that it also seeks to read ancient texts in light of contemporary neuroscience and psychology.

5. As A. A. Long observes, "Stoic doctrine gives human beings a special status in the universe, both in their direct 'kinship' as rational beings with Zeus, and in their interpersonal relationships to other people or other 'divine spirits,'" *Greek Models of Mind and Self* (Cambridge, MA: Harvard University Press, 2015), 182.
6. See Katja Vogt, "Seneca," *Stanford Encyclopedia of Philosophy*, for a consideration of how to characterize Seneca's perspectives.
7. Mikhail Bakhtin, *Problems of Dostoevsky's Poetics*, ed. and trans. Caryl Emerson (Minneapolis: University of Minnesota Press, 1984), 91.

Bibliography

Abegg, Martin G., Jr., with James E. Bowley and Edward M. Cook. *The Dead Sea Scrolls Concordance.* Vol. 1: *The Non-Biblical Texts from Qumran.* Leiden: Brill, 2003.

Adams, Samuel L. *Wisdom in Transition: Act and Consequence in Second Temple Instructions.* JSJSup 125. Boston: Brill, 2008.

Ahearn, Laura M. "Language and Agency." *ARA* 30 (2001): 109–37.

Albertz, Rainer, and Claus Westermann. "*rûaḥ.*" *THAT* 2: 726–53.

Alonso Schökel, Luis. "Sapiential and Covenant Themes in Genesis 2–3." Pages 468–80 in *Studies in Ancient Israelite Wisdom.* Edited by James L. Crenshaw. New York: Ktav, 1976.

Althaus, Rüdiger, Judith Hahn, and Matthias Pulte, eds. *Im Dienste der Gerechigkeit und Einheit: Festschrift für Heinrich J. F. Reinhardt zur Vollendung seines 75. Lebensjahres.* Essen: Ludgerus Verlag, 2017.

Baillet, Maurice. *Qumrân Grotte 4.III (4Q482–4Q520),* DJD 7. Oxford: Clarendon, 1982.

Bakhtin, Mikhail. *Problems of Dostoevsky's Poetics.* Edited and translated by Caryl Emerson. Minneapolis: University of Minnesota Press, 1984.

Bakker, Arjen. "The Figure of the Sage in Musar le-Mevin and Serek ha-Yahad." PhD diss., Katholieke Universiteit Leuven, 2015.

Bandura, Alfred. "Toward a Psychology of Human Agency." *PPS* 1 (2006): 164–80.

Barclay, John M. G. *Paul and the Gift.* Grand Rapids, MI: Eerdmans, 2015.

Barclay, John M. G., and Simon J. Gathercole, eds. *Divine and Human Agency in Paul and His Cultural Environment.* LNTS 335.

Barr, James. *The Garden of Eden and the Hope of Immortality.* Minneapolis: Fortress, 1993.

Barton, John. *Understanding Old Testament Ethics: Approaches and Explanations.* Louisville: Westminster John Knox, 2003.

Bauks, Michaela. "Erkenntnis und Leben in Gen 2–3: Zum Wandel eines ursprünglich weisheitlich geprägten Lebensbegriffs." *ZAW* 127 (2015): 20–42.

———. "Sacred Trees in the Garden of Eden and Their Ancient Near Eastern Precursors." *JAJ* 3 (2012): 267–301.

Berg, Shane. "Ben Sira, the Genesis Creation Accounts, and the Knowledge of God's Will." *JBL* 132 (2013): 139–57.

Blenkinsopp, Joseph. *The Pentateuch: An Introduction to the First Five Books of the Bible.* New York: Doubleday, 1992.

Blount, Benjamin. "Situating Cultural Models in History and Cognition." Pages 271–98 in *Approaches to Language, Culture, and Cognition: The Intersection of Cognitive Linguistics and Linguistic Anthropology*. Edited by Masataka Yamaguchi, Dennis Tay, and Benjamin Blount. New York: Palgrave Macmillan, 2014.

Boas, Franz. *The Mind of Primitive Man*. New York: Macmillan, 1911.

Boehm, Christopher. *Hierarchy in the Forest: The Evolution of Egalitarian Behavior.* Cambridge, MA: Harvard University Press, 1999.

Botterweck, G. Johannes, Helmer Ringgren, Heinz-Josef Fabry, and Holger Gzella, eds. *Theological Dictionary of the Old Testament*. Translated by John T. Willis, David E. Green, and Douglas W. Stott. 16 vols. Grand Rapids, MI: Eerdmans: 1974–2018.

Brand, Miryam T. *Evil Within and Without: The Source of Sin and Its Nature as Portrayed in Second Temple Literature*. JAJSup 9. Göttingen: Vandenhoeck & Ruprecht, 2013.

Brettler, Marc Zvi. "Predestination in Deuteronomy 30:1–10." Pages 171–88 in *Those Elusive Deuteronomists: The Phenomenon of Pan-Deuteronomism*. Edited by Linda S. Schearing and Steven L. McKenzie. JSOTSup 268. Sheffield: Sheffield Academic, 1999.

Brooke, George J. "Body Parts in *Barkhi Nafshi* and the Qualifications for Membership of the Worshipping Community." Pages 79–94 in *Sapiential, Liturgical and Poetical Texts from Qumran: Proceedings of the Third Meeting of the International Organization for Qumran Studies, Published in Memory of Maurice Baillet*. Edited by Daniel K. Falk, Florentino García Martínez, and Eileen M. Schuller. STDJ 35. Leiden: Brill, 2000.

Brunner, Hellmut. *Altägyptische Erziehung*. Wiesbaden: Harrassowitz, 1957.

Buber, Martin. *The Prophetic Faith*. Translated by Carlyle Witton-Davies. New York: Macmillan, 1949.

Bührer, Walter. "The Relative Dating of the Eden Narrative Gen *2–3." *VT* 65 (2015): 365–76.

Burke, Kenneth. *A Grammar of Motives*. Berkeley: University of California Press, 1969.

Callicott, Baird. "Genesis and John Muir." Pages 187–219 in *Beyond the Land Ethic: More Essays in Environmental Philosophy*. Albany: SUNY Press, 1999.

Carmignac, Jean. "Les affinités qumrâniennes de la onzième Ode de Salomon." *RevQ* 3 (1961): 71–102.

———. "Un Qumrânien converti au Christianisme: L'auteur des Odes de Salomon." Pages 75–108 in *Qumran-Probleme: Vorträge des Leipziger Symposions über*

Qumran-Probleme vom 9. bis 14. Oktober 1961. Edited by Hans Bardtke. SSA 42. Berlin: Akademie-Verlag, 1963.

Carr, David M. *The Formation of the Hebrew Bible: A New Reconstruction*. New York: Oxford University Press, 2011.

———. *Writing on the Tablet of the Heart: Origins of Scripture and Literature*. New York: Oxford University Press, 2005.

Carrithers, Michael, Steven Collins, and Steven Lukes, eds. *The Category of the Person*. Cambridge: Cambridge University Press, 1985.

Carson, Anne. *Eros the Bittersweet*. Princeton, NJ: Princeton University Press, 1986.

Charlesworth, James H. *Critical Reflections on the Odes of Solomon*. Vol. 1: *Literary Setting, Textual Studies, Gnosticism, the Dead Sea Scrolls and the Gospel of John*. JSPSup 22. Sheffield: Sheffield Academic, 1998.

———. "Les Odes de Salomon et les manuscrits de la mer Morte." *RB* 77 (1970): 522–49.

———. "The *Odes of Solomon* and the Jewish Wisdom Texts." Pages 323–49 in *The Wisdom Texts from Qumran and the Development of Sapiential Thought*. Edited by Charlotte Hempel, Armin Lange, and Hermann Lichtenberger. BETL 159. Leuven: Peeters, 2001.

Chazon, Esther. "The Creation and Fall of Adam in the Dead Sea Scrolls." Pages 13–24 in *The Book of Genesis in Jewish and Oriental Christian Interpretation: A Collection of Essays*. Edited by Judith Frishman and Lucas van Rompay. TEG 5. Leuven: Peeters, 1997.

———. *The Words of the Luminaries: Critical Edition, Commentary, and Socio-Historical Implications*. DSSE. Leiden: Brill, forthcoming.

Chiang, Ted. *Stories of Your Life and Others*. New York: Vintage Books, 2016.

Christian, Mieke. "The Literary Development of the 'Treatise of the Two Spirits' as Dependent on Instruction and the Hodayot." Pages 153–84 in *Law, Literature, and Society in Legal Texts from Qumran: Papers from the Ninth Meeting of the International Organization for Qumran Studies, Leuven 2016*. Edited by Jutta Jokiranta and Molly Zahn. STDJ 128. Leiden: Brill, 2019.

Clarke, Michael J. *Flesh and Spirit in the Songs of Homer: A Study of Words and Myths*. Oxford: Clarendon, 1999.

Clifford, Richard. *Proverbs: A Commentary*. OTL. Louisville: Westminster John Knox, 1999.

Clines, D.J.A. "The Tree of Knowledge and the Law of Yahweh (Psalm XIX)." *VT* 24 (1974): 8–14.

Clines, D.J.A., and D. M. Gunn, "'You Tried to Persuade Me' and 'Violence! Outrage!' in Jeremiah XX 7–8." *VT* 23 (1978): 20–27.

Cohen Stuart, Geert H. *The Struggle in Man between Good and Evil: An Inquiry into the Origin of the Rabbinic Concept of Yeser Hara*. Kampen: Kok, 1984.

Collins, Billie Jean. *The Hittites and Their World*. ABS 7. Atlanta: SBL, 2007.

Collins, John J. "In the Likeness of the Holy Ones: The Creation of Humankind in a Wisdom Text from Qumran." Pages 609–18 in *The Provo International Conference on the Dead Sea Scrolls: Technological Innovations, New Texts, and Reformulated Issues*. Edited by Donald W. Parry and Eugene Ulrich. STDJ 30. Leiden: Brill, 1998.

———. *The Invention of Judaism: Torah and Jewish Identity from Deuteronomy to Paul*. Oakland: University of California Press, 2017.

Cottrill, Amy C. *Language, Power, and Identity in the Lament Psalms of the Individual*. LHBOTS 493. New York: T&T Clark, 2008.

Crenshaw, James L. *Old Testament Wisdom: An Introduction*. Rev. and enl. ed. Louisville: Westminster John Knox, 1998.

Cross, Frank M. *From Epic to Canon: History and Literature in Ancient Israel*. Baltimore: Johns Hopkins University Press, 1998.

Crouch, Carly L. "*ḥṭʾt* as Interpolative Gloss: A Solution to Gen 4,7." *ZAW* 123 (2011): 250–58.

Damasio, Antonio. *Self Comes to Mind: Constructing the Conscious Brain*. New York: Vintage, 2010.

de Bruin, Tom. *The Great Controversy: The Individual's Struggle between Good and Evil in the Testaments of the Twelve Patriarchs and in Their Jewish and Christian Contexts*. Göttingen: Vandenhoeck & Ruprecht, 2013.

de Jong, Albert. "Iranian Connections in the Dead Sea Scrolls." Pages 479–500 in *The Oxford Handbook of the Dead Sea Scrolls*. Edited by Timothy H. Lim and John J. Collins. New York: Oxford University Press, 2010.

de Waal, Franz. *Are We Smart Enough to Know How Smart Animals Are?* New York: W. W. Norton & Co., 2017.

———. *Peacemaking among Primates*. Cambridge, MA: Harvard University Press, 1990.

Dietrich, Jan. *Kollektive Schuld und Haftung*. ORA 4. Tübingen: Mohr Siebeck, 2010.

DiFransico, Lesley R. *Washing Away Sin: An Analysis of the Metaphor in the Hebrew Bible and Its Influence*. BTS 23. Leuven: Peeters, 2016.

Di Vito, Robert A. "Old Testament Anthropology and the Construction of Personal Identity." *CBQ* 61 (1999): 217–38.

Donald, Merlin. *A Mind So Rare: The Evolution of Human Consciousness*. New York: W. W. Norton & Co., 2001.

Duckworth, Tyler. "Cultivating *Rûaḥ* in the Ethos of Proverbs." Paper presented at the Society of Biblical Literature International Meeting, Helsinki, Finland, August 2, 2018.

Dumont, Louis. "A Modified View of Our Origins: The Christian Beginnings of Modern Individualism." Pages 93–122 in *The Category of the Person*. Edited by Michael Carrithers, Steven Collins, and Steven Lukes. Cambridge: Cambridge University Press, 1985.

Eastman, Susan Grove. *Paul and the Person: Reframing Paul's Anthropology*. Grand Rapids, MI: Eerdmans, 2017.

Edenburg, Cynthia, and Reinhard Müller. "Editorial Introduction: Perspectives on the Treaty Framework of Deuteronomy." *HeBAI* 8 (2019): 73–86.

Ehrlich, Arnold B. *Randglossen zur hebräischen Bibel*, Vol. 6. Hildesheim: Georg Olms, 1913.

Eichrodt, Walther. *Ezekiel: A Commentary*. OTL. Philadelphia: Westminster, 1970.

Ellman, Barat. *Memory and Covenant: The Role of Israel's and God's Memory in Sustaining the Deuteronomic and Priestly Covenants*. Emerging Scholars. Minneapolis: Fortress, 2013.

Elwolde, John Francis. "The Human Spirit and the Holy Spirit in the Qumran Hodayot." Pages 281–315 in *Sacred Texts and Disparate Interpretations: Qumran Manuscripts Seventy Years Later: Proceedings of the International Conference Held at the John Paul II Catholic University of Dublin, 24–26 October, 2017*. Edited by Henryk Drawnel. STDJ 133. Leiden: Brill, 2020.

Engberg-Pedersen, Troels. *Cosmology and Self in the Apostle Paul: The Material Spirit*. Oxford: Oxford University Press, 2010.

———. *Paul and the Stoics*. Louisville: Westminster John Knox, 2000.

Eshel, Esther. "Apotropaic Prayers in the Second Temple Period." Pages 69–88 in *Liturgical Perspectives: Prayer and Poetry in Light of the Dead Sea Scrolls: Proceedings of the Fifth International Symposium of the Orion Center for the Study of the Dead Sea Scrolls and Associated Literature, 19–23 January, 2000*. Edited by Esther G. Chazon, Ruth Clements, and Avital Pinnick. STDJ 48. Leiden: Brill, 2003.

Estes, Douglas, ed. *The Tree of Life*. TBN 27. Leiden: Brill, 2020.

Ewing, Katherine. "The Illusion of Wholeness: Culture, Self, and the Experience of Inconsistency." *Ethos* 18 (1990): 251–79.

Fabry, Heinz-Josef, and Ulrich Dahmen, eds. *Theologisches Wörterbuch zu den Qumrantexten*. 3 vols. Stuttgart: Kohlhammer, 2011–16.

Falk, Daniel. "Barkhi Nafshi." Pages 286–88 in *T&T Clark Companion to the Dead Sea Scrolls*. Edited by George J. Brooke and Charlotte Hempel. London: T&T Clark, 2019.

Feder, Yitzhaq. "Contagion and Cognition: Bodily Experience and the Conceptualization of Pollution." *JNES* 72 (2013): 151–67.

———. "Death, Afterlife and Corpse Pollution: The Meaning of the Expression *ṭāmēʾ la-nepeš*." *VT* 69 (2019): 408–34.

———. "Defilement and Moral Discourse in the Hebrew Bible: An Evolutionary Framework." *JCH* 3 (2016): 157–89.

Feldman, Ariel. "4Q422 (Paraphrase of Genesis and Exodus)." Pages 83–129 in Ariel Feldman and Liora Goldman, *Scripture and Interpretation: Qumran Texts That Rework the Bible*. Edited by Devorah Dimant. BZAW 449. Berlin: De Gruyter, 2014.

Flusser, David. "Qumran and Jewish 'Apotropaic' Prayers." *IEJ* 16 (1966): 194–205.

Fox, Michael V. "The Pedagogy of Proverbs 2." *JBL* 113 (1994): 233–43.

———. *Proverbs 1–9*. AB 18A. New York: Doubleday, 2000.

———. "Who Can Learn? A Dispute in Ancient Pedagogy." Pages 62–77 in *Wisdom, You Are My Sister: Studies in Honor of Roland E. Murphy, O. Carm.* Edited by M. L. Barre. CBQMS 29. Washington, DC: Catholic Biblical Association, 1997.

———. "Words for Folly." *ZAH* 10 (1977): 4–17.

Frevel, Christian. "Person—Identität—Selbst: Eine Problemanzeige aus alttestamentlicher Perspektive." Pages 65–89 in *Anthropologie(n) des Alten Testaments*. Edited by Jürgen van Oorschot and Andreas Wagner. Leipzig: Evangelische Verlagsansalt, 2015.

_______. "'Quellen des Selbst'? Charles Taylor's Einfluss auf die alttestamentliche Anthropologie." Pages 447–63 in *Im Dienste der Gerechigkeit und Einheit: Festschrift für Heinrich J. F. Reinhardt zur Vollendung seines 75. Lebensjahres*. Edited by Rüdiger Althaus, Judith Hahn, and Matthias Pulte. Essen: Ludgerus Verlag, 2017.

_______. "Struggling with the Vitality of Corpses: Understanding the Rationale of the Ritual in Numbers 19." Pages 199–226 in *Les vivants et leurs morts*. Edited by Jean-Marie Durand, Thomas Römer, and Jürg Hutzli. OBO 257. Fribourg: Academic Press; Göttingen: Vandenhoeck & Ruprecht, 2012.

Frevel, Christian, ed. *Biblische Anthropologie: Neue Einsichten aus dem Alten Testament*. QD 237. Freiburg im Breisgau: Herder, 2010.

Frevel, Christian, and Oda Wischmeyer. *Menschsein*. NEBTh 11. Würzburg: Echter, 2003.

Frey, Jörg. "Different Patterns of Dualistic Thought in the Qumran Library: Reflections on Their Background and History." Pages 275–309 in *Legal Texts and Legal Issues: Proceedings of the Second Meeting of the International Organization for Qumran Studies, Cambridge, 1995: Published in Honour of Joseph M. Baumgarten*. Edited by Moshe Bernstein, Florentino García Martínez, and John Kampen. STDJ 23. Leiden: Brill, 1997.

———. "Flesh and Spirit in the Palestinian Jewish Sapiential Tradition and in the Qumran Texts: An Inquiry into the Background of Pauline Usage." Pages 367–404 in *The Wisdom Texts from Qumran and the Development of Sapiential Thought: Studies in Wisdom at Qumran and Its Relationship to Sapiential Thought in the Ancient Near East, the Hebrew Bible, Ancient Judaism, and the New Testament*. Edited by Charlotte Hempel, Armin Lange, and Hermann Lichtenberger. BETL 159. Leuven: Peeters, 2002.

Frey-Anthes, Henrike. *Unheilsmächte und Schutzgenien, Antiwesen und Grenzgänger: Vorstellung von "Dämonien" in alten Israel*. OBO 227. Fribourg: Academic Press; Göttingen: Vandenhoeck & Ruprecht, 2007.

Frymer-Kensky, Tikva. "Pollution, Purification, and Purgation in Biblical Israel." Pages 399–414 in *The Word of the Lord Shall Go Forth*. Edited by Carol L. Meyers and Michael O'Connor. Winona Lake, IN: Eisenbrauns, 1983.

Geeraerts, Dirk. "Deliteralization and the Birth of 'Emotion.'" Pages 50–67 in *Approaches to Language, Culture, and Cognition: The Intersection of Cognitive Linguistics and Linguistic Anthropology*. Edited by Masataka Yamaguchi, Dennis Tay, and Benjamin Blount. New York: Palgrave Macmillan, 2014.

Geertz, Clifford. "From the Native's Point of View." *BAAAS* 28 (1974): 26–45.

———. *Local Knowledge: Further Essays in Interpretive Anthropology*. New York: Basic Books, 1983.

Gerstenberger, Erhard S. "' . . . (He/They) Shall Be Put to Death': Life-Preserving Divine Threats in Old Testament Law." *ExAud* 11 (1995): 43–61.

Gertz, Jan Christian. "The Formation of the Primeval History." Pages 107–35 in *The Book of Genesis: Composition, Reception, and Interpretation*. Edited by Craig A. Evans, Joel N. Lohr, and David L. Petersen. VTSup 152. Leiden: Brill, 2012.

Goff, Matthew J. *4QInstruction*. WLAW 2. Atlanta: SBL, 2013.

Graham, Jesse, Jonathan Haidt, Sena Koleva, Matt Motyl, Ravi Iyer, Sean P. Wojcik, and Peter H. Ditto. "Moral Foundations Theory: The Pragmatic Validity of Moral Pluralism." *AESP* 47 (2013): 55–130.

Greenfield, Jonas C. "The Root 'GBL' in Mishnaic Hebrew and in the Hymnic Literature from Qumran." *RevQ* 2 (1960): 155–62.

Gyatso, Janet. *Apparitions of the Self: The Secret Autobiographies of a Tibetan Visionary*. Princeton, NJ: Princeton University Press, 1998.

Haidt, Jonathan. *The Righteous Mind: Why Good People Are Divided by Politics and Religion*. New York: Pantheon Books, 2012.

Haig, David. "Intrapersonal Conflict." Pages 8–22 in *Conflict*. Edited by Martin Jones and A. C. Fabian. Cambridge: Cambridge University Press, 2006.

Han, Shihui, and Yina Ma. "A Culture—Behavior—Brain Loop Model of Human Development." *TCS* 19 (2015): 666–76.

Harkins, Angela Kim. *Reading with an "I" to the Heavens: Looking at the Qumran Hodayot through the Lens of Visionary Traditions*. Ekstasis 3. Berlin: De Gruyter, 2012.

Harrington, Hannah K. *The Purity Texts*. CQS 5. London: T&T Clark, 2004.

Harvey, Paul B., Jr., and Baruch Halpern. "W.M.L. de Wette's 'Dissertatio Critica . . .': Context and Translation." *ZAR* 14 (2008): 47–85.

Heatherton, Todd F. "Neuroscience of Self and Self-Regulation." *ARP* 62 (2011): 363–90.

Heelas, Paul. "The Model Applied: Anthropology and Indigenous Psychologies." Pages 38–63 in *Indigenous Psychologies: The Anthropology of the Self*. Edited by Paul Heelas and Andrew Lock. London: Academic, 1981.

Heidegger, Martin. "Language." In *Hermeneutical Inquiry*. Vol. 1: *The Interpretation of Texts*. Edited by David E. Klemm. AARSR 43. Atlanta: Scholars, 1986.

Hogan, Karina Martin. *Theologies in Conflict in 4 Ezra: Wisdom Debate and Apocalyptic Solution*. JSJSup 130. Leiden: Brill, 2008.

Holland, Dorothy, William Lachicotte, Jr., Debra Skinner, and Carole Cain. *Identity and Agency in Cultural Worlds*. Cambridge, MA: Harvard University Press, 1998.

Holland, Dorothy, and Naomi Quinn. "Culture and Cognition." Pages 3–42 in *Cultural Models in Language and Thought*. Edited by Dorothy Holland and Naomi Quinn. Cambridge: Cambridge University Press, 1987.

Hultgren, Stephen J. *From the Damascus Covenant to the Covenant of the Community: Literary, Historical and Theological Studies in the Dead Sea Scrolls*. STDJ 66. Leiden: Brill, 2007.

James, William. *The Principles of Psychology*. New York: H. Holt, 1890.

———. *Psychology*. New York: H. Holt, 1892.

Janowski, Bernd. *Anthropologie des Alten Testaments: Grundfragen, Kontexts, Themenfelder*. Tübingen: Mohr Siebeck, 2019.

———. *Das hörende Herz*. Göttingen: Vandenhoeck & Ruprecht, 2018.

Janowski, Bernd, and Kathrin Liess, eds. *Der Mensch im Alten Israel: Neue Forschungen zur alttestamentlichen Anthropologie*. HbS 59. Freiburg im Breisgau: Herder, 2009.

Jassen, Alex P. "Religion in the Dead Sea Scrolls." *RC* 1 (2007): 1–25.

Johnson, Aubrey. *The Vitality of the Individual in the Thought of Ancient Israel*. Cardiff: University of Wales Press, 1949.

Johnson, Mark, and George Lakoff. *Philosophy in the Flesh: The Embodied Mind and Its Challenge to Western Thought*. New York: Basic Books, 1999.

Johnson, Michael. "Reassessing the Genres of the Hodayot: Thanksgiving Psalms from Qumran." PhD diss., McMaster University, 2019.

Kazen, Thomas. "Emotional Ethics in Biblical Texts: Cultural Construction and Biological Bases of Morality." *HeBAI* 6 (2017): 431–56.

Kidd, David Comer, and Emanuele Castano. "Reading Literary Fiction Improves Theory of Mind." *Science* 342 (2013): 377–80.

Kirkpatrick, John, and Geoffrey M. White. "Exploring Ethnopsychologies." Pages 3–32 in *Person, Self, and Experience: Exploring Pacific Ethnopsychologies*. Edited by Geoffrey M. White and John Kirkpatrick. Berkeley: University of California Press, 1985.

Kister, Menachem. "Demons, Theology and Abraham's Covenant." Pages 167–81 in *The Dead Sea Scrolls at Fifty: Proceedings of the 1997 Society of Biblical Literature Qumran Section Meetings*. Edited by Robert A. Kugler and Eileen M. Schuller. EJL 15. Atlanta: Scholars, 1999.

———. "'Inclination of the Heart of Man,' the Body and Purification from Evil." Pages 243–84 in *MSDSS* 8. Edited by Moshe Bar-Asher and Devorah Dimant. Jerusalem: Bialik Institute and Haifa University, 2010 (Heb.).

———. "The Root NDB in the Scrolls and the Growth of Qumran Texts: Lexicography and Theology." Pages 111–30 in *MSDSS* 11–12. Edited by Jonathan Ben-

Dov and Menachem Kister. Haifa: Haifa University; Jerusalem: Bialik Institute and The Hebrew University Magness, 2015 (Heb.).

Klawans, Jonathan. *Impurity and Sin in Ancient Judaism*. New York: Oxford University Press, 2000.

———. *Josephus and the Theologies of Ancient Judaism*. New York: Oxford University Press, 2012.

———. "Josephus on Fate, Free Will, and Ancient Jewish Types of Compatibilism." *Numen* 56 (2009): 44–90.

Klein, Anja. "From the 'Right Spirit' to the 'Spirit of Truth.'" Pages 171–91 in *Dynamics of Language and Exegesis at Qumran*. Edited by Devorah Dimant and Reinhard Kratz. FAT 2/35. Tübingen: Mohr Siebeck, 2009.

———. *Schriftauslegung im Ezekielbuch: Redactionsgeschichtliche Untersuchungen zu Ez 34–39*. BZAW 391. Berlin: De Gruyter, 2008.

Knibb, Michael A. "The Exile in the Literature of the Intertestamental Period." *HeyJ* 17 (1976): 253–72.

———. *The Qumran Community*. Cambridge: Cambridge University Press, 1987.

Koch, Klaus. "Der Güter Gefährlichstes, die Sprache, dem Menschen gegeben . . . ; Überlegungen zu Gen 2, 7." *BN* 48 (1989): 50–60.

Köhler, Ludwig. *Hebrew Man: Lectures Delivered at the Invitation of the University of Tübingen, December 1–16, 1952. With an Appendix on Justice in the Gate*. Translated by Peter R. Ackroyd. London: SCM, 1956.

Kövecses, Zoltán. *Metaphor and Emotion: Language, Culture, and Body in Human Feeling*. Cambridge: Cambridge University Press, 2000.

Kozman, Rony. "Ezekiel's Promised Spirit as *adam*'s Revelatory Spirit in the Hodayot." *DSD* 26 (2019): 30–60.

Kronenfeld, David B., Giovanni Bennardo, Victor C. de Munck, and Michael D. Fischer, eds. *A Companion to Cognitive Anthropology*. Chichester: Blackwell, 2011.

Krüger, Thomas. "Das 'Herz' in der alttestamentlichen Anthropologie." Pages 103–18 in *Anthropologische Aufbrüche: Alttestamentliche und interdisziplinäre Zugänge zur historischen Anthropologie*. Edited by Andreas Wagner. Göttingen: Vandenhoeck & Ruprecht, 2009.

———. "Sündenfall? Überlegungen zur theologischen Bedeutung der Paradiesgeschichte." Pages 95–109 in *Beyond Eden*. Edited by Konrad Schmid and Christoph Riedweg. FAT 2/34. Tübingen: Mohr Siebeck, 2008.

Kuhn, Heinz-Wolfgang. *Enderwartung und gegenwärtiges Heil*. SUNT 3. Göttingen: Vandenhoeck & Ruprecht, 1966.

Lambert, David. "'Desire' Enacted in the Wilderness: Problems in the History of the Self and Bible Translation." Pages 25–49 in *Self, Self-Fashioning, and Individuality in Late Antiquity: New Perspectives*. Edited by Maren R. Niehoff and Joshua Levinson. CRPGRW 4. Tübingen: Mohr Siebeck, 2019.

———. *How Repentance Became Biblical: Judaism, Christianity, and the Interpretation of Scripture*. New York: Oxford University Press, 2016.

Lange, Armin. "Considerations Concerning the 'Spirit of Impurity' in Zech 13:2." Pages 254–68 in *Die Dämonen: Die Dämonologie der israelitisch-jüdischen und frühchristlichen Literatur im Kontext ihrer Umwelt*. Edited by Armin Lange, Hermann Lichtenberger, and K. F. Diethard Römheld. Tübingen: Mohr Siebeck, 2003.

———. *Weisheit und Prädestination: Weisheitliche Urordung und Prädestination in den Textfunden von Qumran*. STDJ 18. Leiden: Brill, 1995.

Lapsley, Jacqueline E. *Can These Bones Live? The Problem of the Moral Self in the Book of Ezekiel*. BZAW 301. Berlin: De Gruyter, 2000.

———. "Feeling Our Way: Love for God in Deuteronomy." *CBQ* 65 (2003): 350–69.

Lemke, Werner E. "Circumcision of the Heart." Pages 299–319 in *A God So Near: Essays on Old Testament Theology in Honor of Patrick D. Miller*. Edited by Brent A. Strawn and Nancy R. Bowen. Winona Lake, IN: Eisenbrauns, 2003.

Leverage, Paula, Howard Mancing, Richard Schweickert, and Jennifer Marston William, eds. *Theory of Mind and Literature*. Purdue, IN: Purdue University Press, 2011.

Levin, Christoph. *Die Verheissung des neuen Bundes: In ihrem theologiegeschichtlichen Zusammenhand ausgelegt*. FRLANT 137. Göttingen: Vandenhoeck & Ruprecht, 1985.

Levison, John R. *Filled with the Spirit*. Grand Rapids, MI: Eerdmans, 2009.

Lichtenberger, Hermann. *Studien zum Menschenbild in Texten der Qumrangemeinde*. SUNT 15. Göttingen: Vandenhoeck & Ruprecht, 1980.

Lienhardt, R. G. *Divinity and Experience: The Religion of the Dinka*. New York: Oxford University Press, 1961.

Lilly, Ingrid E. "*Rûaḥ* Embodied: Job's Internal Disease from the Perspective of Mesopotamian Medicine." Pages 323–36 in *Borders: Terminologies, Ideologies, and Performances*. Edited by Annette Weissenrieder. WUNT 366. Tübingen: Mohr Siebeck, 2016.

———. *Two Books of Ezekiel: Papyrus 967 and the Masoretic Text as Variant Literary Editions*. VTSup 150. Leiden: Brill, 2012.

Lin, Lynda C., and Eva H. Telzer. "An Introduction to Cultural Neuroscience." Pages 399–420 in *The Handbook of Culture and Biology*. Edited by José M. Causadias, Eva H. Telzer, and Nancy A. Gonzales. New York: John Wiley & Sons, 2018.

Lindholm, Charles. "Does the Sociocentric Self Exist? Reflections on Markus and Kitayama's 'Culture and the Self.'" *JAR* 53 (1997): 405–22.

Lock, Andrew. "Universals in Human Conception." Pages 19–36 in *Indigenous Psychologies: The Anthropology of the Self*. Edited by Paul Heelas and Andrew Lock. London: Academic, 1981.

Long, A. A. *Greek Models of Mind and Self.* Cambridge, MA: Harvard University Press, 2015.

Luhrmann, Tanya M. "Prayer as Metacognitive Activity." Pages 297–318 in *Metacognitive Diversity: An Interdisciplinary Approach.* Edited by Joëlle Proust and Martin Fortier. New York: Oxford University Press, 2018.

———. *When God Talks Back: Understanding the American Evangelical Relationship with God.* New York: Random House, 2012.

Lust, Johan. "Ezekiel 36–40 in the Oldest Greek Manuscript." *CBQ* 43 (1981): 517–33.

Lyons, Michael. *From Law to Prophecy: Ezekiel's Use of the Holiness Code.* LHBOTS 507. New York: T&T Clark, 2009.

Lyu, Sun Myung. *Righteousness in the Book of Proverbs.* FAT 2/55 .Tübingen: Mohr Siebeck, 2012.

MacDonald, Nathan D. "The Spirit of Yahweh: An Overlooked Conceptualization of Divine Presence in the Persian Period." Pages 95–120 in *Divine Presence and Absence in Exilic and Post-Exilic Judaism.* Edited by Nathan MacDonald and Izaak J. de Hulster. FAT 2/61. Tübingen: Mohr Siebeck, 2013.

Margalit, Avishai. *On Betrayal.* Cambridge, MA: Harvard University Press, 2017.

Markus, Hazel Rose, and Shinobu Kitayama. "Culture and the Self: Implications for Cognition, Emotion, and Motivation." *PR* 98 (1991): 224–53.

Martyn, J. Louis. "De-apocalypticizing Paul: An Essay Focused on *Paul and the Stoics* by Troels Engberg-Pedersen." *JSNT* 24 (2002): 61–102.

Maston, Jason. *Divine and Human Agency in Second Temple Judaism: A Comparative Study.* WUNT 297. Tübingen: Mohr Siebeck, 2010.

McCann, Clinton. "Psalm 73: An Interpretation Emphasizing Rhetorical and Canonical Criticism." PhD diss., Duke University, 1985.

McCullough, M. E., M. B. Kimeldorf, and A. D. Cohen. "An Adaptation for Altruism? The Social Causes, Social Effects, and Social Evolution of Gratitude." *CDPS* 17 (2008): 281–85.

Mendenhall, George E. "Covenant Forms in Israelite Tradition." *BA* 17 (1954): 50–76.

Merrill, E. H. *Qumran and Predestination: A Theological Study of the Thanksgiving Hymns.* STDJ 8. Leiden: Brill, 1975.

Metso, Sarianna, with Michael Knibb. *The Community Rule: A Critical Edition with Translation.* EJL 51. Atlanta: SBL, 2019.

Meyer, Nicholas A. *Adam's Dust and Adam's Glory in the Hodayot and the Letters of Paul: Rethinking Anthropology and Theology.* SNT 168. Leiden: Brill, 2016.

———. "Born of Woman, Fashioned from Clay: Tracking the Homology of Earth and Womb from the Hebrew Bible to the Psalms of Thanksgiving." *DSD* 28 (forthcoming 2021).

Milgrom, Jacob. *Leviticus 17–22.* AB 3A. New York: Doubleday, 2000.

Moran, William L. "The Ancient Near Eastern Background of the Love of God in Deuteronomy." *CBQ* 25 (1963): 77–87.

Müller, Katrin. "*Lobe den Herrn, meine 'Seele'": Eine kognitiv-linguistische Studie zur næfeš des Menschen im Alten Testament*. BWANT 215. Stuttgart: Kohlhammer, 2018.

———. "Die synthetische Körperauffassung—keine Besonderheit des hebräischen Denkens." Pages 67–77 in *Individualität und Selbstreflexion in den Literaturen des Alten Testaments*. Edited by Andreas Wagner and Jürgen van Oorschot. VWGT 48. Leipzig: Evangelische Verlagsanstalt, 2017.

Müller, Reinhard. "A Prophetic View of the Exile in the Holiness Code: Literary Growth and Tradition History in Leviticus 26." Pages 207–28 in *The Concept of Exile in Ancient Israel and Its Historical Contexts*. Edited by Ehud Ben Zvi and Christoph Levin. BZAW 404. Berlin: De Gruyter, 2010.

Murphy, Roland E. "*Yēṣer* in the Qumran Literature." *Biblica* 39 (1958): 334–43.

Nahmias, Eddy. "Your Brain as the Source of Free Will Worth Wanting: Understanding Free Will in the Age of Neuroscience." Pages 251–68 in *Neuroexistentialism: Meaning, Morals, and Purpose in the Age of Neuroscience*. Edited by Gregg D. Caruso and Owen J. Flanagan. New York: Oxford University Press, 2018.

Najman, Hindy. *Losing the Temple and Recovering the Future: An Analysis of 4 Ezra*. Cambridge: Cambridge University Press, 2014.

Nemeroff, C., and P. Rozin. "The Contagion Concept in Adult Thinking in the United States: Transmission of Germs and Interpersonal Influence." *Ethos* 22 (1994): 158–86.

Newman, Judith H. "Words of the Luminaries." Pages 365–66 in *T&T Clark Companion to the Dead Sea Scrolls*. Edited by George J. Brooke and Charlotte Hempel. London: T&T Clark, 2019.

Newsom, Carol A. *The Book of Job: A Contest of Moral Imaginations*. Oxford: Oxford University Press, 2003.

———. "Deriving Negative Anthropology through Exegetical Activity: The Hodayot as Case Study." Pages 258–74 in *Is There a Text in This Cave? Studies in the Textuality of the Dead Sea Scrolls in Honour of George J. Brooke*. Edited by Ariel Feldman, Maria Cioată, and Charlotte Hempel. STDJ 119. Leiden: Brill, 2017.

———. "A Farewell to the Hodyaot of the Community." *DSD* 28 (2021): 1–19.

———. "'If I had said. . . .' (Ps 73:15): Retrospective Introspection in Didactic Psalmody of the Second Temple Period." Pages 69–82 in *Petitioners, Penitents, and Poets: On Prayer and Praying in Second Temple Judaism*. Edited by Timothy J. Sandoval and Ariel Feldman. BZAW 524. Berlin: De Gruyter, 2020.

———. "In Search of Cultural Models for Divine Spirit and Human Bodies." *VT* 70 (2020): 104–23.

———. "Models of Moral Agency: Hebrew Bible and Second Temple Judaism." *JBL* 131 (2012): 2–25.

———. "Moral 'Recipes' in Deuteronomy and Ezekiel: Divine Authority and Human Agency." *HeBAI* 4 (2017): 488–509.

———. "'The Righteous Mind' and Judean Moral Culture: A Conversation between Biblical Studies and Moral Psychology." Pages 117–34 in *Worship, Women, and War: Essays in Honor of Susan Niditch*. Edited by John J. Collins, Tracy M. Lemos, and Saul M. Olyan. BJS 357. Providence: Brown University, 2015.

———. *The Self as Symbolic Space: Constructing Identity and Community at Qumran*. STDJ 52. Leiden: Brill, 2004.

———. "Toward a Genealogy of the Introspective Self in Second Temple Judaism." Pages 63–78 in *Functions of Psalms and Prayers in the Late Second Temple Period*. Edited by Mika Pajunen and Jeremy Penner. BZAW 486. Berlin: De Gruyter, 2017.

———. "Woman and the Discourse of Patriarchal Wisdom: A Study of Proverbs 1–9." Pages 39–54 in *Rhetoric and Hermeneutics: Approaches to Text, Tradition and Social Construction in Biblical and Second Temple Literature*. FAT 130. Tübingen: Mohr Siebeck, 2019.

Newsom, Carol A., ed. *Seeking Knowledge: The Intellectual Project of Apocalypticism in Cultural Context*. *HeBAI* 5.3 (2016).

Nicholson, Ernest W. *God and His People: Covenant and Theology in the Old Testament*. Oxford: Clarendon, 1986.

Nickelsburg, George W. E. *1 Enoch 1: A Commentary on the Book of 1 Enoch, Chapters 1-36; 81-108*. Hermeneia. Minneapolis: Fortress, 2001.

Niditch, Susan. "Genesis." Pages 27–45 in *Women's Bible Commentary*. 3rd ed. Edited by Carol A. Newsom, Sharon H. Ringe, and Jacqueline E. Lapsley. Louisville: Westminster John Knox, 2012.

———. *The Responsive Self: Personal Religion in Biblical Literature of the Neo-Babylonian and Persian Periods*. AYBRL. New Haven: Yale University Press, 2015.

Nihan, Christophe L. "Ezekiel and the Holiness Legislation: A Plea for Nonlinear Models." Pages 1015–39 in *The Formation of the Pentateuch: Bridging the Academic Cultures of Europe, Israel, and North America*. Edited by Jan Christian Gertz, Bernard M. Levinson, Dalit Rom-Shiloni, and Konrad Schmid. FAT 111. Tübingen: Mohr Siebeck, 2016.

Noort, Ed. "Taken from the Soil, Gifted with the Breath of Life: The Anthropology of Genesis 2:7 in Context." Pages 1–15 in *Dust of the Ground and Breath of Life (Gen 2:7): The Problem of a Dualistic Anthropology in Early Judaism and Christianity*. Edited by Jacques T.A.G.M. van Ruiten and George H. van Kooten. TBN 20. Leiden: Brill, 2016.

Ochsner, K. O., and J. J. Gross. "Cognitive Emotion Regulation." *CDPS* 17 (2008): 153–58.

Oden, Robert A., Jr. *The Bible without Theology: The Theological Tradition and Alternatives to It*. Urbana and Chicago: University of Illinois Press, 2000.

Olyan, Saul. "The Search for the Elusive Self in Texts of the Hebrew Bible." Pages 40–50 in *Religion and the Self in Antiquity*. Edited by David Brakke, Michael L. Satlow, and Steve Weitzman. Bloomington, IN: Indiana University Press, 2003.

Otto, Eckhart. "Die Paradieserzählung Genesis 2–3: Eine nachpriesterschriftliche Lehrerzählung in ihrem religionshistorischen Kontext." Pages 167–92 in *"Jedes Ding hat seine Zeit": Studien zu israelitischen und altorientalischen Weisheit (FS D. Michel)*. Edited by Anja A. Diesel, Reinhard G. Lehmann, Eckart Otto, and Andreas Wagner. BZAW 241. Berlin: De Gruyter, 1996.

Pagels, Elaine. *Adam, Eve and the Serpent*. New York: Vintage Books, 1989.

Pajunen, Mika S. *The Land to the Elect and Justice for All: Reading Psalms in the Dead Sea Scrolls in Light of 4Q381*. JAJSup 14. Göttingen: Vandenhoeck & Ruprecht, 2013.

Pakkala, Juha. "The Influence of Treaties on Deuteronomy, Exclusive Monolatry, and Covenant Thelogy." *HeBAI* 8 (2019): 159–83.

Pedersen, Johannes. *Israel: Its Life and Culture*. 2 vols. Translated by A. Møller and A. I. Fausbell. London: Oxford University Press, 1926–40.

Perlitt, Lothar. *Bundestheologie im Alten Testament*. WMANT 36. Neukirchen-Vluyn: Neukirchener Verlag, 1969.

Pidoux, Georges. *L'homme dans l'Ancien Testament*. Neuchâtel: Delachaux & Niestlé, 1953.

Popović, Mladen. *Reading the Human Body: Physiognomics and Astrology in the Dead Sea Scrolls and Hellenistic-Early Roman Period Judaism*. STDJ 67. Leiden: Brill, 2007.

Porter, Frank C. "The Yeçer Hara: A Study in the Jewish Doctrine of Sin." Pages 93–156 in *Biblical and Semitic Studies: Critical and Historical Essays by the Members of the Semitic and Biblical Faculty of Yale University*. New York: Scribner's, 1901.

Porzig, Peter. "The Place of the 'Treatise of the Two Spirits' (1QS 3:13–4:26) within the Literary Development of the Community Rule." Pages 127–52 in *Law, Literature, and Society in Legal Texts from Qumran: Papers from the Ninth Meeting of the International Organization for Qumran Studies, Leuven 2016*. Edited by Jutta Jokiranta and Molly Zahn. STDJ 128. Leiden: Brill, 2019.

Qimron, Elisha. "Notes on the 4Q Zadokite Fragment on Skin Disease." *JJS* 42 (1991): 256–59.

———. *The Dead Sea Scrolls: The Hebrew Writings*. 3 vols. Jerusalem: Yad Izhak Ben-Zvi, 2020.

Quinn, Naomi. "How to Reconstruct Schemas People Share, from What They Say." Pages 35–82 in *Finding Culture in Talk: A Collection of Methods*. Edited by Naomi Quinn. New York: Palgrave Macmillan, 2005.

———. "The Self." *AT* 6 (2006): 362–84.

Ravven, Heidi M. *The Self beyond Itself: An Alternative History of Ethics, the New Brain Sciences, and the Myth of Free Will*. New York: New Press, 2013.

Reber, Rolf, and Ara Norenzayan. "Shared Fluency Theory of Social Cohesiveness: How the Metacognitive Feeling of Processing Fluency Contributes to Group Processes." Pages 47–67 in *Metacognitive Diversity: An Interdisciplinary Approach*. Edited by Jöelle Proust and Martin Fortier. New York: Oxford University Press, 2018.

Reed, Annette Yoshiko. *Demons, Angels, and Writing in Ancient Judaism*. Cambridge: Cambridge University Press, 2020.

Rey, Jean-Sébastian. *4QInstruction: Sagesse et eschatologie*. STDJ 81. Leiden: Brill, 2009.

Robinson, H. Wheeler. *Corporate Personality in Ancient Israel*. Philadelphia: Fortress, 1964.

Rogerson, John W. "The Hebrew Conception of Corporate Personality: A Re-Examination." *JTS* 21 (1970): 1–16.

Rosen-Zvi, Ishay. "Bilhah the Temptress: The Testament of Reuben and 'The Birth of Sexuality.'" *JQR* 96 (2006): 65–94.

———. *Demonic Desires:* Yetzer Hara *and the Problem of Evil in Late Antiquity*. Philadelphia: University of Pennsylvania Press, 2011.

Ross, Lee, and Richard E. Nisbett. *The Person and the Situation: Perspectives of Social Psychology*. New York: McGraw-Hill, 1991.

Royzman, Edward, Pavel Atanasov, Justin F. Landy, Amanda Parks, and Andrew Gepty. "'CAD or MAD?' Anger (Not Disgust) as the Predominant Response to Pathogen-Free Violations of the Divinity Code." *Emotion* (2014): 892–907.

Samson, Edward E. "The Debate on Individualism: Indigenous Psychologies of the Self and Their Role in Personal and Societal Functioning." *AP* 43 (1988): 15–22.

Sanders, Seth L. "The Appetites of the Dead: West Semitic Linguistic and Ritual Aspects of the Katumuwa Stele." *BASOR* 369 (2013): 35–55.

———. *From Adapa to Enoch: Scribal Culture and Religious Vision in Judea and Babylon*. TSAJ 167. Tübingen: Mohr Siebeck, 2017.

Sandoval, Timothy J. *The Discourse of Wealth and Poverty in the Book of Proverbs*. BibInt 77. Leiden: Brill, 2006.

Sax, William S. "Agency." Pages 473–81 in *Theorizing Rituals*. Vol. 1: *Issues, Topics, Approaches, Concepts*. Edited by Jens Kreinath, Jan A. M. Snoek, and Michael Stausberg. Leiden: Brill, 2006.

Schaper, Joachim. "Elements of a History of the Soul in North-West Semitic Texts: *npš/nbš* in the Hebrew Bible and the Katumuwa Inscription." *VT* 70 (2020): 156–76.

Schipper, Bernd U. *Proverbs 1–15*. Translated by Stephen Germany. Hermeneia. Minneapolis: Fortress, 2019.

———. "'Teach Them Diligently to Your Son!': The Book of Proverbs and Deuteronomy." Pages 21–34 in *Reading Proverbs Intertextually*. Edited by Katharine Dell and Will Kynes. LHBOTS 629. London: T&T Clark, 2019.

Schlimm, Matthew Richard. "At Sin's Entryway (Gen 4,7)." *ZAW* 124 (2012): 409–15.

Schloen, David, and Amir S. Fink. "New Excavations at Zincirli Höyük in Turkey (Ancient Sam'al) and the Discovery of an Inscribed Mortuary Stele." *BASOR* 365 (2009): 203–19.

Schmid, Konrad. "Die Unteilbarkeit der Weisheit: Überlegungen zur sogenannten Paradieserzählung Gen 2f. und ihrer theologischen Tendenz." *ZAW* 114 (2002): 21–39.

Schuele, Andreas. "The Notion of Life: *Nepeš* and *Rûaḥ* in the Anthropological Discourse of the Primeval History." *HeBAI* 1 (2012): 484–501.

Schuller, Eileen M. "Petitionary Prayer and the Religion of Qumran." Pages 29–45 in *Religion in the Dead Sea Scrolls*. Edited by John J. Collins and Robert A. Kugler. Grand Rapids, MI: Eerdmans, 2000.

Schuller, Eileen M., and Carol A. Newsom. *The Hodayot (Thanksgiving Psalms): A Study Edition of 1QH*[a]. EJL 36. Atlanta: SBL, 2012.

Schwartz, Baruch J. "The Ultimate Aim of Israel's Restoration in Ezekiel." Pages 305–19 in *Birkat Shalom: Studies in the Bible, Ancient Near Eastern Literature, and Postbiblical Judaism Presented to Shalom M. Paul on the Occasion of His Seventieth Birthday*. Vol. 1. Edited by Chaim Cohen, Victor Hurowitz, Avi Hurvitz, Yochanan Muffs, Baruch J. Schwartz, and Jeffrey Tigay. Winona Lake, IN: Eisenbrauns, 2008.

Schwartz, Ethan. "The Exegetical Character of 1QS 3:13–4:26." *DSD* 27 (2020): 31–65.

Seely, David R. "Implanting Pious Qualities as a Theme in the *Barki Nafshi* Hymns." Pages 322–31 in *The Dead Sea Scrolls—Fifty Years after Their Discovery: Proceedings of the Jerusalem Congress, July 20–25, 1997*. Edited by Lawrence H. Schiffman, Emanuel Tov, James C. VanderKam, and Galen Marquis. Jerusalem: Israel Exploration Society, 2000.

Seow, Choon Leong. *Ecclesiastes: A New Translation and Commentary*. AB 18C. New York: Doubleday, 1997.

Shweder, Richard A., and Edmund J. Bourne. "Does the Concept of the Person Vary Cross-Culturally?" Pages 158–99 in *Culture Theory*. Edited by Richard A. Shweder and Robert A. LeVine. Cambridge: Cambridge University Press, 1984.

Ska, Jean Louis. "Genesis 2–3: Some Fundamental Questions." Pages 1–27 in *Beyond Eden: The Biblical Story of Paradise (Genesis 2–3) and Its Reception History*. Edited by Konrad Schmid and Christoph Riedweg. FAT 2/34. Tübingen: Mohr Siebeck, 2008.

Skehan, Patrick W., and Alexander A. Di Lella. *The Wisdom of Ben Sira*. AB 39. New York: Doubleday, 1987.

Sklar, Jay. "Sin and Impurity: Atoned or Purified? Yes!" Pages 18–31 in *Perspectives on Purity and Purification in the Bible*. Edited by Baruch Schwartz, David P.

Wright, Jeffrey Stackert, and Napthali S. Meshel. LHBOTS 474. New York: T&T Clark, 2008.

Smith, Mark S. *The Genesis of Good and Evil: The Fall(out) and Original Sin in the Bible*. Louisville: Westminster John Knox, 2019.

Snell, Bruno. *The Discovery of the Mind: The Greek Origins of European Thought*. Translated by T. G. Rosenmeyer. Oxford: Blackwell, 1953.

Spiro, Melford E. "Is the Western Conception of the Self 'Peculiar' within the Context of World Cultures?" *Ethos* (1993): 107–53.

Staubli, Thomas. "Disgusting Deeds and Disgusting Gods: Ethnic and Ethical Constructions of Disgust in the Hebrew Bible." *HeBAI* 6 (2017): 457–87.

Staubli, Thomas, and Sylvia Schroer. *Body Symbolism in the Bible*. Translated by Linda M. Maloney. Collegeville, MN: Liturgical, 2001. Originally published as *Die Körpersymbolik der Bibel*. Darmstadt: Wissenschaftliche Buchgesellschaft, 1998.

Stegemann, Hartmut. "The Number of Psalms in *1QHodayot*[a] and Some of Their Sections." Pages 191–234 in *Liturgical Perspectives: Prayer and Poetry in Light of the Dead Sea Scrolls: Proceedings of the Fifth International Symposium of the Orion Center for the Study of the Dead Sea Scrolls and Associated Literature, 19–23 January, 2000*. Edited by Esther G. Chazon, with Ruth Clements and Avital Pinnick. STDJ 48. Leiden: Brill, 2003.

Stegemann, Hartmut, and Eileen Schuller, with translation of texts by Carol Newsom. *1QHodayot*[a] *with Incorporation of 1QHodayot*[b] *and 4QHodayot*[a–f]*: Qumran Cave 1, III*. DJD 40. Oxford: Clarendon, 2009.

Steiner, Richard C. *Disembodied Souls: The Nefesh in Israel and Kindred Spirits in the Ancient Near East, with an Appendix on the Katumuwa Inscription*. ANEM 11. Atlanta: SBL, 2015.

Stewart, Anne W. *Poetic Ethics in Proverbs: Wisdom Literature and the Shaping of the Moral Self*. Cambridge: Cambridge University Press, 2016.

Stone, Michael E. *Ancient Judaism: New Visions and Views*. Grand Rapids, MI: Eerdmans, 2011.

———. *Fourth Ezra: A Commentary*. Hermeneia. Minneapolis: Augsburg Fortress, 1990.

Storalden, T. *Echoes of Eden: Genesis 2–3 and Symbolism of the Eden Garden in Biblical Hebrew Literature*. CBET 25. Leuven: Peeters, 2000.

Strauss, Claudia. "Analyzing Discourse for Cultural Complexity." Pages 35–82 in *Finding Culture in Talk: A Collection of Methods*. Edited by Naomi Quinn. New York: Palgrave Macmillan, 2005.

———. "Research on Cultural Discontinuities." Pages 210–51 in *A Cognitive Theory of Cultural Meaning*. Edited by Claudia Strauss and Naomi Quinn. Cambridge: Cambridge University Press, 1997.

Strine, Casey A. "The Role of Repentance in the Book of Ezekiel: A Second Chance for the Second Generation." *JTS* 63 (2012): 467–91.

Taylor, Charles. *Sources of the Self.* Cambridge, MA: Harvard University Press, 1989.
ten Hoopen, Robin B. "Genesis 5 and the Formation of the Primeval History: A Redaction Historical Case Study." *ZAW* 129 (2017): 177–93.
Tigchelaar, Eibert. "Changing Truths: ʾĕmet and *qōšeṭ* as Core Concepts in the Second Temple Period." Pages 395–415 in *Congress Volume Stellenbosch 2016.* Edited by Louis C. Jonker, Gideon R. Kotzé, and Christl M. Maier. VTSup 177. Leiden: Brill, 2017.
———. "The Evil Inclination in the Dead Sea Scrolls, with a Re-Edition of 4Q468i (4QSectarian Text?)." Pages 347–57 in *Empsychoi Logoi: Religious Innovations in Antiquity: Studies in Honour of Pieter Willem van der Horst.* Edited by Alberdina Houtman, Albert de Jong, and Magdalena Wilhelmina Misset-van de Weg. AJEC 73. Leiden: Brill, 2008.
———. "Historical Origins of the Early Christian Concept of the Holy Spirit: Perspectives from the Dead Sea Scrolls." Pages 167–240 in *The Holy Spirit, Inspiration, and the Cultures of Antiquity.* Edited by Jörg Frey, John R. Levison, and Andrew Bowden. Ekstasis 5. Berlin: De Gruyter, 2014.
———. "'Spiritual People,' 'Fleshly Spirit,' and 'Vision of Meditation': Reflections on *4QInstruction* and 1 Corinthians." Pages 103–18 in *Echoes from the Caves: Qumran and the New Testament.* Edited by Florentino García Martínez. STDJ 85. Leiden: Brill, 2009.
Trivers, R. L. "The Evolution of Reciprocal Altruism." *QRB* 46 (1971): 35–57.
Turner, Mark, and Gilles Fauconnier. "A Mechanism of Creativity." *PT* 20 (1999): 397–418.
VanderKam, James C. *Jubilees: A Commentary in Two Volumes.* Hermeneia. Minneapolis: Fortress, 2018.
von der Osten-Saken, Peter. *Gott und Belial: Traditionsgeschichtliche Untersuchungen zum Dualism in den Texten aus Qumran.* SUNT 6. Göttingen: Vandenhoeck & Ruprecht, 1969.
von Oorschot, Jürgen, and Andreas Wagner, eds. *Anthropologie(n) des Alten Testaments.* VWGT 42. Leipzig: Evangelische Verlagsanstalt, 2015.
Wagner, Andreas. "Wider die Reduktion des Lebendigen: Über das Verhältnis der sog. anthropologischen Grundbegriffe und die Unmöglichkeit, mit ihnen die alttestamentliche Menschenvorstellung zu erfassen." Pages 183–99 in *Anthropologische Ausbrüche: Alttestamentliche und interdisziplinäre Zugänge zur historischen Anthropologie.* Edited by Andreas Wagner. FRLANT 232. Göttingen: Vandenhoeck & Ruprecht, 2009.
Wallace, Howard N. *The Eden Narrative.* HSM 32. Atlanta: Scholars, 1985.
Weinfeld, Moshe. "The Covenant of Grant in the Old Testament and in the Ancient Near East." *JAOS* 90 (1970): 184–203.
Weinfeld, Moshe, and David Seely. "Barkhi Nafshi." Pages 255–334 in *Qumran Cave 4. XX: Poetical and Liturgical Texts, Part 2.* Edited by Esther G. Chazon et al. DJD 29. Oxford: Clarendon, 1999.

Werman, Cana. "What Is the *Book of Hagu*?" Pages 125–40 in *Sapiential Perspectives: Wisdom Literature in Light of the Dead Sea Scrolls: Proceedings of the Sixth International Symposium of the Orion Center for the Study of the Dead Sea Scrolls and Associated Literature, 20–22 May, 2001*. Edited by John J. Collins, Gregory E. Sterling, and Ruth A. Clements. STDJ 51. Leiden: Brill, 2004.

Wernberg-Moller, P. *The Manual of Discipline*. STDJ 1. Leiden: Brill, 1957.

Westermann, Claus. *Genesis 1–11: A Commentary*. Translated by John J. Scullion, S.J. CC. Minneapolis: Augsburg, 1984.

White, Geoffrey M. "Exploring Ethnopsychologies." Pages 3–32 in *Person, Self, and Experience: Exploring Pacific Ethnopsychologies*. Berkeley: University of California Press, 1985.

Wibbing, Siegfried. *Die Tugend- und Lasterkataloge im Neuen Testament und ihre Traditionsgeschichte unter besonderer Berücksichtigung der Qumrantexte*. BZNW 25. Berlin: Töpelmann, 1959.

Wikan, Unni. *Managing Turbulent Hearts: A Balinese Formula for Living*. Chicago: University of Chicago Press, 1990.

Williams, Bernard. *Ethics and the Limits of Philosophy*. Cambridge, MA: Harvard University Press, 1985.

Witte, Markus. *Die biblische Urgeschichte: Redaktions- und theologiegeschichtliche Beobachtungen zu Genesis 1,1–11,26*. BZAW 265. Berlin: De Gruyter, 1998.

Wold, Benjamin. *4QInstruction: Divisions and Hierarchies*. STDJ 123. Leiden: Brill, 2018.

———. "Genesis 2–3 in Early Christian Tradition and 4QInstruction." *DSD* 23 (2016): 329–46.

Wolff, Hans Walter. *Anthropologie des Alten Testaments: Mit zwei Anhängen neu herausgegeben von Bernd Janowski*. Gütersloh: Gütersloher Verlagshaus, 2010.

———. *Anthropology of the Old Testament*. Translated by Margaret Kohl. Philadelphia: Fortress, 1974. Originally published as *Anthropologie des Alten Testaments*. München: C. Kaiser, 1973.

Woźniak, Mateusz. "'I' and 'Me': The Self in the Context of Consciousness." *FP* 9 (2018): 1–14.

Yoder, Christine Roy. "The Shaping of Erotic Desire in Proverbs 1–9." Pages 148–63 in *Saving Desire: The Seduction of Christian Theology*. Edited by F. LeRon Shults and Jan-Olav Henriksen. Grand Rapids, MI: Eerdmans, 2011.

Younger, K. Lawson, Jr. "The Kulamuwa Inscription." *COS* 2.30: 147–48.

Zenger, Erich, and Frank-Lothar Hossfeld. *Psalms 2: A Commentary on Psalms 51–100*. Translated by Linda M. Maloney. Hermeneia. Minneapolis: Fortress, 2005.

Subject Index

Ancient Source Index

Hebrew Bible

Rabbinic Literature

Ancient Near Eastern Literature

Hebrew Key Word Index